*To Tracey Allan
With Best wishes
William 2013*

THE WAY WE WERE

William S. Smith

Published by

MELROSE BOOKS

An Imprint of Melrose Press Limited
St Thomas Place, Ely
Cambridgeshire
CB7 4GG, UK
www.melrosebooks.co.uk

FIRST EDITION

Copyright © William Smith 2012

The Author asserts his moral right to
be identified as the author of this work

Cover designed by Teri Smith

ISBN 978-1-907732-77-5

All rights reserved. No part of this publication may be reproduced, stored in a retrieval system, or transmitted, in any form or by any means electronic, mechanical, photocopying, recording or otherwise, without the prior permission of the publishers.

This book is sold subject to the condition that it shall not, by way of trade or otherwise, be lent, re-sold, hired out or otherwise circulated without the publisher's prior consent in any form of binding or cover other than that in which it is published and without a similar condition including this condition being imposed on the subsequent purchaser.

Printed and bound in Great Britain by:
TJ International Ltd, Padstow, Cornwall

DEDICATED
to my dearest wife,
Mary

Oh! What would I be!
Where would I have gone!
Without this lovely lady
To devote my life upon

Contents

PART ONE

100 Years to my birthday	1
Growing up in the Thirties	25
War, Sadness and Love	61
Follow your Heart and Hope Reaching for the Mid-Fifties	251
Epilogue	301

Part One

100 Years to my birthday

Yesterday I played a game of snooker with my grandson Daniel. I am fortunate enough to possess my own full-sized table, due in part to the foresight of my younger son Barry.

The year is 2003. The day, the Sunday before August Bank holiday Monday, the weather is overcast but very warm and during the recent weeks it has been very hot, one day the hottest on record at just over 100 degrees Fahrenheit. Of course if these writings are ever read by future generations of Smiths, they may not understand the term Fahrenheit, for the simple reason that for my wife Mary and me and our generation, this has been a period of much change.

I write at this time because both Barry and Daniel came to Mary and I on this particular Sunday, Barry to utilise our small workshop to repair Daniel's friend Max's car, so whilst here Daniel was happy to challenge his grandfather. There are exactly fifty years between Daniel and me, and Daniel was gallantly pleased when I managed to win by one point after he had just missed potting the black after obtaining an excellent pink.

During this rare game with young Daniel we spoke of my life and times, something of which Barry had touched upon that very same day. Each confessed how nice it would be to see things that perhaps only I would be able to remember written down for the future. So today I thought I might just try and do that. It could be rather daunting but here goes.

In composing this history, if that's what one can call it, I shall endeavour to fill in various life happenings across the world, as well as uncovering the lives of those close family members around me. Naturally I shall take you back as far and accurately as possible in this search, thereby granting as much perspective on our forebears as possible.

I have found that as one gets older the tendency is, particularly in my case, to want to read more and more about our past. You suddenly get the feeling that life is really quite short, which of course it is, especially when

THE WAY WE WERE

one compares it to the span of life on the planet as a whole. It is humbling to note that the dinosaurs were around for approximately 140 million years against man's, to date, mere three million.

The thing that strikes most when looking at the twentieth century in particular, is how it became after thousands of years of gradual change pitched into a fervour of rapid progress.

The consequence of this is that I find of all the centuries to have been born in, perhaps the twentieth was the most rewarding. However, having expressed that view, it is highly possible that previous ancestors probably felt the same about their time on earth, as they had never been able to experience anything different. Another point about getting older is that it is often felt that not everything called progress is necessarily so, as many ideas and values from the past are often sadly missed! But once again exactly as our ancestors could not miss what they never had, so too does this dictum apply to later offspring who never experienced something that has gone forever!

Mind you one can imagine what life may have been like without certain advantages that we have come to take for granted. Good plumbing springs to mind. I would have hated to live in a world such as the eighteenth century, where populations and cities were expanding without the valued inventions of flushing loos and running water on tap. So when I explain that I was born in an age before bathrooms as we know them—no electricity for many people only gas lighting—you will understand more what I mean.

As a boy many were the times I saw the man come round to light up the gas mantle in the street lamps. In the morning he would arrive with a long pole complete with hook and proceed to place the hook in one of two rings and pull down a chain thus cutting off the gas supply to extinguish the mantle. Afterwards carrying the pole like a lance he would jump on his bike and cycle to the next and so on. Gas lighting in many ways was a soft form of lighting; it certainly lent itself to a comforting feeling and gave off a lovely glow on snow-covered roads and sidewalks.

Many vendors would come round the streets with wares, not just the horse drawn milk float, but a chap selling bread and cakes, another selling meat and fish, others would sell groceries, and yet another offering to sharpen your knives and scissors for a penny. Always in the summer would be the "Stop Me and Buy One" man on his tricycle with front carrier full of ice, selling ice cream and iced lollies. Not forgetting of course, the ever-present rag and bone man who for a few coppers would buy anything you wanted to

William S. Smith

get rid of, or perhaps you might make a purchase!

When I was at least ten years old, and being cared for by my eldest sister Ciss at her new home in Romford, I would for a couple of freshly baked buns help the bread seller cover all the local avenues. I can always remember how the horse knew exactly when to start and stop without ever once being directed by the baker.

Naturally there were no such things as televisions or washing machines, fridges or freezers. Few private telephones were available, and born as I was in 1927, there were certainly very few private motor cars.

Our family home at my birth was number 62 Usher Road, Bow, in London, and rented from the London Council. I am unable to remember all the roads around, but I do recall that the main thoroughfare running across the top end of Usher Road was called Roman Road. On the corner where these roads met, some fifty yards or so away, stood a pub. This must have been a favourite haunt of Grandfather, who lived upstairs. I can see him now, this slightly portly, grey mustachioed figure shuffling along in his carpet slippers, jug in hand, to retrieve his daily pint of beer, which he would bring home to sup.

This was my paternal grandfather, who was born on the 3rd November 1854 and christened William Henry, after his father before him, William Burn Smith.

Now William Burn gave his profession as "Mariner"; I am sure he was actually a pastry cook aboard coastal ships that plied the seas around our coasts. This was very often the favoured mode of transport when travelling long distances, rather than the hard ride afforded by stagecoach on gravel byways. Eventually he married Anne Thomson, giving his abode as No. 5 Cutbank, Newcastle-on-Tyne.

And so it was that young William Henry, who had also trained as a pastry cook in the footsteps of his father, decided one day when only about nineteen years old, to leave his mum and dad, William and Anne, and journey to London to seek a better fortune! The only trouble was he had no money, and he had no footwear either. Nevertheless he was determined, especially because as the story goes, he had had a very bad falling out with his dad. With resolve he would go forth, just like that!

Well maybe not quite so immediate, for someone recently suggested to me that about this time there had been a large exodus of people walking from the north, and it is quite possible grandfather was amongst these. Such a feat

THE WAY WE WERE

seems hard to believe today but man of course has travelled many hundreds of miles in times gone by without anything to protect his feet, and when the gold of London's streets beckoned, most adventurous young men and women of the day would not have hesitated.

William Henry never found a fortune as such, although it was rife in the Smith clan through a story handed down, that he was offered by a Mr Peak to join him and a Mr Frean in starting their own biscuit-making business.

For whatever reason Grandfather declined this offer, maybe he was already gainfully employed and he felt the risk too great. Unfortunately as it transpired, Peak Frean Biscuits went on to become a household name, which if it were true of course, could so easily have been Peak Frean and Smith.

He did however find love and when he was just twenty-one years old married Sophia Webb on the 16th April 1876 at St Thomas Church in Stepney. His address given as 18 Thomas Street, Stepney.

Sophia was almost two years William Henry's junior, having been born on the 17th of March 1856, this being St Patrick's day and one day removed from my own birth date of the 18th March. Sophia's father, also a William, surname Webb, was born in 1827 and held a profession known as "Journeyman/Housepainter", whilst her mother named Elizabeth came from the family surnamed Bills, and was born in 1829.

They were married on the 12th of August 1855, and as dear Sophia my grandmother was born only seven months and one week later it looks very likely that some hanky panky had been going on a little while before Elizabeth said "I do". At the time of her marriage Elizabeth had reached the ripe old age of twenty-six years, which in those days was quite unusual. The Webb family was also resident near William Henry, at 2 Middle Stores Street, Stepney, Mile End, Old Town!

All was now set for Sophia, aged twenty, and William Henry, twenty-one, to start a family, remember there was no television, no radio, and no electric light, and above all no duvets or electric blankets. Man rose with the dawn and snuggled down just after dusk, if he wasn't working! The first child born was a boy, guess what he was called! Correct: William Henry. some six years after they were married came their second son John George My father and your paternal ancestor, born on 29th August 1882. Then Jessie, I remember big Aunt Jessie, she was quite a rotund lady, and then it was Arthur, and Bertie Edwin, before finally Florence. Six children in all. However it is highly likely that fighting got in the way of the conceiving and giving birth to some of the children, for along with many others of the period the Smiths were destined to be a military lot.

Before the turn of the century fighting had started in South Africa when Dutch peasants known as Boers rebelled against the authority of Her Majesty Queen Victoria. Such a thing was intolerable, for our Queen ruled over the greatest empire ever known. Why, even when I went to school most of the world atlas was shaded pink to represent all the territory controlled by Great Britain.

Men rallied to the cause and Grandfather, William Henry, who thought nothing of walking from the north barefoot, was one of those stalwarts to answer the call to colours. It is highly possible, but unable to be substantiated, that Grandfather was also in the King's Royal Rifles, for my father John George joined this regiment at the outbreak of WWI, and in all likelihood did so on the recommendations of his father. Should this be the case then Grandfather could have been involved in the relief of Mafeking, which the King's Royal Rifles became part of.

On January the 22nd 1901 Queen Victoria died at the age of eighty-one, one year and four months before the Boers surrendered. Edward VII now sat on the throne with his wife Queen Alexandra.

The fourth and sixth children, Arthur and Florence, each went to live in Canada after WWI and both with their respective spouses returned to visit the old country a couple of times. These journeys would be quite protracted because it meant sailing both ways. (No fast jet travel in those days.)

Florence married a chap called George and they set up home on Vancouver Island, a far cry in both distance and environment from the areas around Mile End in London. My recollection is of Florence and George's son Robert paying a visit to my sister Ciss, her husband Jack and myself at Romford during WWII. He was a Canadian soldier, a tall, quite striking looking lad, not unlike my grandson Daniel. He came on leave with a fellow soldier for just a couple of days as he had promised his mum, Florrie, that he would endeavour to look up her relatives in the old country.

Not long afterwards Lord Louis Mountbatten commanded a seaborne landing at Dieppe in which mostly Canadian troops were used. Tragically, Robert along with many other Canadian soldiers was lost in this action. Although Florrie and George had been the bearers of nine children, the loss of dear Robert proved to be a heavy cross to bear.

In the nineteenth and early twentieth centuries two things seemed to prevail when it came to continuity of family. One was that in most instances the first born son would inherit his father's first names and secondly all sons unless strongly willed otherwise would continue in their fathers' footsteps when it came to their choice of profession.

Likewise the eldest daughter of a family invariably took on her mother's first names, the whole exercise becoming fraught with confusion when trying to decipher who was who back down the years. Conversely of course the complication of trying to sort full family relatives from half family members in this present day could be considered a nightmare hardly worth the exercise, so much has family tradition been eroded.

Who knows then if this attempt at trying to establish where our recent roots lay may be the last possible opportunity to do so! Being the second son, Dad escaped his father's name but he certainly trained to be a professional pastry cook.

My father, John George Smith met my mother Harriet Horne sometime before March 1906, because on the 11th of that month they were married at St Benets Church in the Parish of Stepney. Mother was just eighteen years old for she was born on the 16th February 1888. Dad, at this time being some five and a half years older, would still have been twenty-three in March 1906.

Harriet was of Irish descent, her father, whose profession is listed as a Traveller, which could quite so easily mean a kind of Romany, was, to confuse matters further, also another William Henry. He had married a Harriet Burke, but we have no dates relating to this or their births. Many Irish records were lost when record offices were burned down during a later period of Irish history. We do however have the story passed down to my sister Irene by mother, telling her daughter Irene that she knew that her Grandfather "Patsy" Burke fell whilst acting as a steeplejack and as a result was killed. He, she said, had a real Old Irish funeral with all their relatives and friends invited to attend a drinking party to wish him farewell, whilst "Patsy" stood, resplendent in Sunday suit propped up inside his coffin against one corner. I am sure that the area the Burkes were associated with was County Cork, but unfortunately I have no addresses.

Dad was now residing at 69 Bridge St, Mile End, Old Town, with Harriet virtually on his doorstep at 38 Single Street of the same parish, so I guess William Henry and Sophia must have moved from 18 Thomas Street, Stepney.

However after Dad and Harriet wed they moved to Cordown Road, Bow. Then to two addresses in Malmesbury Road, Bow, before finally finishing up at 62 Usher Road, Bow. This would not have been a long journey for both the Boroughs of Stepney and Bow are quite close to one another. There is one big difference however: if you resided in Stepney you were strangely enough within earshot of Bow Bells which was not the case if you lived in Bow, and it was this fact that definitely made you a Cockney of London Town. All you needed was to have been born within the sound of Bow Bells; a requirement that all Cockneys are proud of, but it was certainly not the wealthiest area to be born into at the turn of the century. I have been given to understand that 62 Usher Road became the home of Grandfather William Henry and Grandmother Sophia during WWI.

Dad was a very upright, tall, quite handsome, athletic man, as many of his photographs portray. Unfortunately I have been unable to find any early pictures of my mother, Harriet, but those I possess show a very proud straight-backed attractive woman. I can so easily imagine father being completely bowled over by this fiery, vivacious, seventeen-year-old colleen using all her wiles to woo him. More is the pity that I was never able to know her for sadly the year I was born, so Mother died. This was exactly 100 years from the birth of my great-grandfather who was Sophia's father, William Webb. The family tell me that mother had needed to go into hospital with a suspected appendicitis, and whilst there they took me to see her so that she might hold me, her new nine-month-old son, murmuring sweet nothings as gently she rocked me in her arms.

Following my visit tragedy struck the very next day as mother was rushed into emergency surgery for peritonitis, with a "burst appendix", and at the young age of thirty-nine she died. It was the 7th of December 1927.

The century of more rapid progress was now upon us, and the first child born into it was Harriet Florence. However as she grew up and became a young lady with courtship on her mind she was strong willed enough to insist on being called Cecilia, which swiftly became shortened to Ciss! Ciss has already been mentioned in my writing and with the loss of mother would play a big part in my life. The shortened version of Harriet was Hetty and it became a name Ciss could not wait to discard, but she never officially changed it leaving her with the irony of having to use Harriet whenever official papers needed her signature, such as marriage records and cheque payments.

My eldest sister was born twenty-one years before me on the 29th June 1906. There seems little doubt that our fiery Irish colleen was heavily

THE WAY WE WERE

pregnant with her daughter at seventeen and well before marrying Dad.

This year was marked in April, the nineteenth to be exact by the San Francisco earthquake. A thousand people perished in this catastrophe which also created a firestorm, reducing many buildings to ashes.

By 1908 Harriet had given birth to a son, John George, naturally, with a further daughter on the 5th June 1913, Elsie Lillian Susan. Elsie had actually been a twin of a boy, Bertie Edwin, named after Dad's younger brother, of whom I know little; but sadly this twin died at birth.

By now the streets of London were beginning to encompass a few of the new motorised vehicles as gradually after thousands of years the horse began to be replaced. Railway journeys were also becoming the norm enabling people's horizons to widen.

In 1907 the first dreadnought battleship sailed from Gibraltar at a speed of seventeen knots, and the government had ordered three more. It was actually discussed in Parliament to construct a railway tunnel under the channel, but the proposal was defeated as a threat to national security. It all went to show how the twentieth century was picking up speed, and to cap it all the first heavier-than-air craft flew a closed circuit round a field near Paris, bringing Henri Farman the French aviator a coveted £5000 prize. It had been only three years earlier that the American army chiefs had discarded the idea of utilising the Wright brothers plane as irrelevant.

New discoveries began taking place almost daily as life started to gather apace; we had gone through the industrial revolution, it's true, but people's lives had changed very little other than now working more in factory areas as opposed to rural.

Wireless had been invented but as yet was not universal, one discovery at the end of 1909 brought that possibility nearer when a Belgian chemist accidentally discovered the formula for making Bakelite whilst searching for a substitute for shellac. The mixture of phenol and formaldehyde would be poured over a mould and when it set could withstand great heat, and being a good insulator of electricity became ideal for the various components needed to build radio receivers.

In 1910 the thoughts of war were already beginning to occupy some peoples minds, for in February it was stated that horses for the armed services in the event of hostilities would need to number 170,000 and be renewed by that number every six months. It was pointed out that Germany and Austria spent £200,000 each annually on horse breeding whilst Britain spent less than £5,000.

I mention these facts to give some indication of daily news brought to young John and Hetty as steadfastly they set about bringing up their young family.

Without a doubt the East End of London where they resided was one of the poorest areas imaginable, but despite this and given the maxim that what you have never known you do not miss they enjoyed a happy existence. Neighbourliness was a very important part of their life, where everyone within your street or road knew everyone else. Communal baths in Roman Road witnessed the daily scenes of adults carrying towels and soaps in order to cleanse themselves, whilst the children shared the tin bath in front of the coal fire or hob in the kitchen, eldest first, youngest last; toilets were always nearest the small garden area, and sometimes completely separate from the main building. In wintertime it was the venue to escape from as quickly as possible, and more often than not toilet rolls were small squares of old newspaper stacked into a pad or placed on a spike.

In May 1910 King Edward VII died and King George V succeeded to the throne, and then in August of the same year Florence Nightingale, our lady with the lamp, finally passed away at the age of ninety-one.

It was then on April the fifteenth 1912 that more than fifteen hundred passengers out of a total of two thousand three hundred and forty perished in the terrible disaster that befell Great Britain's "unsinkable" liner, the newly built *Titanic*.

The shock and disbelief that swept across the nation were overwhelming, leaving many questions to be answered in Parliament, such as: How was it that White Star's managing director won reprieve in the first lifeboat, and who of those rescued was responsible for pushing other poor souls back into the icy waters? And why in god's name, despite dire warnings of iceberg activity, was *Titanic* sailing at full speed?

These and other questions would cause this tragedy to reverberate down the century.

My second eldest sister Elsie was born on the 5th June 1913, one day after one of the suffragettes, a certain Emily Davison, threw herself under the King's horse Anmer and suffered fatal injuries at the Derby races.

Also in August concern was mounting over the number of fatalities being caused by motorised buses, even though the speed limit around Hyde Park Corner was limited to ten mph.

THE WAY WE WERE

Elsie was barely a year old when on June 28th 1914 the Archduke of Austria, Franz Ferdinand, and his wife the Duchess of Hohenburg, were both gunned down and killed as their open car slowed to negotiate a corner whilst visiting Serbia.

As Austria and Serbia glared at one-another over this tragic act by one man, assassin Gavrilo Princip, the whole of Europe braced itself for the start of the Great War.

The declaration of war against Germany took place on August the 4th and almost immediately Dad joined the ranks of the King's Royal Rifles.

Because of my date of birth and separation from the rest of the family during most of my young life I had very little opportunity to learn of Dad's involvement in war over these four terrible years.

In later life I did learn that like many men who took part in those awful battles, he suffered severely from shell shock and succumbed to attack by gas. Harriet, to keep body and soul together, became, apart from mother to two daughters and one son, a postwoman, having to carry the heavy canvas bag of mail on foot from door to door.

It must have been a traumatic time with so many Ministry letters arriving telling of lost ones. And how awful to wonder each day whether you might be the recipient of the next one.

Dad eventually came home on leave in the September of 1916, I know this because sister Irene Blanche Sophia was born on June the 5th 1917, and coincidentally the same date as Elsie four years earlier. It was to be Irene's eldest daughter Maureen, when giving birth in turn to her daughter in the year 1990, who would name her newborn child Harriet and thus perpetuate our mother's name.

It was now that mother felt overwhelmed having to cope with a newborn child and look after an eleven-year-old, nine-year-old and four-year-old at the same time, although to be fair eleven-year-old Harriet (Ciss) was now helping her mum with most of the daily chores as well as attending school and learning to play the piano, something that would stand her in good stead when she began accompanying the silent movies at the local cinema. So Mum gave up her heavy tiring job and at William Henry and Sophia's insistence moved into 62 Usher Road so they might all the more help young Harriet and reduce her cost of living at the same time.

On June 14th, nine days after the birth of my sister Irene, the Germans launched a raid against the East End using aircraft for the first time. They had previously used Zeppelin airships which were a bigger target to hit. This time approximately fifteen aircraft dropped bombs for about fifteen minutes, with one bomb hitting a school and killing ten children. Another hit a railway station and damaged a train.

All this time people were climbing on roofs or anywhere to get a better view of proceedings. Later, government officials wondered if sirens or hooters should be sounded to warn the public of possible danger, but it was thought this may lead to more chaos with the warnings used as an excuse to vacate their place of work. Such was the thinking of those days! The family was to remain at Usher Road until after the Second World War.

Dad finally returned in one piece, "Thank God", in November 1918, not having seen his latest daughter for eighteen months, just one of the fortunate few to survive four years of the most horrendous wars ever fought.

It had been a war to end all wars, but less than twenty-one years later it was to start all over again. It was also to be a homecoming for heroes, and if ever there was a hero, surely Dad was, but his home and family would be hard to support as civilian work became more and more difficult to find. The best he could do was as an Usher in the new entertainment of silent films. With the advent of this American import cinemas began sprouting all over the country, and would eventually see off the popular music hall as the poor man's pastime.

Revolution was rife in Germany and still the main preoccupation in Russia as the ordinary populace let fly with their frustrations towards pompous overlords.

Only in Great Britain were we prepared to accept our lot with reasonable grace, and get on with the task of keeping body and soul together.

It was Great Britain that achieved the first Atlantic flight from America when Alcock and Brown landed their Vickers Vimy biplane in a bog near the Irish coast in June 1919. When my wife Mary and I visited southern Ireland in the 1980s we saw the actual site marked with a monument to the two aviators. Then almost a week later the German skeleton crews left aboard their armistice impounded ships at Scapa Flow in the Orkneys, pulled the sea-cocks and scuttled all seventy of them. I guess they lay there still on the bottom, even today!

On April the fourteenth 1920 my second eldest brother was born, destined to become one of the most loved and admired members of our clan. Mum and Dad named him Leonard Alfred.

THE WAY WE WERE

Ciss was now nearly fourteen years old and to all intents and purposes a young woman, having to help Mum do all the chores and assisting with the growing family. Our eldest brother John was now twelve, Elsie seven and Irene three, and of course newly born Leonard.

This is how the family continued, Dad remaining as an Usher, and as soon as possible after giving birth to Len, Harriet our mum becoming cashier at the same cinema.

Life for the richer set gradually took on the aspect, which would become known as the roaring twenties, as a strong American influence began to take hold. But for Mum and Dad this period would become a daily slog to make ends meet.

It was a time of the miners' strike, of government controls against food hoarding and bloody conflicts in Ireland involving the IRA, which at the time of writing is, believe it or not, although not actually shedding blood, still trying to be resolved.

By February 1921 many ex-servicemen were reduced to hawking wares in the streets. Unemployment stood at over one million, which was a shocking statistic for the times, and unemployment benefit was a new 75p a week for men and 60p for women.

In America in May this year of 1921 concerns had been expressed about the rising hems of womens' skirts and the heavier use of make-up, it tended, so the authorities argued, to reduce the moral standards of the day. This sentiment was probably unjustified then, but here over eighty years later I personally think there is a strong element of truth in that thinking when associated with current customs.

Seaside postcards of the time showed family outings in the new open-topped Charabancs as everyone who could journeyed to the coast. On August 1st that year it became the fiftieth anniversary of the Bank Holiday. Now so many people who had been unable to travel and enjoy themselves because of war and lack of the means to move around, crammed steam trains and the advancing development of motorised transports, that places like Blackpool began displaying signs saying "Town Full".

My sisters told of how the poor from the East End "which included our family" would all go down to the Kent hop-fields, and spend a fortnight picking hops, which they were paid a few shillings for, and live in wooden huts especially built for them. Everyone thoroughly enjoyed themselves and used to look forward to the annual event, meeting up with old friends and everybody's kids having a high old time of it!

Ciss had left school now, as we all eventually would, at the responsible and worldly-wise age of fourteen years, and apart from carrying out gainful employment, kept herself busy helping Mum with all the housework and looking after younger brothers and sisters. She still continued her piano practice, with Brother John taking up violin lessons. So despite a constant lack of money, Mum and Dad still found the where-with-all to encourage their kids in the arts.

Soon it would become a family ritual to have a singsong while Ciss and John performed a duet. This would continue for many years and even after both were married they would meet on occasion for a musical evening whilst we watched and listened.

Before long Ciss was accompanying the silent movies, no doubt encouraged and helped by both our cinema-working parents. Having to watch the film from way down near the front and literally thump the heavy chords when the villain approached and then play lightly over the keys as the heroin escaped. It was the era of Charlie Chaplin and Rudolph Valentino, and when Charlie returned to London, the city of his birth, in September 1921, the crowds went wild.

This was also the decade of dictatorships, When Mussolini first started to enter the stage, his Fascist party managed to get thirty-five of its followers elected to the Italian Parliament. Communication proper had finally arrived, when in November 1922 the newly formed BBC began a regular news broadcast, although most listeners would have to use headphones, as speakers as we know them had yet to be produced.

On the 27th January 1923 Adolf Hitler the ex-corporal now leading the National Socialist Party in Germany held his first public congress showing the new crooked cross emblem of the swastika, a symbol of an ancient eastern device.

Oblivious to all these ominous signs, the new craze in America was dancing until you drop for high prize money; the problem was taxing American legal minds as couples were severely injuring themselves. In Cleveland one female contestant, whose ankles had swollen to twice their size, had worn out five male partners, while others had been dancing non-stop for as much as fifty-three hours before being stopped by police.

Young brother Len had reached the age of nearly three and a half, when there was a terrible earthquake in Japan which killed upwards of 300,000

THE WAY WE WERE

people in Tokyo and Yokohama, leaving a further two and half million homeless in September of that year. Ex-corporal Adolf Hitler was also arrested on November 11th at a village called Essing, after leading a failed coup to overthrow the German Government.

The collapse of the German currency was also helping to fuel the sympathy surrounding Hitler and his followers. The price of a loaf of bread had reached two billion marks!

On 21st January 1924 Lenin the great Russian revolutionary died, and within the dictates of his testaments he declared Stalin unworthy as a successor. It would become ironic therefore that Stalin the dictator should slaughter millions whilst holding onto power.

Meanwhile on April fools day of that same year, Hitler received a timid slap on the wrist by German judges, when he was sentenced to five years in prison for high treason, but told he could be paroled after six months.

The whole direction of European dictatorships would have a lasting effect on our country, our family and particularly brother Len as he approached his fourth birthday.

By the end of 1925 radios had become so popular there were now about ten million Households that possessed them. The BBC stressed that all their announcers were definitely trained in the correct use and pronunciation of the English tongue.

Since the harnessing of electricity the country had been trying to get to grips with its distribution, and it was to this end on January the 15th 1926 that the Prime Minister, Stanley Baldwin announced the linking of a national grid. At 62 Usher Road though, gas lighting would remain the norm for a few more years yet.

By Christmas 1926, Mother had been carrying me for six months or so and twenty-year-old Ciss was becoming more like a mum, taking responsibility for discipline within the family. Brother John, now eighteen, had started work as a fitter of roof tiles, having to clamber around and over rooftops, but still setting off to work in a suit and bowler hat to avoid giving the impression of one who laboured with his hands. Thirteen-year-old Elsie had become the high spirited one quite prepared to answer her elder sister back if she thought it warranted it. A somewhat more docile nine-year-old Irene was less of a handful, whilst six-year-old Leonard began to feel the freedom of his feet.

Usher Road sloped down slightly from the main thoroughfare Roman Road, and ran on for some 300 yards. Each house was joined to the next in a string of two story yellow bricked terraced houses. The street as I remember did not appear to be unduly narrow, with reasonable sized paving stone footpaths either side and a further set of similarly terraced houses opposite. One thing you could always rely on was plenty of horse manure, meaning one of the off-springs duties was to retrieve said droppings to propagate Dad's roses if nothing else.

Fronting each house was a very small paved area no more than two paces deep cordoned off in turn from the pavement and the adjoining neighbour by an iron railing. Iron railings seemed to be very popular and most streets in and around where we lived seemed to be full of them.

After entering our front door you were confronted by a dark passage, with perhaps four steps in on the left a fairly steep set of stairs leading to an upper landing, also in virtual darkness.

The first door to the right from the hall led into the front room, with its stone-constructed bay window facing Usher Road. This was the parlour, and only to be used on Sundays and high holidays, such as Christmas. Here Ciss had her piano, and John could practise his violin. Unfortunately Dad could not withstand the strident tones of Brother John's practising, for which John never forgave him; Dad apparently also fiercely criticised his son's snobbishness in going to work in a suit and having to change when arriving. In fairness to John he had initially trained as a draughtsman, but apprenticeships in those days for these professions were poorly paid. He finally turned to the more lucrative building trade, being forced to dress accordingly, therefore I do not think my brother acted out of snobbishness, I rather admire him for being smartly dressed whenever he could. I always remember him as totally pristine, a worthy trait!

To continue through the house, the next door on the right enclosed the dining room, with one stone-clad flat window overlooking a small paved area, with our also stone-clad kitchen window on the left, and wooden boundary fence on the right. This narrow section opened out to quite a decent sized garden beyond, complete with large trees and low boundary stone wall standing between our neighbours rear garden and us. As opposed to the upright piano, settee and armchairs of the front room, the dining room was modestly furnished with just long wooden table and chairs and one sideboard.

Straight ahead at the end of the passage was the door leading to the kitchen. Here on the left as you entered built into a recess stood a black coal-burning range, nothing like a modern Aga of course. You fed the Range by

THE WAY WE WERE

lifting circular cast iron lids that possessed recesses complete with straddling bar. This was achieved by placing a cast iron lever under the bar of the recess and levering upwards to display the fiery embers to which you could then add more coal. You could also set the lid to one side and place a heavy iron kettle immediately over the hole to thus heat water quicker. The oven was a large black door, which you opened by using the same lever to raise a heavy catch. It never paid to touch anything by hand! This masterpiece of ingenuity was meticulously black-leaded every day, as was the front step continuously white-washed to uphold the pride within the household.

Either side of the range and set into shallower recess's stood cupboards for food and china. Above the range and facing more forward into the room, if memory serves me correctly, was a narrow shelf holding various ornaments with a big clock, which you wound each and every day, lodged at the centre.

Opposite the range stood a large wooden table, which invariably if there was no more than four or five eating at a time, would serve as a dining table to save disturbing the tidiness of Cissy's dining room.

A further door beyond the end of the kitchen invariably left open, lead to our washroom, with a big butler sink to the right, and next to that a large tub for heating and washing clothes etc.

Beyond this again lay the coalhouse, where once a week the coalman, having traversed through our dark hall into the kitchen and past the washhouse, would deposit two or three hundredweight of coal, whilst Ciss or Mum fussed over the possible mess created. Life was never easy!

Everything had to be transported this way to get to the rear of the house, as no other access was possible. The loo could only be reached by going into the garden through a door adjacent the coalhouse, and entering it via another plain, latch only, wooden door, no locks, to the left. It seems to dwell in my mind that all these doors were painted brown, but I believe we did merit wallpaper on the interior walls of kitchen, hall, living and bedrooms. Walls to washroom, toilet etc. would be whitewashed.

Gas lamps were provided in the kitchen and scullery/washhouse, and living rooms, but I do not recall any in the hall, stairway, or landing or the loo come to that! which you invariably frequented in total darkness, unless cupping a candle in both hands to save being blown out by the wind!

Everybody washed either at the butler sink in the washhouse, or as was often the case with the likes of Ciss and Mum in a specially prepared bowl in their bedrooms.

William S. Smith

During this period our eldest sister met up with a bit of a rough diamond. Now Ciss had a reputation for being pretty fastidious in most things, always looking neat and clean and expecting everything around her to exude the same attributes. So it came as a bit of a shock when she took up with Jack, because he was very much the opposite, delving into oily mechanics, which initially, meant Ciss having to contend with Jack's other love, motorbikes!

His family resided at a close London Borough called Plaistow. It consisted of his mum and dad and four other brothers. Jack being the second eldest of the five and the only one at that time involved in mechanics, which for obvious reasons was still very much in its infancy.

How she and Jack met I am not sure, it could quite conceivably have been through the auspices of the cinema. But Ciss certainly became one of the few girls of the period to be riding pillion, a position she more than once vacated when Jack's enthusiasm got the better of him. Not only thrown from the pillion, but a sidecar as well when her beloved failed to negotiate a bend at the bottom of a steep hill.

Jack I am afraid was a bit of a daredevil, though his driving skills outshone most peoples, as I was to testify in later life.

He would play a big part in my upbringing, and because of it would inevitably affect my children and in turn theirs too.

This was the year of the General Strike, when workers everywhere came out in support of the miners, when open-topped buses would be seen crowding the London streets, and you could watch the conductor climbing up and down the winding stair protruding at the back of the bus, unprotected from all weathers. When Rudolph Valentino died at the age of thirty-one, due primarily to a ruptured appendix coupled with a complicated gastric ulcer. That Gertrude Ederle a nineteen-year-old New Yorker swam the English Channel in the record time of fourteen hours thirty-one minutes. And England regained the Ashes from Australia for the first time in fourteen years. How strange that Harry Houdini should also succumb to a burst appendix, on the 31st October 1926.

Not only was the new century expanding and accelerating at discovering new ideas, but so also was everything gathering momentum on the ground and in the air. By February 4th 1927 Malcolm Campbell had successfully broken his own land speed record in his car Bluebird for the third time, reaching 174.224 mph on the Pendine Sands of Carmarthen, in Wales. Yet before I was two weeks old Major Henry Segrave had increased this speed to

THE WAY WE WERE

203.841 at Daytona Beach, Florida. At the time the car remained unnamed, but would later become known as the Golden Arrow. Then just over two months after my birth Lindbergh touched down at Le Bourget airport near Paris on the 21st May, as the first man to fly solo non-stop from New York.

Usher Road was more than just a road; it was a community, where everyone knew everybody else. Hardly ever was a front door locked, and in fair weather most of them remained open. Most families consisted of five or six children, but because of the Great War many had suffered terrible losses, sometimes fathers, sometimes sons, and sometimes both.

But for the most part our neighbour's were a happy lot. At evening time hardly any traffic entered the road which, despite nearby parks and open areas became, a children's playground. For the older ones there were the roller skating rinks, evening cinema or swimming baths. But many of the up to twelve-year-olds would congregate in the road to test their home made scooters, fashioned from odd pieces of flat wood and cast-off roller skate wheels gleaned from the local rink. Slices of broom handle were lashed to upright stakes which in turn slotted through the foot platform to produce a swivel action acted as steerage. They would line up across the road and scoot like mad down hill with no brakes to stop them.

The only obstacles might be the odd vendor's cart parked at the kerbside.

Girls would be chalking the pavements to claim territory for their game of hopscotch whilst others would be skipping as fast as they could twist their ropes. Younger lads would hold marbles tournaments all along the gutter, following the gradual downward slope of Usher Road.

When they went to school no one would bat an eye when some of the more adventurous lads ran and grabbed the tailboards of passing lorries to gain a lift to the classroom. Len became adept at this. Tall fatherly figures of policemen patrolling their beat would sometimes admonish the young tearaways; perhaps taking them by the ear and depositing the miscreants at the school gates, extolling a dire warning against such behaviour in the future. It represented a hands-on method of discipline, which worked extremely well and taught each and every one of us a salutary lesson in how life should be conducted. All such practices have now disappeared, which is one advance seen as a backward step by my generation!

Another passion for boys in particular was building carts from orange boxes and old pram wheels. A long plank supported the box seat at the back and a swivelling piece of wood with a smaller wheel each side acted as front steering. The idea was you sat on the box with one foot pressed against each side of the front swivel which in turn had a continuous piece of rope running from one stub axle through your hands and to the next stub axle, this you held onto tightly. So by pushing with your feet and pulling with your hands you could steer very accurately indeed. Other boys would act as pushers and god help you if you didn't keep a decent straight line, as these contraptions could do a barrel roll in the wink of an eye! One or two of the more clever lads would fit makeshift brakes operated by a lever on one side of the crate. These could work after a fashion, but it meant trying to steer with one hand as you reached for your safety handle, a somewhat dextrous manoeuvre!

It can easily be seen that life was very innovative and very tough, no Nanny State held your hand or interfered with your god given right to injure yourself.

By now Dad had managed to get himself accepted as a Greater London Council employee, it may not have been over-glamorous but it gave surer security and pension rights, which meant an awful lot in those days. It was definitely a step up the ladder.

The description was Handyman/Gardener, which in essence involved looking after the grounds and boilers of a children's home. Today they would probably call him a Thermal Heating Engineer and Ground Artisan. In any event he maintained his position as usher at the local cinema each evening.

With twenty-one-year-old Ciss and nineteen-year-old brother John working, plus fourteen-year-old Elsie about to leave school and contribute towards her keep, life for our household began to get a little easier.

Children at the Greater London Orphanage began calling Dad by the nickname Pop! It was an endearment that was to stick with him until his passing at the age of ninety-four; sometimes it would be Ginger Pop to reflect his mop of ginger hair. Despite his various occupations, including the growing of most of the children's home's vegetables, he never forgot his training as a pastry cook, and not only ours, but most of our neighbours' birthday and other anniversary cakes were made and iced by Pop. You can imagine how much input dear old Pop would have had on all those orphaned kids birthdays!

The only bit of news I can find on the day I was born involved a possible Mexican revolution announced on 18th March 1927 owing to hostility towards their government's anti-clerical policies. But a much greater blow did occur on the tenth when the Bavarian government lifted its ban on Hitler speaking in public.

THE WAY WE WERE

On October 6th 1927 the first talking movie made its debut starring Al Jolson in *The Jazz Singer*, and for Ciss the writing was on the wall for her cinema piano accompaniments. But it wasn't going to be just Ciss's life that was about to change because before Christmas arrived poor Harriet, our dear mother, passed away in hospital when her appendicitis turned dramatically to peritonitis.

William S. Smith

1898. Mother Harriet Horne and Irish family. County Cork.

*1914. John Smith.
Portrait World War I, age 32.*

THE WAY WE WERE

1916. Possibly my aunt Florrie's wedding.

*1920! Portrait.
Grandfather, William Henry.*

William S. Smith

*1920! Harriet.
Cameo portrait.*

*1923. Ciss at 17 years,
with Harriet 35 years.*

THE WAY WE WERE

1920!
Ciss with William Henry.

1926. Ciss 20 years with 19-year-old brother John.

Growing up in the Thirties

Initially Ciss had to act as mum, life had become hard again, and it didn't help being saddled with a baby brother. Dad still needed to continue working as much as ever, meaning my eldest sister, although remaining gainfully employed, had to look after and prepare meals for all of us. It was a tough task. My other sisters would strongly argue that they did their fair share, which I am sure they did, but my earliest recollections were of terrible rows between fiery Elsie and authoritative Ciss. It cannot be easy taking up the role of mother and expecting your brothers and sisters to accept obedience.

I am not suggesting I remembered such episodes from the age of nine months, these images must stem from a later age when I was transported from time to time back to 62 Usher Road, but before Ciss was married, so I could have been no older than four.

Being very young and impressionable, I guess these traumas were exaggerated in my little mind. In any event with Ciss courting quite strongly now, and even Brother John walking out with one of four sisters called Ivy, the situation demanded a resolution for yours truly. It came in the guise of a family friend who was prepared to take me under her wing and care for me alongside her very young daughter.

Where I lived I am unable to substantiate, I can only say that I vividly recollect playing within a very small paved back garden, if you could describe it as such, for I have no recollection of flowers or borders. This allowed me to enjoy steering my tiny red pedal car in tight circles as chubby legs swept furiously back and forth, without actually damaging anything.

When glancing to one side during these gyrations all I could see was a high red brick wall, on top of which thundered every so often a steam train pulling a dozen carriages. On the other side lay the bane of my tiny existence! The outdoor loo. I say the bane because not only was it cold and uncomfortable, I seem to remember having to spend a lot of time there owing to my inability to perform correct bodily functions to satisfy my surrogate mother.

THE WAY WE WERE

In all fairness to the woman [whose name I have since learned could have been Henrietta Stringer as that is the name used by Brother Johns wife Ivy when alluding to my mother], I must have been a frustrating child, especially when she hadn't given birth to me, so didn't really deserve such agony's, bless her!

I do not recall her daughter but as there is a photograph showing quite clearly the two of us laughing together, not only was she real but obviously good company too. In this particular shot one can also see the strong influence of Al Jolson when he sang Sonny Boy to a youngster on his knee in his latest movie, showing the upside down pudding basin haircut that had then been thrust upon me to emulate the films young star. Here I would remain until approximately the age of four or five.

During this period the world had moved on, including part of my family.

In August 1928 one of the biggest jokes of history took place when Britain and fourteen other nations signed a Treaty outlawing war, Germany being the first to sign.

The age of the private car was beginning to make its impact when in November 1928 a government white paper showed that there had been 133,943 road accidents in the year of my birth, and 5329 deaths.

The legendary Marshall of Dodge City, Wyatt Earp, died in his sleep on January 13th 1929 age eighty years. And the worst Gangland killing in Chicago took place on Valentine's Day the same year, when seven members of Al Capone's mob were gunned down by sub-machine guns.

In June that year proof was shown of the possibility of colour television, but any practical application was a long way off, when it was discovered the size of the image was no bigger than a postage stamp.

Another air milestone was breached when Germany's airship, the mighty *Graf Zeppelin* girdled the Earth in twenty-one days, seven hours and twenty-six minutes. She carried thirty-seven crew and sixteen passengers, and made only three stops in her 19,500 mile voyage.

By Sept 7th Great Britain had won the Schneider Trophy for the third time in succession with a speed in excess of 300 mph and became the outright owner of the Trophy.

Then on 24th October came the great Wall Street crash where some individuals actually threw themselves from skyscrapers unable to endure their disastrous losses.

As the bells chimed in the New Year of 1930 Mahatma Gandhi

proposed complete independence from British rule for India, which was overwhelmingly passed by the All India National Congress the following day.

The world was changing as it had never changed before. I have stolen some writings from a magazine I read in the year 2000, just to give some idea of the gathering pace of change. It declares the unknown factors that applied to those born before 1940; obviously these can apply in even greater measure to those born before 1930!

We were born before television, before penicillin, polio shots, frozen foods, Xerox, contact lenses, videos and the pill. We were before radar, credit cards, split atoms, laser beams and ballpoint pens, before dishwashers, tumble dryers, electric blankets, air conditioners, drip dry clothes, central heating and before man walked on the moon.

We got married first and then lived together (how quaint can you be!). We thought fast food was what you ate in Lent, a "Big Mac" was an oversized raincoat and "crumpet" we had for tea. We existed before househusbands, computer dating, and "sheltered accommodation" was where you waited for a bus.

We were before day-care centres, group homes and disposable nappies. We never heard of FM radio, tape decks, artificial hearts, word processors, or young men wearing earrings. For us "time sharing" meant togetherness, a "chip" was a piece of wood or fried potato, "hardware" meant nuts and bolts and "software" wasn't a word.

Before 1940 "Made in Japan" meant junk, the term "making out" referred to how you did in your exams, "stud" was something that fastened a collar to a shirt and "going all the way" meant staying on a double-decker bus to the terminus. In our day, cigarette smoking was "fashionable", "grass" was mown, "coke" was kept in the coal-house, a "joint" was a piece of meat you ate on Sundays and "pot" was something you cooked in. Rock music was a fond mother's lullaby, "Eldorado" was an ice-cream, a "gay person" was the life and soul of the party, while "aids" just meant beauty treatment or help for someone in trouble.

I hope for the sake of our children and grandchildren Mary and I did adapt over the years to these remarkable changes. Previous generations changed so slowly, that very often people saw scant difference between their birth and death, apart from maybe just one or two innovations, such as the advent of steam railway, or perhaps when gas lighting first became available.

THE WAY WE WERE

Suddenly as the twentieth century progressed everything began to gather pace and you became swept along with it.

Brother John was the first to marry, after a short engagement, walking young Ivy down the aisle on the 15th February 1930. This Christmas, 2003, Mary and I received a Christmas card from her declaring that although somewhat frail she had reached a venerable ninety-four, seventy-three years since she wed John at the tender age of twenty-one. Poor Ivy has had to survive widowhood for thirty-seven years after losing her beloved husband at the age of only fifty-eight in 1966.

I am unsure of Ivy's family, but I do recall her three sisters, Maud, Maisie and Vera because they more or less fell in love with my swashbuckling brother Len, who became a Spitfire pilot.

John and Ivy had three children, a daughter Peggy, the eldest, then two sons, Rodney and Raymond.

Brother John himself became a very accomplished musician able to not only play the Violin, but Piano, Clarinet and Saxophone as well. Another trait that seemed to permeate consistently through the Smith dynasty was the ability to draw reasonably well, at which John excelled, and fast catching up was brother Len. After WWII in which he served in the RAF as a ground technician, he promptly formed a dance band and at the same time secured himself a position within White Horse Whiskey Distillery, London. In this he was helped by one of his sisters-in-law, Maud, being the one who obtained a job for him as store-man, a foot on the rung from which John eventually rose to become manager.

Indeed it is my niece Peggy's humble opinion that because her dad portrayed such a gentle kindly soul, that it was the severe cut and thrust of business that undermined his health at such a young age! It has often been stated that the villain of life, "cancer", lies dormant in all of us just waiting for the right catalyst to set it free. So it was with Brother John.

In its wisdom the Government Housing Committee decided about this time to allow Ribbon Development to take place outside the London area. This meant the swallowing up of green land with fingers of roads and new housing stretching outwards from the capital in various directions. One of these creeping encroachments headed in a north-easterly direction towards the villages of Romford and Hornchurch within the County of Essex.

After Ciss and Jack tied the knot in the summer of 1931 they headed out to Romford, and there in a lovely tree-lined avenue Jack put down a small

William S. Smith

deposit to secure the new and only property in Norwood Avenue that had sufficient space alongside it to house a garage. At the time other brand new attached houses cost the princely sum of £500. In Ciss and Jack's case, their semi-detached property with this added feature cost £600.

It would be during this period that I found myself transferred from my temporary home with one garden wall acting as a railway viaduct, to live with and be brought up by Jack's mum and dad. Here I would share a room with his youngest brother Frank, who would have been about six, and approximately one-year-older than I.

I have fond memories of Jack's kindly father whom we all seemed to also call Pop! His profession was a salesman for a prestigious wholesaler called Lovell & Christmas. I remember he was the proud owner of his own car. Whether this was supplied by his company or not, I do not know, but each evening this chubby faced mustachioed man would sit at the head of a long scrubbed wooden table in the big kitchen and fill out his order books. Once again I remember the big iron range alongside one wall where his wife, the matriarch of the house, we called Ma, would be forever busy. Other people would couple her married name, referring to her as Ma Rouse!

The house was much larger than our one in Usher Road and although I cannot recall the actual address other than it was in the Borough of Plaistow, I do remember it being an end house. This allowed it to contain a large piece of wooded ground running down its left-hand side and round the back. All this to us kids seemed like a small forest, which equated to heaven when playing cowboys and Indians.

Just to one side of the kitchen stood a fairly large annex, and in here chained by one foot to a five foot high perch was Pop's cockatoo. Beneath him the floor was littered with sunflower seeds. Constantly this noisy bird would tack from one side of his perch to the other; I think he used to utter the occasional word between picking up seeds from his tray and holding onto them with one foot whilst he proceeded to remove the husk with his vicious looking beak.

Wending one's way through the woods round the side of the big three story house you would suddenly come across a greenhouse, which would be full of growing tomato plants, amongst others. Jack's grandfather seemed to be the keeper of these, and that's all I ever knew him as, "Grandfather Rouse", a nice old boy, slightly built, clean shaven with strong hands and sinews, at one time a master builder, and I believe before that a blacksmith

THE WAY WE WERE

and farrier. One of the treasured memories of him was when he built a switch-backed decorative wall to edge off the front garden of 86 Norwood Ave. Another task Jack asked of him was to chip off pronounced corrugated sections from a concrete wall Jack had built between his newly constructed garage and the next door boundary, having used corrugated sheeting as shuttering.

His neighbour, a certain Mr Winch, objected strongly to Jack's arbitrary action declaring that each corrugation protruded into his territory by all of one-inch. It meant this encroachment had to be removed by poor old Granddad painstakingly smoothing out these waves. A few years later when the Rouse family had acquired holiday land at a place called Stone on the river Blackwater, some thirty-six miles away, it was not unusual to see Jack's Grandfather peddling there on his three wheeled bike.

Right at the top of the house was Jack's eldest brother Ted's room. It was like a large attic, where I only remember venturing just the once. What greeted me was a mystery display of wires, valves, knobs and dials. Ted it transpired when I was old enough to understand was a radio ham, and someone who could actually send messages over the airways. He could also send signals right across the country using Morse code. Needless to say his domain became strictly out of bounds!

Jack's dad, being the owner of the freehold, had brought the house more up to date by having electricity installed, so we did not have to constantly ignite mantels and put them out again, not withstanding the superior light we enjoyed. Also just past the outside loo he had erected an addition to house a bath; a big white affair that stood high on its feet, but how we got hot water into it I cannot recall!

Frank and I slept on the first floor in our own room, also on this floor but strictly private as far as Frank and I were concerned was Pop and Ma's room, brother Bob's and brother Jim's room, and of course Grandfather's.

The downstairs was taken up apart from the kitchen and annex by a large living and dining room. Once again there was only the one loo, plus of course the scullery adjacent to the kitchen where everyone dived under cold water taps at the big butler sink unless Ma Rouse had been kind enough to us kids and boiled water on her range. Fortunately by the time Frank and I got there all others in the household had disappeared to work or whatever.

I distinctly recall spending one Christmas there, because apart from the usual sock full of apples, oranges and nuts, I can remember Frank and I each receiving one of those Russian dolls, the type that got smaller and smaller as you disembowelled them.

As 1930 progressed so did Hitler's Nazi Party, by September the National Socialists had increased their representation in the Reichstag ninefold, from twelve deputies to 107, and become the second largest party in Germany. This meant the Nazi vote had gone up from 800,000 in 1928 to 6,409,000.

Within one month anti-Jewish demonstrations were taking place in Berlin and chants of "down with the Jews" could be heard as stores owned by them had their windows smashed. At the same time Communists rallied against the Nazis in bitter rivalry.

That October was the month the R101 airship crashed in a fireball killing forty-four passengers.

Ghandi in India was promoting civil disobedience until complete independence was granted, but Churchill was favouring a solution put up by the Indian Princes, and decided to resign at the end of January 1931.

In February Captain Malcolm Campbell surpassed the current speed limit at Daytona Beach in America, by achieving 245 mph in poor visibility.

By May the Swiss professor Auguste Piccard with a fellow scientist had soared to 52,462 feet in a specially enclosed aluminium gondola.

At the same time in New York President Hoover opened the world's tallest building. The Empire State Building has 86 floors, and stands 1,245ft tall.

The latest census published on June 5th put the British population at 44,790,485, and showed a marked tendency for people to migrate south. Also the death toll for the 1920s was thirty percent lower than the 1900s. Progress indeed!

My second eldest sister, Elsie, had reached the age of eighteen and within a year would be married to her fiancé, Walter Faul.

Unfortunately Wally had contracted rheumatic fever as a child, and this had led to a rheumatic heart condition, something that would affect the course of his life.

For some time after they married both he and Elsie lived on at Usher Road, with their first child Derek being born in 1933. Elsie and Wal, as we came to know him, would continue to have sons, whether it was for the want of trying for a daughter I do not know, but they ended up with six fine boys. They certainly made up for Ciss who by now had discovered that she would

THE WAY WE WERE

not be able to bear children. Such a phenomenon may of course have been a fault within the Rouse protégé, as the only brother out of Jack's family of five who bore any offspring would be our radio ham, Ted.

Dear Wal, who found work at the well known pharmaceutical company May and Baker, still going to this day, finally managed to get council accommodation near this enterprise in Dagenham, not far from Romford and thereby quite near Ciss and Jack.

During WWII, although classed as unsuitable due to his disability, Wal would insist on his patriotic right to help all he could and worked hard in the Civil Defence Service. Involved in many tiring tasks such as search and rescue in the heart of London, whilst still resident at Usher Road, Bow.

After the war and only six months from the birth of their last son, Wal would succumb to the dreaded illness tuberculosis. The years were 1948/9, a tumultuous time for all the family, which I shall come to later.

By 1933 Sister Irene had reached the beautiful age of sixteen with Brother Len touching thirteen and one year from leaving school. Ciss, John and I of course no longer resided at Usher Road and Elsie had taken command with her new husband.

Hitler was now Chancellor of Germany and I was within one year or so of my next move as Ciss made final preparations to receive me. In the first instance after 86 Norwood had been purchased, John had stayed there with his young wife Ivy, until such time as they were able to acquire a new home just outside Hornchurch Aerodrome and within three miles of Romford. This home in Lancaster Drive, Hornchurch, is still in this current year 2003, the residence of ninety-four-year-old Ivy!

One of the latest biplanes, a Westland Wallace, had succeeded in flying over Mount Everest, whilst Marlene Dietrich the glamorous German actress started a new fashion for women by wearing men's clothes.

I do not recall ever experiencing visits from my brothers or sisters during my temporary home venues or from Dad come to that, but that is not to say I was forgotten. In fact at about the age of six or seven, I was being strongly discussed by all the family.

Apparently, so I was informed in later life, Ciss and Jack wanted very much to adopt me as their own. This idea being heavily contested by everybody else, it could even have been the cause of the upsets I witnessed between Ciss and Elsie.

I can quite understand Jack wishing to pursue this course. Unable to have a son of his own, if he were going to be lumbered with me, surely it would be better. Also, at one and the same time, it might avoid any undue pressure from outside, as to how I was brought up! In the end of course Jack lost and knowing how persevering my eldest sister could be, I guess he had no alternative but to accept responsibility for me purely as her baby brother.

Sister Irene had found a job at Clarnico's. This was a sweet factory, which she thoroughly enjoyed, especially when the girls were able to take some of the goodies home. Such a possibility endeared her no end to our brother Len. His final report on the 25th July 1934 from Fairfield Road School at Bow had shown him to be of honest and hard-working character with an aptitude towards sport and art including metalwork.

The sought after mode of transport was the bicycle and as soon as you started work the effort was to obtain one. Kiddie's cycles were not made as such yet and youngsters would have to borrow Mum's or their sister's because without crossbars they could ride them between the forks. Bouncing up and down on pedals below a saddle too high to reach. In many ways fortunate that traffic was reasonably scarce in side roads!

Front gardens and hallways became homes for every kind of two-wheeled machine. Locks for these were unheard of, whether they were left outside homes, shops, or even over the recreation grounds while you went off to play.

Joining a cycle club quickly became the norm and it was not unusual to see dozen's of these groups all heading out to the countryside, perhaps covering as much as 100 miles there and back in a day.

On top of this Irene also joined a walking club, where annually a race would be held from London to Southend, a distance approaching something like thirty miles. A fast walk was very difficult to accomplish, you couldn't help smiling at the gait of the walker as they swung their arms in concentration and locked their knees to avoid the disqualification of a semblance of breaking into a trot.

My sister performed well in these events, and I believe she won some trophies.

Len I know, used to cycle miles and regularly cycled to Southampton to catch the Ferry to the Isle of Wight for his annual holiday. Then proceed to encompass the entire island. This on top of swimming and roller skating, plus drawing and model making, made up most of his hobbies. At all times he seemed to possess a natural ability of rhythm and balance, couple this with

THE WAY WE WERE

a photographic memory and leaning towards art and you can see he would be a tough act to follow! But the aptitude that really had us all in stitches was when he started to copy the speech of Walt Disney's Donald Duck, something that would endear him to us and comrades alike, throughout his short life.

By 1934 President Hindenburg was dead at the age of eighty-seven and Hitler now ruled supreme. Already the ugly face of Nazism was changing the way Germans lived and eventually the rest of Europe. Hitler had decreed that in order to produce a pure Aryan Race imperfect Germans would be sterilised without course of appeal. In fact no aspect of new German law would be subject to appeal.

Before the end of 1933 he had quit the League of Nations, and at last Britain began to wake up when the government announced a reversal of their defence spending and agreed to provide the armed forces with some badly needed cash.

By the age of seven I had been firmly installed at 86 Norwood Avenue, I am sure of this by the type of school I attended. It was a junior school but had a senior school adjoining, so I would not be going anywhere else for some time.

Rush Green School stood within walking distance of number 86. If you traversed to the right after leaving the house and walked for some 100 yards to the main road, then swung sharp left you soon approached a cross roads. Here lay various shops which, quite quickly I would come to recognise as day after day even sometimes during school lunch breaks; I collected my sister's shopping requirements. I did not object to this and very soon began to build up books of coloured stamps received from various traders which, I could, come Christmas time, exchange for cash and purchase presents with.

Across this junction and some half a mile further on, past farmers' fields, stood our school. A newly built red brick building full of noisy kids milling around in the playground, and tucked behind, lovely big playing fields with wide open country beyond. It was all a far cry from Bow and Plaistow and I revelled in the wide-open spaces. Vaguely I recall attending school at Plaistow, but this must have been more like a kindergarten for all I can envisage is lying in the open on some sort of camp bed, under trees in full leaf with the sun shining through, and high railings running alongside me. There must have been a requirement for little ones to have an afternoon nap!

At Rush Green each pupil had his or her own desk with flip-up lid. All books and accoutrements needed for a full day's schoolwork lay enclosed. Seldom did we need to move, as on most occasions teachers of different subjects came to us. The only time I remember leaving class was for the playing fields or science teaching, when journey's to the lab became necessary.

Number 86 constituted a new world, now I had my own bedroom. True it was the smallest room in the house, but to be fair I was the smallest person. Called the box-room, its one window overlooked the avenue above the front door. Next to me sprouting a big upstairs bay window was Ciss and Jack's bedroom, and behind theirs another bedroom overlooking the quite large garden. The main staircase ran from the right hand side of the hallway to join the landing that swung left at the top to allow access to the three bedrooms, but if you turned right we had our dream, an indoor loo complete with hand-basin and bath! The beauty of this of course stemmed from all these new properties having built-in hot water tanks complete with electric immersions. So for the very first time we were also able to enjoy hot water straight from the taps!

The downstairs comprised the front room with bay window facing the avenue. A room once again designated as at Usher Road, for Sundays and special occasions only, housing a posh green leather suite and Ciss's upright piano. The dining room lay underneath the back bedroom, and like it, faced rearwards overlooking the garden.

Each had doorways leading off to the left as you traversed the hallway, where towards the end you finally entered the kitchen.

Here we had not only gas for cooking, but also electric light and sockets. Implanted in skirting boards these would be available to accommodate all those modern inventions gradually coming on stream, so now we could plug our new mains radio straight into any wall.

The garden stretched for about 150 feet and because of the extra space for a garage ended up the largest plot in the avenue.

But without a doubt the greatest joy was to come, for after passing through a rustic gate at the bottom of Ciss's garden you entered what I can only describe as a child's paradise. Today the vista opening before me would be sealed off, such has become the interference of the state, but fortunately for me no do-gooders had yet surfaced, and would not for at least another twenty years.

Firstly there stood a field of wild grass stretching a distance equal to the

THE WAY WE WERE

entire avenue. To my young eyes it appeared quite wide, wide enough to play any sort of game you could think of. Not that the normal games could be played, for one step into the grass and you became lost as the seeded ears sprouting from the tops of the blades closed around your head.

After wading through this wonderful forest you reached giant oaks, chestnut, ash and hawthorn trees. Thick hedges sprouted between them opening up all sorts of possibilities for places to play hide and seek. Yet beyond all this a vast area sprawled, full of lakes supporting little islands covered in vegetation, bulrushes and reeds grew in tumultuous profusion around the edges. The whole wonder must have extended to twenty acres or more, and winding throughout its entire perimeter ran a disused narrow track railway.

At intervals along this still usable track, clustered small, perhaps just four feet long, open topped v-shaped cast iron swivel bucket trucks. If you really heaved hard you could tip them to one side or the other, yet it was still possible to climb in and get shoved along without any feeling of becoming destabilised.

The whole area was actually one gigantic disused sand and ballast pit! I guess the water table must have been pretty high too, enabling lakes to form probably something to do with the local topicality. After all Romford obviously meant a ford over the river Rom!

In any event having utilised all the goodness beneath the ground for the development that had taken place for miles around, the powers that be had now vacated the whole site, and judging by the mature growth that had ensued had probably not come near nor by for some years.

Here I would grow up with other equally lucky children who happened to live on the edge of this man-made assault course. Tree climbing, building grass encampments from the tall grasses, giving one another rides on the trucks, making rafts from anything we could lay our hands on. Firing home made arrows tipped with old darts high into the air from home made bows, having to step smartly out of the way when they came whistling down again embedding themselves into the ground. Chasing butterflies as they cavorted amongst the wild flowers and watching fascinated by the angular geometry of the grasshoppers rubbing both back legs together before leaping into the undergrowth.

We created gangs and would have horrendous home-made sword fights with one another, leaping from our hidey-holes to attack rival members.

Invariably I came home with some injury or other. I remember one particular fracas when foolishly laughing during a battle; the other guy's sword stabbed me in the roof of the mouth.

At all times Ciss showed great concern, but Jack was a tough nut, and expected everybody to be likewise, not that I remember crying that much. To be fair, although he may have been a hard taskmaster, he never asked anything of anybody he wouldn't tackle himself, but then I can think of very little that he wouldn't tackle!

His job now entailed driving a Green Line coach. In the beginning he drove double decker green buses whose journeys were of shorter duration and carried more stops. But later drivers were selected to cover greater distances in single decked coaches, travelling from the centre of London to outlying districts some thirty or forty miles away. Jack was known to be able to squeeze through a gap only two inches wider than his coach.

I do remember a couple of stories about boys getting trapped in the reeds and actually ending up being drowned, which I suppose would have been avoided if the whole place had been fenced off. But then we wouldn't have grown up as tough as we were, and who knows, if our youth of that era had been constantly wrapped in cotton wool the Nazis might be ruling us today!

Fortunately for us, the authorities just asked parents to make sure their kids were aware, and we all went on leading the life of Riley.

As I approached the halfway mark to my eighth birthday, Hitler's Gauleiter of Bavaria was proudly proclaiming that the German form of life had definitely been settled for the next one thousand years!

By 1935 Mussolini was preparing to invade Abyssinia and Britain began increasing its defences to counter any German threat as Herr Hitler marched into the Saar.

Two weeks after King George V celebrated his Silver Jubilee, so it was announced the RAF was to treble in size within two years. We would need to reach 1500 aircraft to match Germany's forecast strength.

About the same time an icon of the century so far, Colonel Lawrence of Arabia was killed when swerving on his motorbike to avoid two boy cyclists.

Malcolm Campbell's Bluebird car smashed the 300 mph barrier at Bonneville Salt Flats in Utah, just as Hitler announced all Jews were to be banned from any form of public life.

By October Abyssinia had fallen and Attlee became the new leader of the Labour Party.

THE WAY WE WERE

Jack was now the proud owner of a garage alongside his home, and Grandfather Rouse was in the throes of helping him build a conservatory to the rear. Already Ciss had planted quite a few fruit trees, including two we would come to cherish. A lovely Victorian Plum and a delicious Black Cherry. To edge the garden, wooden posts were driven in at six-foot intervals carrying angled sections forming a Y to support a top rail running lengthways along each boundary. Then to cut the garden in half, Jack had instituted the same pattern, to which Ciss swiftly introduced climbing roses.

In the first half Jack soon had constructed a circular path that enclosed a plinth supporting a cherub stone statue complete with birdbath. Pathways leading from the circle ran backwards to the new conservatory, and onwards to the upper half of the garden where our non-stop worker would eventually create a vegetable patch.

Our first trip to Devon consisted of a safari of at least four cars. Jack's mum and dad carrying Grandfather Rouse and Brother Jim. Jack's big 1929 Morris with he and Ciss filling the front, Len and Rene sprawled in the back and Frank and I ensconced on occasional seats that folded down from behind the front bench seat. This meant now having to travel all the way to Devon backwards. Bob with his latest lady acquaintance travelled in his small two-seater and Brother Ted brought up the rear in his prized three-wheeled Morgan.

These were halcyon days of exploration and the unexpected at every mile. Nobody worried about possible problems so far from home, Jack would conquer them all. I have witnessed us pulling onto the grass verge miles from anywhere because a big end had gone on the Morris.

With Dad and Ma Rouse busy brewing up on the Primus, Jack would slide beneath the engine, and in no time have the sump drained and off. Undoing and dropping the offending shell bearing he would then journey in his Dad's car to the nearest garage, perhaps some twenty miles distant and obtain a replacement. Every garage stocked parts of this nature for most makes of vehicle.

Setting up his small workbench always carried for just such an occasion, he'd establish his small vice; offer up the bearing to the crankshaft and after applying Blue paste would crank the engine by hand. After a few turns he would remove the bearing and study it to determine where any high spots might be.

Placing the two halves of the shell in the vice he would then proceed to reamer each carefully where the blue had been disturbed, before carrying out the whole procedure again.

You could bet your life before long everyone would be on the move again none the worse, while to Frank and me it had all been part of the holiday adventure.

If we encountered a steep hill, like Porlock or Canterbury, it would be a case of everybody out and push, whilst Jack stayed at the wheel to keep her going, and when he did it meant the rest of us having to walk to the top.

This was especially so in later years before the war, when Jack had devised the first fold up caravan. A two wheeled trailer that when you opened the double flaps covering its top they could be supported by chains fixed to upright steel posts inserted into the trailer ends. With a horizontal bar running between these posts to form the apex of a roof. Now all you had to do was cover the whole framework in canvas and you had a tent atop a trailer with seating and two side beds formed by the flaps.

Needless to say he had allowed for a small back door in the trailer for easy entry, plus of course the means for cooking and washing, including an Elsan toilet. The whole invention worked a treat.

Us young ones still lived in tents directly on the ground, but Ciss and Ma and Pa Rouse were well catered for, because at a pinch it could sleep four.

Our base was invariably Brixham, right on top of the cliffs, where from the owner's field a winding path had been created, curving down through the gorse to cliff bottom and grey shingle sand.

I vividly recall the sea being awash with jellyfish, but we had some great times here. There were always more than enough bodies to form a game of rounders or cricket.

Throughout the years we journeyed to this field I do not recall ever seeing more than about three or four other families and very often the same ones. Some forty years later I drove out of my way to find this exact spot. It was like another world, totally unrecognisable. So packed had it become with vehicles, caravans, and people that I could not get away from it quickly enough.

Most of the highways and byways in those days were quite narrow with just grass verges and you could very easily travel two or three miles before setting eyes on another vehicle. Whenever we did pass someone going the other way, we would all wave in friendly recognition of another adventurous traveller.

THE WAY WE WERE

To fill up with fuel entailed a lengthy process, not only did the petrol pump have to be hand cranked sucking up one a gallon at a time, but the stop always meant checking the engine for oil and radiator for water. The temperature gauge consisted of a round calibrated glass unit screwed into the top of the radiator which needed to be large enough and clear enough to read from the driver's seat.

Each pump, of which there might be only three, was of a different variety, with their own proudly displayed emblem on top. For some reason or other Jack always preferred the symbol showing Cleveland, if he could get it. The average price per gallon, if I remember correctly, varied from about an old currency ten pence to eleven and a halfpenny for premium grade!

The Hood of the Morris folded down so you were able to enjoy the scenery in good weather. Side windows were constructed of layered celluloid supported by sidebars and top rail. These you lifted out of their sockets and stored close by if you wanted a better view. All packing cases would be stacked high, covered with a waterproof sheet and tied onto the rear rack, which also housed a spare wheel beneath. Jack repaired most punctures himself, over the years he taught me countless ideas on how to keep a vehicle on the road. A lesson in self-reliance that never left me!

In 1936 we lost our Grandmother Sophia who was still living upstairs at 62 Usher Road with Grandfather William Henry Smith. She had reached the age of eighty, yet despite all those years on earth, I have been unable to find a photograph of her, unless she bides there in some group that I am unaware of. Four years later William Henry would follow her at the age of 86 and although I do not remember attending any funerals, these deaths would be the first in the family my young life would be touched by.

Towards the end of 1935 a devise had been tried that promised to detect objects at some distance, by the sending of radio signals that fanned out in waves. Whenever these met a solid subject a rebound signal would immediately be returned to the sender. It would prove invaluable in the years ahead, and become known as Radar.

By November the Tories had been swept back to power with a huge majority, and although not much used as a plank in the election, made clear that defence spending would increase. It proved how so easily the world could have taken a different turn.

Since the kidnap and subsequent killing of his first child, Charles Lindbergh arrived by ship with his wife Anne and their second son, two-year-old Jon. Having been plagued by threats of similar treatment to Jon, Lindbergh had decided to leave America and start a new life in England.

Within two days of the New Year, Hitler was busy telling the League of Nations to mind its own business on his treatment of the Jews, and then on the 28th of January King George V was laid to rest at Windsor. King Edward VIII now became our monarch, but before long all us kids at school would be singing "Hark the Herald Angels sing, Mrs Simpson stole our King"!

Whilst on the subject of children, I must let you know of those elated urchins rampaging with me over our paradise playground. These included, young Olive, one year older than me, from number 84, daughter of Mr and Mrs Dear, and Bob & Babs, older and younger than me respectively, offspring of Mr and Mrs Underwood from number 82. Mr and Mrs Winch our right hand neighbours and bane of Jack's life, at number 88, to my knowledge did not have any offspring.

There were others naturally, but their names escape me. All of us including the girls were adroit tree climbers, but us boys I have to say invariably reached higher. On a particular day I sought to retrieve an arrow shot way up into an oak, having to precariously reach far out on an extending limb within striking distance of the treetop. The effort brought its reward, but I must admit if I saw one of my grandchildren trying to emulate the feat I would scold them and forbid it.

A favourite pastime was gathering as much of the tall grass as you could, and building a circular den. This we would build higher and higher until we could hardly see over the top, having left just a small entrance to creep through and snuggle inside.

One day I found myself alone with little seven-year-old Babs Underwood in this retreat, whereupon she proceeded to wrap both arms around me in a most affectionate manner, and plant a great big kiss on my cheek. To say I was taken aback would be a slight understatement. At eight years old I was definitely into battles with toy soldiers and even a bit of aircraft modelling, but unfortunately Babs was a bit premature when it came to me and girls. I have often wondered what kind of little temptress she became in later life!

It was never more fortunate that as Hitler's troops marched into the Rhineland, so Mitchell's Spitfire was rolled out for public viewing for the first time at Eastleigh Aerodrome, Southampton.

This took place in March 1936 when nearly sixteen-year-old Len had the unenviable task of taking care of his little kid brother. The opportunity

THE WAY WE WERE

arose when Ciss had taken me to visit our old home and decided to leave me for a few days, no doubt because she and Jack needed some free time together. So big brother took me to the swimming baths, not that I could swim, but he could! Performing swallow dives from the top board while I watched and admired from a safe distance at the shallow end. At least I had him to thank for not throwing me in at the far end, which he could so easily have done considering what an absolute prankster he was. He would have Irene and her Clarnico chums in hysterics leaping out from dark corners each time they entered Usher Road's dim passageway.

Another highlight of his was walking all the way up Usher Road on his hands; something I witnessed on more than one occasion.

Other times he would reluctantly drag this nine-year-old problem to his local roller skating rink. Here after plying me with the hired boots already fitted with skate wheels, he would dash off with some scantily clad female to generally cavort and gyrate in the centre of the rink.

I remember thinking how pretty these girls were, all wearing short skirts and colourful blouses with lovely white skating boots, not unlike they wear when ice skating today.

Even at my young age I became envious of my talented brother, but unfortunately all I could do was cling perilously to the side rail and pull myself along.

At home he excelled at carving models, he had made a beautiful reproduction of the piggy-back Mayo and Mercury flying boats, all whittled from solid wood, no plans, just a perceptive eye. The whole thing stood about eighteen inches high with the larger four-engine Mayo about three feet across, perfect in every detail. I have often wondered what became of it! Only quite recently when talking to my now fifty-six-year-old niece, daughter of Irene, did she tell me that she had come across one of Len's leather carvings which he used to do with sharp scalpel tools, called marquetry.

Now the Spitfire had entered the scene Len would busy himself drawing its beautiful lines from every angle, as well as making many miniatures of this and other aircraft.

By the middle of the year Fascists in Spain had started a civil war; it gave Hitler a golden opportunity to assist and allow his pilots to gain valuable experience for what might lay ahead as he began flexing his muscles throughout Europe.

William S. Smith

Having been launched, the *Queen Mary* took no time in sailing back and forth across the Atlantic to regain the Blue Riband for Great Britain. She'd managed the single crossing in three hours, thirty-one minutes less time than France's latest liner *Normandie*.

On August the 16th 1936 the Berlin Olympics closed amid much chagrin for the Nazi Regime when Hitler was forced to recognise the prowess of Jesse Owens. This American black sprinter had won four gold medals against much flaunted German competition. All their Dictator could do was to disappear before the final curtain.

At this moment in time I am the proud possessor of a 1935 Ford V8 Cabriolet. This vehicle with its owner actually attended the 1936 Berlin Olympics and it bears a commemorative badge affixed to its glove compartment in recognition of the event.

If you walked to the far end of Norwood Avenue past a long curving bend, you would eventually meet up with Rush Green Road again, turn left here and continue for a short distance before crossing and hey presto! Behold our local Scout Hut. Here, most evenings, any youngsters interested would be able to watch for a halfpenny, silent cartoon movies.

These would include Felix the Cat and The Man in the Inkwell. I realise in today's sophisticated world these early beginnings must seem pretty pathetic, but to us kids they denoted a magic well worth watching.

I can still see the pen drawing taking shape on the screen and waiting for the black outline to suddenly become animated, jumping from the page to perform all sorts of antics, even grabbing the pen and drawing something himself that he desired maybe a horse that our cartoon figure would then start to ride. To be perfectly honest I would not be ashamed to entertain today's very modern young child with the same formula.

But within another year we would all be marching in the opposite direction down Rush Green to reach a cinema about two miles away at Becontree Heath. With two pennies given by Ciss, I could now buy a bag of sweets and purchase a ticket for the Saturday morning matinee, proudly presenting Tom Mix and his horse Silver, Tonto the Indian Brave or The Lone Ranger. Together these champions of all that was good could outwit any number of bad men throughout the whole of the Wild West. Such entertainment was only put on for kids, which was just as well because the noise was deafening!

Even over here in Britain we had our Fascists, under the leadership of

THE WAY WE WERE

Sir Oswald Mosley. Dressed in black shirts, and known by that name, 7,000 of them clashed with 100,000 of the public in Cable Street on 11th October 1936. Within five weeks of these riots the Great Exhibition Hall of Crystal Palace came tumbling down in one of the greatest fires ever seen in London. Pilots were claiming the firestorm could be seen halfway across the channel.

Before the years end us school kids would be chanting the loss of King Edward VIII to Mrs Simpson and George VI sat on the throne. As a lad I invariably curled up in the winter months, on the hearth next to the coal fire in Ciss's dining room, listening intently to the radio. I well remember amongst other important announcements soaked in from this position, the faltering staccato voice of our poor unwilling Prince Albert as he declared his lifelong fealty to Britain and the Commonwealth.

If one ever wonders about the Basques in Spain and their pursuit of independence, let them recall Hitler's assistance to Spain's General Franco, when in a forerunner to WWII he sent his Heinkel 111 and Junkers 52 bombers, protected by fighters, to destroy their spiritual city of Guernica.

This was Spain's Civil War, but cynically Hitler required first hand experience for his pilots and what better way to achieve it! Slowly the drums of war were beginning to increase their beat!

But those of us nearing the time to leave junior school and start senior classes were mostly oblivious to these far off happenings. Our days were taken up with lessons and play, and sometimes a journey to the River Blackwater. Here at a place called Stone, maybe because what shore there was looked like pebble beach, Jack's dad had bought a plot of land. This gradually became a nucleus for the Rouse and Smith families, as one after another, even right through the coming hostilities we would migrate to this quiet haven.

Both Jack and Bob would eventually own land here and even Mary and I would come here for our honeymoon.

Right now Pop Rouse had purchased for himself a do-it-yourself home. In these more forgiving days you could buy a piece of land that was not in the general area of development and armed with plans and materials in kit form erect your own home!

Not just a holiday home, but one you could live in all year. So with the help of their five sons and Grandfather Rouse, Ma and Pa Rouse built themselves a riverside home they could commute to at weekends, and at the same time a possible retirement home as well.

William S. Smith

Hitler would soon be boasting of his German Autobahn, well we had a dual carriageway too! It ran from Romford to Southend-on-Sea, and what is more, alongside the carriageway in each direction ran a special cycle track. These were wide enough to take three cycles abreast. This highway became a gateway not only to Southend-on-Sea, but the Blackwater River resort of Stone.

If you took a left about two thirds of the way along what is now the A127 and headed for Battlesbridge, then followed a general north easterly direction through the country lanes you would eventually come to the village of Steeple. This is the nearest village to Stone that itself lies quite close to St Lawrence Bay. Unfortunately at the time of writing our one-time family haven has been totally commercialised by the advent of a vast marina.

I had now reached an age where I could achieve some independence. With a bit of effort I could actually earn the odd sixpence or two doing a paper round very early in the morning, and helping the baker at the weekend, although as I have already indicated he preferred to pay me with a couple of doughnuts.

One of the toy guns that Bob Underwood brought into our garden definitely caught my eye. Of all things it was made in Germany, they were certainly difficult to beat when it involved exquisite engineering. This particular gun very much resembled a German 88-millimetre. There was a very lifelike breech, and the shell had its own casing enclosing a spring. The idea was you attached the shell to the spring-loaded case, then inserted the whole thing into the breech and closed it. Taking careful aim you snatched a lanyard and the thing launched the shell a good ten yards.

On one occasion having hung one of my lead soldiers up by its head, Bob took aim and the shot literally took the body away leaving the head behind. We had some good sport with this particular elaborate toy. Setting up our armies in little scooped out valleys then firing into them to see how much devastation we could cause. We might have been horrible kids, but at least it wasn't hurting anybody unlike happenings throughout the world around us.

Another airship bit the dust when in May 1937 the *Hindenburg* exploded in a ball of fire as it approached its mooring mast in New Jersey. Hitler and Dr Goebbels were immediately informed that their flagship of ten transatlantic journeys had been destroyed. This airship once flew very near Romford on its flight over London. I can visualise it now, a huge bloated

THE WAY WE WERE

monster flying quite low and travelling terribly slowly, its engines sending out a throbbing pulsating beat as it droned along well below cloud level.

This same month Neville Chamberlain took over from Stanley Baldwin as Prime Minister of the day; a man that would soon be waving a paper signed by Herr Hitler declaring peace in our time!

It is hard to select news items of the day for the world was in turmoil.

Eight Soviet Generals facing the firing squad.

The demise of Jean Harlow at 26.

The Japanese bombing of Shanghai.

Campbell shattering the world water-speed record.

Hitler and Mussolini together on the same rostrum.

Non-Nazi parents to lose their children.

A proposal in parliament to issue all of us with air raid shelters: something Churchill had been calling for over the last three years!

Then in 1938 Walt Disney gave us *Snow White and The Seven Dwarfs*, a masterpiece requiring two million drawings and taking three years to make. One hot weekend we were paddling along the edge of the river Blackwater (I'm sure its name must have been derived from the fact that the bed of the river oozed black mud) when Jack suddenly said, "Time for you to learn to swim, Libby!" I had won the name Libby from the Rouse family because Bob Rouse had started this craze for speaking back-slang! Back-slang is when you read something backwards, very often when we sat down for a meal he would say "Pass the T-las please", this was reverse for Salt. However as it was impossible to reverse Billy, he reversed the Bill to Libb then added the Y on the end. All a bit confusing really and in retrospect somewhat foolish, but it was part of my growing up and seemed to stick for many years!

Although I thought nothing of shunting home made rafts around our deep-water disused sand and gravel pit, I still harboured a dread of swimming. Now I come to think of it I guess Ciss used to have kittens each time I ventured out towards our wild playing area.

However Jack being the type he was would not stand on ceremony, once he'd made his mind up, yours truly found himself carried into deep water and dropped while Jack held onto my hair to save me from drowning. Left to flounder around, like this, I felt absolutely petrified. Then he would entice me to lie on my back with the back of my head in water as he placed one hand under my chin. This went on for some time, until he suddenly declared. "You're on your own," at which point I promptly sank.

I would then be brought to the surface, and the whole procedure re-enacted. After about thirty minutes of this I began to feel a bit more confident, and could actually be left alone for as long as five minutes before going under.

From this moment on I never looked back, as gradually I overcame my fear. I never felt ill towards Jack, although at the time if I had been big and strong enough I could so easily have bopped him one!

Jack was forceful in both mind and body, and he exuded competence and reliability and although very tough he could also be fair, imperceptibly over the years these qualities began to rub off on me and I thank him for that.

When I was born, most of Europe was in turmoil, and Germany in particular seemed riven with dispute and discord. Having lost the Great War her surrender terms declared she could never have a standing army, air force or navy again. On top of this the currency had crumbled, and everyone became totally demoralised. Yet by the time I had reached the age of eleven Hitler had turned his country around. With resolute force he had systematically purged Germany of Jews, foreigners, gypsies, the disabled, mentally sick and dissidents.

It had been a well known fact that on Hitler's orders on June 30th 1934, one of his henchmen and staunch supporters, Ernst Röhm, having unfortunately shown his own regard for power, suddenly found himself dispatched along with 200 of his followers, in the Night of the Long Knives!

Everyone in Germany, it would appear, had to be strong and fit in both mind and body, if they wanted to be part of the superior Aryan race. Huge arenas could be seen on newsreels showing hundreds or even thousands of energetic young people all exercising in unison and dressed in identical gym clothing.

Pilots were being prepared under the noses of the League of Nations, by developing large numbers of glider clubs. Secret factories were building Germany's future air force. Hidden dockyards were busy laying down the keels of what would become some of the most modern and devastating warships ever seen, the notorious pocket battleships! Not to count the vast resources committed to submarine construction. All the while huge numbers of selected elite young men were being banded into special units just waiting for the day when they could be brought to the fore as the new Wehrmacht.

THE WAY WE WERE

Even Germany's industrial leaders began underhandedly producing the machinery of war for these very men, the biggest and best tank, massive artillery pieces and every means possible to move an army at speed.

By 1938 all pretence had evaporated and when Hitler marched his troops into his native Austria the populace went wild. Everywhere now it seemed, people wanted and worshipped Hitler the miracle worker.

There was nothing more positive to show how tyrannical things had progressed, when one of Germany's own ex-U-boat commanders, Pastor Niemöller, who had rallied some opposition to the Nazi regime, left court after being fined £180, only to be immediately arrested again and sent to join 3,000 others in Sachsenhausen concentration camp for re-education!

Domestically things at number 86 had started to improve. Ciss now had a washing machine that actually heated the water, even if you did have to agitate the clothes by turning a handle and an early electric iron, which saved all that heating on ranges or gas cookers. We now also possessed a record player. I think it was in 1938 that Jack managed to buy one of the first televisions, a miraculous machine giving a picture about nine inches across. In the car field, Rileys had decidedly caught his eye, and would remain a favourite long after the war.

In the meantime Len had obtained employment in the warehouse of an asbestos suit manufacturer, which was the latest thing for fire fighters. But the joy of his life occurred when he accidentally ran into a chap who had joined the Civil Air Guard, "CAG" as it became known.

Armed with this knowledge he didn't let the grass grow under his feet, especially when he realised this was a government-sponsored scheme and you were expected to supply only your helmet, goggles and speaking tubes. Coupled to this, the guy had actually offered to drive him to the field each time they flew.

During this period I received my first ever letter from him, for years I managed to keep it safe until eventually it became misplaced. But I still remember a couple of passages. He spoke of the machines, De Havilland Puss Moths, and how he had soloed in just five and half hours, that was a course record so far, he enthused. Then later during his training the instructor had wanted him to dive towards a steamer in the Thames Estuary. "When I pulled out," he said, "the boat was still a long way off and so did my stomach seem like!"

Once I found myself in his company at Usher Road again, this time there seemed to be an electric light in the kitchen, just the bulb, no shade or anything. I remember he had a friend with him and they were playing about with a bowl of water and an electrode. His friend had dropped a coin into the water and was egging Len on to retrieve it.

Obviously with electric current passing through water the experience would be traumatic, even so Len never hesitated and gritting his teeth plunged in his hand, only to quickly pull it out again. The pain was tremendous and his whole body went rigid. Yet, never one to be beaten, after recovering he tried again, thrusting his hand to the bottom and fighting to close his fingers around the coin which he just managed before withdrawing his hand, sweat streaming down his face and grinning like a Cheshire cat.

"You try it Billy," he said; "it won't hurt you!"

Not to look chicken in front of my hero, I tentatively offered my hand to the water. One touch and I quickly withdrew as pain shot up my arm. That was enough for me. "I don't think so," I said nervously. "I can't stand it." He'd beaten me again, but to be fair I was seven years his junior, yet somehow I knew that if I had been ages with him, I would still have lost!

Some Britons were getting decidedly edgy and began searching around for the latest type of gas mask. Gas having been used to some effect in the trenches, they thought, not unreasonably, should war come again, this time with greater air power the Germans may resort to it sooner rather than later.

September the 27th saw the launching of the largest liner so far, the 80,000-ton *Queen Elizabeth*, but things nearly didn't go smoothly when restraining timbers gave way and she started to slide prematurely. Keeping her wits about her, Queen Elizabeth, who had been chatting to the two princesses on the launching platform, hastily let go the bottle to name the ship and just managed to catch the tip of her bow as she gathered speed.

Two days later Mr Chamberlain returned from his historic meeting with Herr Hitler, declaring "Peace in our Time", and waving the document signed by the dictator from the balcony of Buckingham Palace. Under this agreement, he declared, Czechoslovakia would be ceded to Germany in return for peace.

However, many MPs were muttering sell-out, including I am sure Winston Churchill!

On October 5th Hitler walked over the border, strutting into his latest conquest without a shot being fired. I wonder what the Czechs were thinking; certainly the Jews amongst them must have been shaking in their shoes!

THE WAY WE WERE

About a month before my twelfth birthday it had been announced that the RAF was now taking delivery of 400 new aircraft every month, even so this number still only represented two thirds of Germany's intake of 600. Latest estimates also gave the Third Reich 4,500 front line aircraft.

I remember quite clearly Brother Len buying me a model plane for this twelfth birthday. Called a Frog it was made of something similar to wax cardboard, each flying surface had movable sections that you could bend up or down, or in the case of the rudder from side to side, so you set these before flight. The undercarriage was made of sprung wire and its lubricated multiple rubber band motor could be wound quite quickly when inserted back into its box.

Placing the fuselage lengthways with the wings supported by side slots allowed the propeller to enter a forward compartment housing a reduction gear winder. When you engaged the prop and gear together, each time you turned an external handle just once, the prop revolved about five times. This produced a powerful motor so that when you held the prop as you placed it on the ground the plane would shoot forward and take off happily on its own. Setting a slight bend on the rudder would send it off in wide circles, but if you kept it straight there was a strong chance of losing the Frog altogether as it gained height and distance. Not until I had reached the age of fifty and flew radio controlled models with son Barry did I enjoy model flying so much.

Only this last year I spied one being shown on the television *Antiques Road Show* which was in mint condition and reportedly worth a great deal of money. I have a sneaking suspicion it was made by a German company!

Franco had virtually won his revolution in Spain, so along with Mussolini, Stalin and Hitler, most of Europe seemed to be run by Dictators now, which was leaving us in Britain a little anxious. Free air raid shelters were in the throes of being distributed to those thought to be in vulnerable areas and by April our government had voted to introduce conscription for twenty-year-olds.

That year Jack decided to take us all to Wales on holiday. There were lots of places he wanted to visit and with his tried and tested trailer tent felt well equipped to do the grand tour. Strangely enough throughout all the intervening years and many thousands of miles behind me, I have never really seen as much of Wales as I remember seeing on that holiday. We visited Cardiff, Carmarthen, Manorbier and Pembroke Castle. Then through the National Parklands of Mynydd Presli, right up to Snowdonia and walked to the very top of the mountain itself.

I have vivid recollections of beautiful castles and lots of armour, wonderful sandy beaches stretching for miles and being surrounded by mountains as we journeyed almost alone along narrow winding roads. We were able to stop almost anywhere, just pull over and have a picnic, I do not recall a bad weather day, but I guess there might have been for one tends to remember the best of times. This trip Jack had used a black Austin 16-hp with hard top and blue leather upholstery, although his first love was still a Riley, which he eventually acquired. Apart from visits to Stone this would be our last proper holiday together.

When our air-raid shelter arrived, at first Jack kept it to one side, but with one eye on current events and nervous soundings from the Government he finally decided that perhaps we had better make preparations. (So much for peace in our time!)

Whilst we had enjoyed our holiday the Germans had been busy attacking Poles in the city of Danzig. Although to all intents and purposes this port sitting at the mouth of the Vistula was confirmed as a free city, German infiltrators had been treating it as one of their own: and the interference could spark an opening to war. Britain and France had declared we would come to the aid of the Poles if their sovereignty were to be breached, so already the writing stood out starkly on the wall!

Jack started by digging a hole at the bottom of the garden, just inside the gateway to our universal playground. Messrs Dear, Winch and Underwood were all about to do the same. Mr Dear in particular was a nice portly gentleman and so was his wife, a comfortably built lady who showed much kindness to us kids, their daughter Olive being the apple of my eye! On the other hand Mr Winch portrayed pinched rather sinister features, he, we were told, had registered as an air-raid warden. Typical, I thought, for he oozed the officious type.

Air-raid shelters consisted of corrugated iron sheets about two feet six inches wide and about six feet tall, curving inwards at the top. Depending on requirements, these could be any number to affect the overall length. Each flat end was just over four feet wide with one cut away to form an entrance.

Together Jack and I dug down about three feet, shaping an oblong hole approximately six feet by four. Fortunately despite my earlier thesis to a high water table, we did not reach this element, but just to be prudent and to allow for rain incursion Jack did carve out a deeper sump area. We then made some three or four cutaway steps to reach the bottom and finally set all the sheets into our handiwork. The side corrugations overlapped nicely to line up with predetermined holes made to receive nuts and bolts. After this it was a case of establishing each end, which I think were just propped against the sides. All back filling would hold things in place, and boy! Was there plenty of that, as a young lad I was amazed at the amount of material we had excavated from such a moderate sized hole.

When it was all finished and our huge piles of earth had been shovelled back over, we went inside and had a good look round. It didn't seem too bad, but of course Jack had all sorts of ideas for improvement. Which was probably just as well for within a year we would be practically living down there.

On the way to school we began to notice ominous signs of things to come, workmen were piling sandbags on street corners, and shop windows suddenly sprouted sticky paper in the form of criss-crosses. This we were told was to stop splintered glass from falling out. Some of the children were also talking about possible evacuation; in fact, some more well to do parents had already sent their offspring to the country there was even talk of being able to go abroad like Canada or other countries belonging to the Empire.

Sister Irene, or Rene as everybody called her, who had reached the age of twenty-two, became very fond of one of her cycling fraternity and she told Ciss it could be serious. His name was John McCarthy: he, she said, had an elder brother called Charlie, and two younger brothers, Jimmy and young Dennis, a bit younger than me; he also had a sister Cathleen about my age. The whole family were descended from Irish immigrants and lived with their mum and dad near the docks in Cable Street. This was an area full of tenement blocks and where the Black-shirt Fascists of Oswald Mosley had clashed with thousands of the ordinary public in late 1936.

Len on the other hand seemed to have girls galore, although Rene swore that even at nineteen he; was still mightily shy of the opposite sex. She used to boast about the time her and one of her work-mates caught this wayward prankster and taught him a lesson, holding him down while they smothered his bare chest in condensed milk and strawberry jam. Already a giggler, the cries of Donald Duck ensuing from 62 could be heard far and wide.

Personally I recall seeing him with different girls each time he went swimming, roller skating, cycling, or preparing to go out dancing.

William S. Smith

He'd called in to see us at 86 ostensibly to visit Ciss. She was fast becoming his number one girl, and he loved the way her husband would tackle anything, as far as Len was concerned, nobody could touch Jack when it came to mechanics. "Cissy," he'd voiced, looking somewhat serious, "Cissy, I am thinking of volunteering for the RAF, I know my experience with the CAG will hold me in good stead, but I have to pass a selection board and I'm a bit nervous about my maths capability." Ciss would sympathise with him and well understood his difficulty, having left school at fourteen.

Most people selected for aircrew training were going to be graduates or at least secondary school boys, it wasn't going to be easy having been brought up in Bow and leaving school at an early age trying to compete with those types!

Len's answer would be to cycle all the way to Abridge Aerodrome about ten miles north of Romford. There ensconced on a high point, he would watch RAF Tiger Moths take off and land as he studied algebra, logarithms and trigonometry, forcing his brain to absorb and understand these difficult subjects.

One Sunday I had settled myself at my favourite position, squatting on the tiled hearth next to a nice blazing fire. I probably liked this spot because being the fetch and carry guy, I guess I was forever keeping it topped up with coal and couldn't resist its tempting warmth.

The radio was on and someone said the Prime Minister was going to speak. I was all by myself, but I knew Ciss hovered somewhere in the house, Jack was definitely not around and could have been on duty, as his driving job entailed some shift working.

Our clock had just chimed twelve noon when the announcer introduced the Prime Minister Neville Chamberlain.

"Hitler," he said, "marched his troops across the Polish border shortly before six am on Friday morning after submitting the Polish people to a heavy bombardment. We therefore..." he continued "...sent an urgent message to Herr Hitler telling him that unless he immediately stopped all aggression towards that country and withdrew from their borders by eleven am today ..." He paused, and you could sense the reluctance in his voice; "... we shall have no alternative but to declare that a state of war exists between our two nations."

"Finally," he continued, "I am afraid I have to inform you that no such undertaking has been received and that therefore a state of war now exists

53

THE WAY WE WERE

between us, along with our French allies, against Germany."

So that was it, the war to end all wars that Dad had been involved in, had lasted just over twenty years. Enough time and no more for my nearest brother in age to grow up, fifteen minutes later the sirens sounded, an up-and-down wailing that so soon would become part of mine and everyone else's life.

Suddenly Ciss appeared, entreating me to make for the shelter, yet before we could get anywhere near it there was Mr Winch charging along the back of everybody's fence exhorting us all to take cover, his Air Raid Warden's hat on and gas mask slung over one shoulder. But unfortunately he beat everyone to it when he stumbled into one of our children's games potholes and disappeared from view. We needn't have worried it was a false alarm in fact so false it would be some time before we ever heard it again

Poor Poland as if one invasion wasn't enough, now uncle Joseph Stalin decided he ought to have a slice, at least it would keep Hitler's hordes further from his borders. Any help we could give the Poles was of necessity short lived

The world began lining up to take sides, but at twelve and half years old a heck of a lot of it would go over my head. This first winter I can only recall how black everything was once the sun went down. How we had to constantly worry about pulling the black out curtains, and be mindful each time we opened a door or a window. To remember to carry my gas mask with me everywhere I went, although we kids usually ended up putting them on just to scare the girls. They smelt all horrible and rubbery and were very claustrophobic.

Jack's Green Line Coaches were to be used as ambulances when not in service and he would have to take his turn at night duty to cover this emergency.

Brother Len to his utter delight did manage to beat the daunting three-officer selection board and get accepted for aircrew training in the category of pilot, but whether at the controls of a fighter or bomber would at this moment in time be an unknown quantity. As it happened the powers that be wanted him to continue his work at the fireman's clothing factory, so much to his disgust they put him on the deferred list, at least until he had reached the respectable age of twenty.

Rene began looking at her options and felt she would like to become a switchboard operator in the Auxiliary Fire Service. They would be looking

William S. Smith

towards women to fulfil many roles previously occupied by men and living as she was in the centre of London they were going to be badly needed.

Jack had done us proud in the shelter stakes. We now had a wooden slatted floor, which Ciss had promptly carpeted. Two very nice bunks the top one being earmarked for me, and he had run an electric cable down the garden to provide us with light and in case of colder weather even an electric heater. We also had tea making facilities and a radio, in fact all the comforts of home.

By October we had 158,000 of the BEF (British Expeditionary Force) established in France, and with the impenetrable French Maginot Line to protect us, there was no way we could lose, or Hitler could win! People openly forecast the war could be over in a matter of months. We received our first shock six weeks after hostilities had begun. A German submarine having penetrated our home port of Scapa Flow promptly sank the *Royal Oak* battleship as she lay at anchor. This first lesson had been an expensive one; nobody thought it possible for a submarine to breach our defences, or a torpedo to penetrate the ships armour. Out of approximately 1,200 souls only 396 are thought to have survived.

After Hitler's blitzkrieg of Poland, he spoke furiously of Britain and France's refusal to negotiate his peace terms. On the 24th October 1939 he had the audacity to suggest war in the West was not necessary and cited the allies as warmongers. Chamberlains reply stated the obvious; Herr Hitler and his government could not be trusted to honour any agreement that the West might reach with them.

As the year struggled to reach its end, at least we all cheered at some good news, when it was announced on December 17th that Hitler's pride and joy, his prized flagship, the 10,000 ton, 3.75 million pound pocket battleship *Graf Spee* had been forced to scuttle herself. Holed up in the River Plate and denied time by the Uruguayan authorities to carry out badly needed repairs, she had been ordered to put to sea or be interned.

Unfortunately for its Captain Hans Lansdorf, waiting for him outside were the three British cruisers which had put him there, the *Exeter*, *Ajax* and *Achilles*. Rather than face the inevitable battle, Hitler himself ordered Lansdorf to blow up the ship.

I at least knew where my future lay; certainly in my young innocent mind all seemed crystal clear. I would now study and try everything I could to emulate my brother Len. He had been accepted for pilot training and so

THE WAY WE WERE

could I. Only one thing held me back, our age difference. It was a millstone hard to overcome, but I was determined to become a pilot, and not just of any old plane, but a Spitfire. Little did I know at the time, which was probably just as well, that ninety percent of all young boys in the British Isles and throughout the Empire cherished the same thought!

But I would have one advantage over most of them, being resident west of Hornchurch and therefore facing the prevailing wind, I personally would be witness to history in the making as Spitfire after Spitfire flew right over my head after taking off from Hornchurch Aerodrome.

It wouldn't happen yet, but the time was coming and until then our life at 86 continued virtually unchanged.

William S. Smith

1929. Billy boy 2 years with Ciss.

1931. Irene 14, Len 11, Billy 4.

THE WAY WE WERE

1931. Ciss with Laddie in garden at 62 Usher Road.

Sister Irene, 16.

Sister Elsie, 17.

Walter Faul, 18.

William S. Smith

1931. Ciss and Jack wedding.

1931. Billy Boy farmed out to possibly lady known as Henrietta Stringle and here photographed with her daughter.

THE WAY WE WERE

Above: 1937. 17-year-old Len the athlete fresh from swimming.

Right: 1938. Len with Dad.

Below: 1939. Sister Ciss at the piano in her new home at No. 86 Norwood Avenue, Romford.

War, Sadness and Love

Two teachers stood out in my mind now I had joined the ranks of school seniors, our middle-aged, short of stature, slightly balding, bespectacled male maths teacher, and our lithesome fair-haired youngish lady English teacher. Of the two I coveted the lady. It wasn't really my hormones, because I am sure she knew exactly what she was doing when addressing the class. Placing her backside firmly against the front edge of her table, she would deliberately raise one foot towards the boy's desk before her. Then slightly hitching a tight hem to allow her remaining knee to rest over the straightened leg would dangle the other provocatively in front of my hapless chum's eyes. Finally in a soft voice she would begin the lesson. To say concentration could be difficult would be an understatement.

On the other hand maths drove all lurid thoughts from susceptible minds, as nervously we watched our bespectacled master creeping up and down desk aisles, wielding his twelve-inch ruler. Sir had a rather nasty habit if he thought you weren't paying enough attention, of bringing this weapon hard down across bare knuckles.

One other classic that emerges from my school days was being got at by a particularly horrible bully. This loathsome oaf seemed to delight in pushing me around, especially when we were journeying home and out of range of teachers and other kids likely to stick up for me. Now I wasn't unduly small for my age or particularly nervous, but I was pretty tolerant and cherished no desire to aggressive behaviour unless sorely provoked. On this occasion I must have felt enough was enough as far as this lout was concerned and decided to lash out. I remember feeling a sense of deep satisfaction as blood oozed from his nose.

I'm sure it was the first time I ever really lost my temper, obviously a little of my Irish mother's spirit lurked somewhere within me, which I was mightily glad of, because I do not recall being pestered by this particular individual, or anyone else come to that, ever again.

THE WAY WE WERE

Brick-built air raid shelters had been erected on part of our playing fields. Corresponding to home types, these stood half-submerged with the excavated material being shovelled on top. It can so easily be forgotten that this was a time before mechanical diggers as we know them, so in nearly every instance work needed to be carried out by hand.

Inside had been installed bench seats running lengthways, with electric bulbs suspended at intervals from the roof. Each entrance took a ninety degree turn round piles of sandbags acting as a blast wall. Practice drills would be performed, with everyone alerted by the school bell. Then following in orderly fashion as each teacher lead the way to their class's shelter. Don't think for one moment that you were going to miss a lesson, for after we had all settled down and been counted as present, teacher would open his or her books, smile confidently, and say, now where were we!

We still consumed our school milk every day and school meals remained available if you wanted them, which I devoured quite often. Some rationing had been introduced for the general public, although cafes and restaurants were so far exempt. You could only purchase four ounces of butter, four ounces of uncooked bacon or ham and twelve ounces of sugar with meat being rationed the following month! So now, when I ran to the shops I needed to remember our ration books. Unfortunately television broadcasts had been suspended for the duration, so before we had any chance to become accustomed to our nine-inch black and white, this new medium had become extinct.

But I very much liked radio, I used to sit in my favourite position at the edge of the fire and allow my imagination to wander as adventurous or dramatic sequences were enacted over the air. I have always felt, even after decades of television, how much better it is to use your own imagination, rather than have images implanted by this box in one corner of a room.

Sometimes we would catch the nasal tones of Lord Haw Haw. This was a one-time compatriot of Lord Mosley who had turned traitor and now broadcast from Germany. Throughout the whole of the war years he would subject the British people to his insidious propaganda, earning the derogatory nickname in the process because of his speech inflection. After the war William Joyce would be hung for his sins, a well deserved and fitting end.

To give them a strategic advantage Russia had invaded poor frail Finland, but to date this gallant little nation was holding the great bear at bay.

All shipping, declared Hitler, was legal prey for his U-boats; even charting a zigzag course was sufficient reason for a sinking. His idea of course was to divert all shipping to Germany; any vessel using a British port even without carrying contraband was automatically a target. They must in essence use Germany as a clearing house for their cargo. Norway, although neutral, stated that Nazi U-boats and aircraft had already sunk fifty of her ships!

On February 26th a German tanker, the *Altmark*, was boarded in a daring raid by our destroyer the *Cossack* who managed to track her into a Norwegian fjord. Found below decks were 300 British seaman captured from ships sunk by the *Graf Spee*.

I couldn't wait to celebrate my coming thirteenth birthday, with only one school year to go and the chance at last to wear long trousers when I started work. But in Finland on March 13th they finally surrendered to overwhelming superior forces. Their fourteen-week fight was now over, Denmark's and Norway's just beginning when on April 9th Nazi forces swept into both countries.

Our Prime Minister was optimistic; he reckoned Hitler had missed the bus because we had reached agreement on trade barriers against Germany with most neutral European governments, including Denmark and Norway! I think it was a case of, if you can't skin a rabbit one way, do it another. Hitler tended to ignore such overtures and just sent in his stormtroopers. How many lessons did we need? Within four weeks despite Britain sending help to Norway the fight was all but over, it had been another blitzkrieg and our Government was in disarray.

By May 10th Churchill was sworn in as leader, but was it too late? Already British and French forces were falling back as Hitler swept through what was once neutral Belgium. Before the end of the month Belgium and Holland had surrendered and we had our backs to the wall as gradually we became encircled. Fortunately at least our field commanders could see what might happen as the advancing German army of 750,000 poured through the Belgium gap. They had totally ignored heavy French defences whose guns now all pointed the wrong way.

At least British forces had a slim chance of rescue, fighting a fierce rearguard action as they fell back towards the French coast and Dunkirk. This time a problem for the Germans could come to our aid, soft marshland being a feature of this part of France, forcing the German high command to show concern at losing heavy tanks and artillery if they give chase to the

THE WAY WE WERE

fleeing British Expeditionary Force.

Churchill spoke movingly and warned of dire times ahead, but promised that everything was being done to bring our troops home. I sat with Ciss and Jack, listening daily to dramatic news; somehow I did not feel scared, only excited, as with each new broadcast my young heart urged everyone to succeed. Surely it was impossible not to win.

Each day now I rushed into the garden at the slightest sound of aircraft engines—the roar of Rolls Royce Merlins was unmistakable—shielding both eyes to stare after Spitfires and Hurricanes as they wheeled above my head before joining into formation, watching as they grew smaller, climbing and heading south toward the coast and on across the English Channel.

Preparing for unknown future losses, the Air Ministry decided to relent, forwarding Len his official call-up papers. It took a long time to train a pilot even though the whole process would be speeded up. Immediate omens did not look promising; however, when he wrote from his induction centre at Blackpool, trying hard to explain a spell of imposed confinement: "Just because one or two of us during parade whistled at some popsies, as if it was our fault they insisted on waving from the roadside." Never mind depressing war news, nothing was going to affect my brother's morale.

We claimed a victory; out of the jaws of annihilation 338,226 fighting men had been rescued from the beaches of Dunkirk. Many would say they never saw the RAF, but if it's any consolation I can vouch they definitely leapt into the sky from my end.

Some thirty years later when Barry and I controlled our own vehicle repair business, an elderly gent going by the name of Bob Moore, who incidentally was not afraid of getting his hands dirty, asked if we had any odd jobs going. After having completed every mundane and debilitating task set him, he one day confessed to serving with the British army as a major. One of his duties, he told us, was to sort out all our forces arriving in England from the Dunkirk beaches. He had been given this horrendous burden by his commanding colonel who knew Major Moore could be entrusted to make absolutely certain nobody missed out on being well nourished, re-clothed, and decently housed, before sorted into proper groupings prior to rejoining their units.

All this Bob achieved by cutting through official red tape, and lambasting everybody's ear that controlled the release of goods and chattels he so badly needed. Even though so many years had passed, it was still good to know we had such forceful characters around at the time, able to get things done in such a forthright manner!

Ciss, Jack and I listened intently to the daily bulletins. There would be no hype, no heavy music or loud voices. No dramatic pronouncements, with cross-talking journalists, no picking over bits and pieces to analyse each minute detail. It would come over clear and concise.

"This is the BBC Six O'Clock News and this Alvar Lidell reading it. The French have been forced to sign their armistice in the same Railway Coach as the Germans did in 1918.

"De Gaulle says the flame of French resistance must not go out.

"Mussolini has declared war against the Allies.

"Reichsmarschall Hermann Goering, the ex-WWI pilot who took over command of Von Richtofen's Circus during that war and now commands Germany's Luftwaffe, has declared he will destroy the RAF.

"Already he is attacking and sinking our ships in the Channel.

"Churchill along with Admiral Sir James Somerville express deep regret at the loss of up to 1000 French lives, because these sailors would not or could not surrender before we were forced to sink their fleet whilst at harbour in Algeria. We were left with no other option to avoid such ships falling into Axis hands.

"Winston also extols the nation to fight on. We will fight on the beaches, the fields, and in the towns, in the forests and the hills, we will never surrender.

"The Home Guard is standing by at the ready.

"German forces have already landed on the Channel Islands."

Cryptic news hiding a thousand heroes and heroines and untold stories that may never see the light of day: maybe some, perhaps, in a dozen years or so, but others will be forgotten forever, except in the memories of those most nearest and dearest to them.

How poignant it all seems now, when compared to the, so frequently, small, unimportant, very often fatuous material, thrust from our living room screens and current newsprint.

Then one bright morning the sirens sounded in earnest, long before time for school. Already a fierce sun burned the heavens, not a cloud disturbing azure blue. I know, because yet again my neck craned backward, hand's held to shield the glare as desperately I struggled to observe the slightest speck. Several Spits had already banked round above me clawing for altitude, when within minutes I spied what appeared to be small metallic glints way up in the sky. Here they came then, the first tentative strikes to clobber our airfields.

Ciss had already hurried past, encouraging me to follow, but there was no way that I was going to miss this. To pacify her concerns I did edge closer to the shelter, but all the while strained an aching neck. This group appeared to be seeking another target, for silently and ever so slowly they crawled across the sky from northeast to southwest.

I experienced a wave of disappointment as though I relished the thought of having to duck from bombs, how daft can you get! Yet at one and the same time apprehension swept through me in case that was exactly what transpired. But I need not have worried, for no sooner had they flown beyond the vertical, then ominous cotton wool puffs appeared and I watched fascinated as these shell bursts began following the German formation. The whole scene seemed so strange and surreal, until abruptly brought back to earth by the sharp crack of anti-aircraft guns. It was uncanny how you never heard the shells explode in the sky, I guess Jerry must have been at about 20–25,000 feet and always our gunners shots trailed far behind the tiny silver reflections.

By now everyone had crowded into his or her garden, close to air raid shelters its true, but nobody had shown the slightest inclination towards entering them.

About fifteen minutes later with the aircraft virtually out of sight, the first wisps of white vapour began to materialise, quickly transforming into giant circles, creating fantastic spidery patterns. Patterns in the sky that we would soon come to accept as an everyday occurrence. Imperceptibly these would change, becoming strung out and ragged, as the high altitude winds took command, tearing and ripping them apart. Then Bob Underwood gave a yell: "Look!" he cried; "there's one coming down." We all swiftly swung round to gaze where he was pointing, somewhere towards the southwest of London, and sure enough there was what looked like a single engine aircraft literally slicing towards the earth in perfect plan view, one wing pointing straight at the ground.

We never saw or heard it hit, it was much too far away for that, but a little later we did spy a parachute, about 8–10,000 feet up, you could just discern the tiny figure hanging on the end. It was floating down in close proximity to the aircraft we had just seen, so guessed it must have been the pilot, but whether friend or foe we were never able to establish.

A little later the All Clear sounded and it was a case of back to normal and prepare for school. To us youngsters it had all been a great adventure, something to talk about in the playground, and if you'd managed to spot something other kids had missed, a strong bragging point.

But before that day ended, we would be in and out of our school shelters again and again, as the Germans began their all out attack on fighter airfields in earnest. Unfortunately under the care of school staff you didn't get the same freedom of opportunity to watch the war's progress, having to huddle together listening to the crump of bombs and crack of guns. But at least it was nearly the end of term so we had everything to look forward to.

Many parents of course were very worried for their children and evacuation was being stepped up. I considered myself one of the lucky ones who had managed to stay behind. Ciss had contemplated sending me away, and I remember her arguing whether to have me shipped to Canada. However with the Atlantic U-boats wreaking havoc to our shipping she had second thoughts, which suited me fine, even though Canada at the time sounded great.

Being so close to Hornchurch airfield Brother John's eldest daughter Peggy, aged eleven, had been evacuated to Birmingham, a venue she hated and within ten weeks would be back home again with the whole family once more reunited. With her remaining two very young boys, Ivy temporarily hastened out of danger, to reside with her sister Maud. These precautions did not prove unnecessary when in one particular bombardment, John and Ivy's house suffered severe damage, with every pane of glass shattered and roof tiles that now swept upwards in distinct waves, necessitating complete removal before re-fixing.

With her first three offspring, Derek, Ron and Brian, Sister Elsie had already been entrained to Norfolk, and were now well clear of possible danger. Husband Wally, however, needed to stay in London, earning a living, and remaining on standby for possible rescue operations.

By now of course most newlyweds in their early twenties were already suffering separation that would in all probability last for many years.

One Monday morning before the beginning of our annual holidays, casually sauntering past farm fields on the way to school, we spotted three shallow craters carved out of the soft earth. Each one was only about twelve yards from where we now stood gazing in disbelief. Three 500-pound bombs dropped by a Heinkel 111, one of our gang volunteered! When pressed, he warmed to his subject. Dad, he boasted, had been on air raid duty the day before and saw it happen. The German came from the direction of the airfield and Dad saw it jettison the bombs. He reckoned it was so they could make a quick getaway. His chest was fair bursting with the prior knowledge he now glowingly imparted.

Incidentally, these twenty-foot wide craters lay only about 600 yards from our school.

Rene's fiancé, John McCarthy, had been called up and now served in the RAF attached to a refuelling section. She herself was on the verge of joining the Auxiliary Fire Service, and would win commendation in the coming Blitz on London.

Although outside the age limit for compulsory military service, Brother John was soon volunteering to join the ranks of the RAF, enlisting into a technicians section and ending up as an electrical engineer. I remain unsure of Dad's whereabouts or the orphans' during this period. I do know that at the time of the Blitz on our capital city, he went along with everyone else to the south coast resort of Littlehampton, where they were billeted in a large white building called a lido.

We eventually heard from Len again, saying how he was now encamped at an ITW, these capital letters standing for Initial Training Wing. In his letter however he did not sound a very happy chap. "If this is the RAF," he wrote, "then it must be wingless; I have not laid eyes on an aircraft since joining and am totally brassed off with studying and exams."

But this period of training was well known to consist of nothing else and until you satisfied your examiners, your progress through the curriculum could very easily stop short of ever stepping into an aircraft.

My initiation into this field would shortly begin when prior to leaving school; I managed to enrol into the RAF cadet corps, known as the ATC (Air Training Corps). Initially as schoolboys we were handed a forage cap and sash before we earned a uniform, I had been hoping to wear long trousers at last, but not quite yet. Strangely enough it taught us appreciation, nothing was ever taken for granted in the process of growing up, and every step on the ladder was graciously acknowledged as recognition of achievement, even if that achievement was just succeeding in reaching another age.

Designated Eagle Day, August 10th was the date Marshal Goering had predicted the RAF would finally be defeated, by then our losses would have been so great in men and machines, nothing could stand in the way of Germany invading our tiny island.

School summer holidays had so far been glorious; I could never remember such constant warm sunshine. Each day you awoke, so the sky beckoned you with a cobalt clearness that just invited thoughts of raft building and frolicking on water. Sirens and air raid wardens were there to be ignored, Spitfires and Hurricanes departed and returned at almost monotonous regularity. But they were different, each time a joy to see!

Before the sun had a chance to climb, our heavenly canvas had become a backcloth on which friend and foe alike wove their intricate patterns of white filigree. Pure and unadulterated entertainment granted to young English blood gazing skywards from their green and pleasant land. It was all too good to hand over to the likes of Nazi jackboots and their sadistic masters.

So Goering didn't get his Eagle Day, then or at any other time. I could have told him that, because I saw our fighters without fail, forever streaking above our garden and playing fields. Most times, so low we could wave enthusiastically to the pilots crouched behind their controls.

Never in the field of human conflict, spoke Churchill, had so many owed so much too so few. Yes! A summer I shall never forget, and as I recall it now after sixty-three years, I know through hundreds of contacts throughout my life, a summer that no one living at the time could ever forget.

Going about our business, such as it was, deep in concentration as to whose conker had smitten the most, or which cigarette card you flicked the furthest, how many marbles did I win today, swapping *Hotspur* for *Dandy* comics. Most of us would be oblivious to small wartime changes. Sure we couldn't help but be involved in following air activity, including the daily ritual of raising and lowering of barrage balloons, but on the whole a lot of life could pass you by. So it came as a bit of a shock when workmen appeared and started to dismantle the pit site disused railway, including the removal of all our precious rolling stock.

We'd obviously missed that bit about local communities gathering all the iron they could to help factories churning out vast numbers of tanks and armoured vehicles. Ciss even chose to give away some of her precious aluminium saucepan's to help build aeroplanes, and this after I had spent umpteen hours polishing the damn things. This happened each time her and Jack visited the pictures, giving me the opportunity to earn a sixpenny piece.

Something else we'd noticed was the reclaiming of wasteland to create a huge ambulance park not far from the Hospital, this area had been surrounded by heavy wire and lay in almost a direct line from 86 on the far side of our adventurous playground.

THE WAY WE WERE

Now when Jack drove us to Stone for the day or weekend using some carefully preserved coupons, I couldn't help noticing how all the fields had suddenly sprouted vertical poles that stuck straight up from the ground. "It's to make it difficult for gliders to land," explained Jack; "we are still preparing for a possible invasion."

When arriving at our riverside retreat and wanting to stroll near the water's edge, you were barred from doing so, because huge coils of vicious barbed wire stood in your way. Then to cap it all great big concrete blocks, standing four or five feet had been embedded deep to deter enemy tanks from striking inland. Other things caught my eye, like large square or hexagon shaped concrete pillboxes so far unmanned, but ready to be so at the slightest provocation.

Once as we journeyed back and forth to our haven near the Blackwater River, we spied a crashed German Messerschmitt fighter. Lying on its belly, it had made a wheels-up landing on a narrow stretch of grassland. Apart from bent propeller blades the machine looked perfect, there were a few people peering over the hedge, so we stopped to join them, but as luck would have it a couple of Home Guard stood strategically between us and the plane.

Sometimes though you could accidentally be near things you didn't want to be, like the time I passed Ciss's small pear tree, planted alongside the garden path, as I walked towards the conservatory.

An air raid was in progress and the usual puffs of anti-aircraft fire could be seen, although not immediately above us. Something unusual caught my eye, hard to describe really, a sort of blur passing vertically through the branches of the tree. I glanced down, and there at its base, about twelve inches from where I walked had appeared a small hole. Bending low, with bare hands I clawed to reach whatever had caused the phenomenon, but after excavating about six inches without unearthing anything, I gave up. Obviously a piece of anti-aircraft shell had penetrated deep. That was the nearest I ever came to shrapnel without a tin hat on, how ironic to have been snuffed out by one of our own guns.

Quite soon you began to realise how everybody appeared to be in uniform, something that as each year progressed would become more and more pronounced, until not to be in uniform classed you as odd man or woman out.

This then portrayed the scene through young eyes during the battle of Britain. Fortress Britain, Churchill called it, and although I never appreciated

William S. Smith

it at the time, a Britain that stood alone in the world. The only bastion left to fight a ghastly tyranny.

Before the turn of the century, Hornchurch, where John and his family now lived, was probably just a hamlet, comprising the obvious church and a small collection of farm dwellings.

My hometown, on the other hand, had existed for some hundreds of years and became established and well known for its cattle market. From 86 you would need to travel the road right round either to the left of our lakes and islands, or to the right, following Rush Green to the north before turning west to enter town, or on the opposing route taking a southerly course before heading west, past two gasometers reclining behind our large modern Oldchurch Hospital.

The first main thoroughfare you came to from either direction was our High Street that in turn lead you to the wide open market place. At the head of the High Street ran the main LNER railway. This stood for the London and North Eastern Railway. The marketplace itself was large enough to have most of its cattle pens left in position all week. Each Wednesday and Saturday, these would be filled with domestic farm animals: pigs, sheep and cattle.

I have good reason to describe my hometown because from the enemy's point of view railway lines and gas works represented prime targets. However, if you journeyed across our old excavations as the proverbial Crow flew, the shortened distance would still represent something in the order of half a mile. A crucial buffer when related to sought after targets.

1940 was the year we lost William Henry, and although I was his youngest grandson, born of his second eldest son, John, and had been given the honour of perpetuating his name, I still knew little of my illustrious grandfather.

Because of mother's loss, and thereby my constant change of abode, there had been precious little opportunity for us to bond. So he passed from my life without any real ache on my part, which I sincerely hope will not be the case with my own grandchildren. They do say that having lost Sophia he pined a lot and on his death-bed asked for his sister Jessie, unfortunately Jessie couldn't get there for she was seriously ill in hospital and died only twelve hours after William Henry. Within two months his eldest son William also died!

Never would I visit 62 Usher Road again, only Rene lived there now, with occasional visits from Dad. Elsie's Wal had found accommodation nearer his

THE WAY WE WERE

work at Dagenham and whenever Len came home on leave he would treat Ciss's home as his own. This naturally struck a cord with me; already he evoked hero worship which could only strengthen once he started to fly.

On August 25th the Luftwaffe bombed London in daylight, this had been the first attack directed towards the city, but years after the war had ended, this episode would be described as an error on the part of the German pilot. But such is the pursuit of war that mistakes can so often lead to terrible consequences.

Incensed by the German action, immediately Churchill chose to retaliate. For nearly three hours the following weekend, British bombers flew over Berlin dropping bombs and propaganda leaflets.

The die had been cast. Irate and apoplectic, Hitler resolved that Great Britain, having sown the wind, should reap the whirlwind. By late afternoon of September 7th, 300 bombers attacked our dockland in the East End, killing 400 and injuring a further 1,600. It heralded the start of the Blitz.

Another piece of historic fact to later emerge would acknowledge that this switch of tactic from attacking our vulnerable airfields to the bombing of civilians actually gave badly needed respite to the RAF and allowed it to gather strength. Threat of invasion gradually declined as all attention became thrust on the execution of our great city. Before long, as dusk fell, the nightly trek to bomb shelters would become the norm. Daylight activity started to wane and our autumn sky's only echoed to the tune of war after dark.

Usually you could guarantee that as the sun set so the sirens sounded. This episode did not lend itself to the bravado acceptance of remaining in the open, or sleeping in your own bed of a night. Anything could happen and bombs could fall anywhere. Sometimes we would stand outside the Anderson shelter watching the hundreds of searchlights sweeping the blackness and see crimson flashes as our shells burst way on high.

Deep red and orange glows silhouetted against the inky blackness barely ten miles away foretold of horrendous damage being wrought to London. All night long you would hear the rumble of exploding bombs and staccato cracks of gunfire.

During the day of course we could still carry on with our schooling, now conveniently uninterrupted, although we couldn't help worrying about our sister Rene, stuck in the thick of it. Jack drove us to parts of the city that had suffered the night before. Driving the Green Line coaches he knew which routes were still open, and I was amazed to see the bombed buildings, and how all the streets were covered in fire hoses. These showed a tangled mass criss-crossing one another, with whole roads completely cordoned off to save vehicles accidentally driving over them. I wondered how on earth they could ever be unravelled.

At my weekend ATC classes I studied hard. I loved the fact that our commanding officer wore wings; he was quite elderly, and had flown in the First World War. Our first task had been to study aircraft recognition; this entailed knowing every German, Italian and British aircraft off by heart. Not just being able to recognise the whole plane, but small sections of it, maybe a portion of tail or wingtip. We would be given pages of black silhouettes to study and then tested by our instructors. The funny thing was, we happily buried ourselves in these directives, no coercion ever needed as opposed to normal schoolwork.

The next requirement meant studying the Morse code so Bob Underwood and I rigged up some wires with small wireless batteries to run via the playing field to our respective shelters. Each night after the sirens sounded we would retire to our underground dens and busy ourselves sending Morse messages back and forth to one-another. The enforced shelter worked well and progress in this field gave us remarkable agility, as with forefinger on the sprung loaded key we speeded to sending thirty words a minute and receiving something in the order of twenty-five.

Wearing glasses Bob knew there was virtually no chance of him ever being involved in flying, but he was happy to learn Morse and be very adept at it. With his sights set on joining the Merchant Navy he soon realised high speed in Morse could stand him in good stead. He succeeded too! Being one year older than me, I became quite envious when one day he came home dressed in his wireless artificer's uniform.

We who lived in and around London were at a loss to understand what had happened on the night of November 30th, when for the first time in almost two months no bombers appeared. So used to the nightly raids had we become, it felt uncanny not to see or hear anything, we couldn't believe the Germans had given up.

They hadn't, for the next morning we learnt that Hermann Goering had switched targets and attacked Coventry. He'd sent 400 bombers to obliterate the city, dropping over 600 tons of bombs plus several thousand incendiaries. From now on he would reduce the number of aircraft attacking London, and send large formations to hit places such as Birmingham, Sheffield,

THE WAY WE WERE

Manchester and Glasgow, hoping to destroy our factories. After that he began going for the ports.

Speaking in the House of Commons, Churchill described how during the first week of the nightly bombings our casualties had been as many as 6,000 killed, but now they were running at about 3,000 per week.

But still they came, having spent a tentative Christmas mostly above ground, on the night of Sunday December 29th London was once more engulfed. Apart from 10,000 firebombs the Germans now dropped parachute mines, a huge canister type device armed with protruding detonators. The size corresponded extremely well with one of our red postal pillar boxes. The idea allowed the mine to explode on impact with the ground instead of digging a hole, thereby causing as much lateral damage as possible.

This night as Rene with a couple of other Auxiliary Fire Service girls manned their switchboard, their station suffered direct hits with firebombs, including a high explosive one that miraculously failed to detonate, burying itself right outside their station door. Undeterred all three girls continued to man their switchboards, directing fire crews to where they were needed, and in so doing helped save many homes from total destruction.

All three were to receive commendations and mention in the following days press. Over Christmas Len had enjoyed a long awaited leave, disregarding nightly air raids as most young servicemen did (after all, air raid wardens and fire fighters amongst others had to) he would be constantly out enjoying himself.

Dance halls and cinemas still operated during late evening despite air raids; in fact it wouldn't be long before Ciss actually started work as an usherette again. He did own up to a little nervousness, but that was purely because where he had been billeted they never experienced nightly bombing.

Studying till early hours, trying desperately to keep abreast of his more educated colleagues, he had finally passed all his exams; something he freely admitted had been a bit of a nightmare for him.

Able at last to let his hair down, it wasn't long before he met a few girls; they all knew that airmen who wore white inserts in their forage caps were aircrew trainees. This fact alone seemed to attract the prettiest of them. Seldom did he return to 86 before two or three o'clock in the morning.

Realising less concentration was now being placed on attacking London, we had all but given up on our nightly treks to the shelter. Often we would take our tea and sit down there listening to the evening's bombardment, then when things quietened down, return once more to the house.

This afforded Ciss an opportunity to play pranks on our wayward brother who now slept in the back bedroom usually until about midday. She would sew up the bottoms of his pyjama legs, and make what we used to call an apple-pie bed, folding the bedclothes in such a way as to make it virtually impossible to climb in-between them. After that we would all hide, waiting patiently for the miscreant to return, and ending up in hysterics as he stumbled around cursing like his favourite duck, swearing he would tan his sister's backside in the morning.

An unfortunate setback did annoy him somewhat, caused by his own talent. Officers at his previous station had noted his artistic ability, something the RAF was always on the lookout for. "I'm being posted to Torquay," he moaned; "that's all I need, just as I was about to start flying. Several of us have been requisitioned to paint the interior walls of hotels taken over by the RAF. This is so types can learn aircraft recognition while eating in the mess or studying in the lecture rooms. Boo hoo!" he'd cry, immediately invoking the wrath of Donald again.

Early December had seen the first British advance in North Africa against the Italians when we swept into Sidi Barani, taking 1000 prisoners and killing a general.

For us food shortages were getting worse, it was announced that most Britons had used carrots in their Christmas puddings owing to the lack of dried fruit: no more bananas were to be had and oranges, lemons and onions were to be very scarce. Coal supplies began to suffer too, as quite a lot came by sea and Hitler was threatening to increase his U-boat activity to ferocious levels.

To be honest, I never actually noticed food shortages; all I can remember is what a smashing cook my sister was. Her stew and dumplings were out of this world; thank goodness my wife Mary emulated her. But Ciss used to make a delicious apple sponge with custard that when withdrawn from the oven had risen to a golden brown lustre, light as a feather and a favourite of Jack and Len's as well as me. We would always refer to it as our greedy pud, because none of us could ever get enough of it. She would also show me how to make puff pastry, so I could help with her steak and kidney pies.

Placing a large portion of ordinary pastry on a board, she would get me to roll it out flat going this way and that to produce a nice thin layer. After this I would be instructed to apply small scallops of lard onto one half of the layer before folding it over and rolling the whole lot out again. Having carried out this procedure some four or five times we would be ready.

Whilst preparing this, our filling would have been simmering on the stove, so smoothing our rolled pastry into a nice oblong dish and planting an upturned ceramic eggcup in the middle, we would then pour the piping hot meats all round it. To complete the pie, another portion of duly prepared puff pastry would be placed over the dish and eggcup and the whole creation then sealed by pressing a fork along the outer rim. Finally Ciss would glaze this with egg yoke and trim off surplus pastry.

Extra material gleaned in this way would be conjured into gingerbread men.

When removed from the oven you could sniff the aroma from the bottom of the garden and the taste in my opinion has remained unsurpassable.

Whilst on the subject of food, I did experience whilst under the dubious care of my elder brother some years before the war, my first takeaway. By ourselves: in Usher Road, Len decided to take his charge to the local pie shop in Roman Road. Armed with two plates each and some muslin cloth we reached a queue standing beneath a large awning and in front of a long marble worktop. This was where they served piping hot portions of meat and potato pie, boiled potatoes with cabbage and for the other plate generous helpings of plum duff and custard.

You would pass your three-pence before getting served, to the helper, who dropped the coins into a wooden drawer. The pies were straight from the back oven of the shop and cut into quarter pound portions on the slab before you. Pushed from stainless steel tubes fresh from steamers, the duff slid out in long shiny white-hot cylindrical shapes. Sliced into hand sized pieces it was then smothered in custard. Covering both our overflowing plates with the muslin we would hurry back to number 62.

I remember Rene coming home with our tea in a bag, a dozen of the best cream cakes she could buy.

Having finally made a collective decision to stay in the house all night to avoid any cold damp conditions while able, Ciss had decided to transfer me to the back bedroom. Now whenever my erring brother returned on leave armed with the usual kitbag full of washing for his number one girl, we would be sleeping together. Amongst other things it afforded him an opportunity to show off his prowess and muscle strength by pinning me to the bed using one strong arm. He certainly portrayed power, and would kid Ciss along by placing one thumb in his mouth and pretending to blow hard as he flexed his biceps like a balloon.

After his stint at Torquay he began writing from Peterborough: here, eight days before my fourteenth birthday, he flew a Tiger Moth for the first time.

Peterborough, in the east of Britain, near the Wash, was the home of No. 13 EFTS (Elementary Flying Training School): here, he would study and fly. Fly and study, a concentrated course prior to switching over too more advanced aircraft. Subject to your ability and demeanour this was where the RAF would decide whether you were suitable to fly a fighter aircraft, demanding a single-minded aggressive approach, or a multi-engine bomber, which usually required the more serious studious type of individual: I felt there was little danger of Len being selected for the latter.

By May 8th he'd completed twenty-seven hours solo including six hours on instruments and passed above average. Two episodes of war stayed with me during brother Len's flying activities away from intruding Germans. One entailed Jack and I driving to Stratford some eight miles on the road to London, during an ensuing air raid. Our necessary journey was in order to collect Ciss from work where meticulously she showed wartime Londoners to their cinema seats, air raid or no air raid.

I remember vividly how intense sky activity was that evening. Searchlights stabbed the sky everywhere. At one point Jack stopped the car for us to get out and take a closer look. Two or three bombers had been caught in various cross beams. Once centralised in these, pilots had great difficulty in shaking loose from them. We could clearly see the bombs leaving the underbellies of the bombers, tumbling and breaking open to expose myriad's of smaller incendiary devices falling in the shafts of light. Fortunately they were not directly above us, but we knew there were plenty of other planes up there that we couldn't see.

After collecting my sister we drove back home to where things were quieter and still went to bed in the house. It was amazing how familiarity had bred contempt, but worse was to come.

This occurred after I had gone to bed one evening leaving both Ciss and Jack reading downstairs. Whether I had actually entered the land of Nod, I do not know, but if I had, I was soon wide-awake. In an instant the whole room, even accounting for our blackout curtains, became filled with an intense white light, to be swiftly followed by a vivid orange glow. Before you could say 'what the!' I had leapt from bed and shot downstairs straight under the dining

THE WAY WE WERE

room table, just as the crash came. Ciss was already there crouching as best she could whilst Jack for some reason had dashed to the kitchen. Everything shook, windows rattled, even the ground seemed to heave, but thankfully all remained in one piece. We learned next day that the new ambulance depot sited just half a mile away, had been hit by two parachute landmines. How many lost their lives we never discovered.

The upshot of this as I swung next morning round the corner of Norwood Avenue on the route to school and final exams, was to almost bump into a conspicuously sinister looking object lying near the middle of the road. Large and cylindrical in shape, it was attached to rigging lines and a parachute. Amazingly adults as well as children were gathered all round it, some already desperately trying to cut away pieces of the parachute.

As far as I could tell, no person in authority had yet cordoned the thing off. So I too joined in and managed to retrieve a piece of the rigging before carrying on to school. When I looked back, people were still crowding round it; the whole contraption bristled with four-inch long detonators sticking out along its sides, any one of which could have been alive. I was probably too naïve to appreciate the danger, but adults should have known better.

Had this particular parachute mine gone off, I dread to think how 86 would have fared, let alone most of the rest of the Avenue?

My first job meant cycling the eight miles to Stratford, working from 8 am to 6 pm and then cycling back home. This was Monday to Friday plus Saturday morning. I stuck it for one week and then promptly gave a week's notice. Jack had found it for me but that didn't mean I had to like it. Packing blue overalls in cardboard boxes for nine hours a day, not counting our one-hour lunch-break, was soul destroying. Ciss and Jack's only concern was that I should now earn my keep and as this particular past time paid the princely sum of only ten shillings (fifty pence) for the fifty-hour week, I reckoned I could do better. Standing out in my mind during this short two weeks was noticing a double-decker bus lying almost vertical against a bombed building near my workplace, and still seeing it there at the end of my employment.

Spying an advertisement for an errand boy wanted at the International Stores, Upminster, lying some six miles in the opposite direction, without further ado I leapt on my bike and shot after it. Here was a small kindly looking manager of what seemed to me then a very senior age. In truth he probably wasn't much more than forty, but certainly well past any call up years.

William S. Smith

There would be two errand boys including myself, to deliver goods prepared by twelve young girls, on one side of a very long counter reaching to the back of the store, and eleven boys down the other. All were between the ages of sixteen and eighteen. Anything older than this and they would be itching to get into uniform.

At the end of what must have been these thirty foot long counters, nestled our storeroom, where piled along the floor stood sacks of sugar, cereals, rice and all sorts of foodstuffs. When weighing these goods out, the boys and girls dextrously formed blue paper cones, scooping material directly into them before setting the results onto brass scales using solid round weights of varying dimension.

At the right-hand counter as you looked into the store, rested large squares of butter and cheese waiting to be cut up by the boys. Slicing into the soft butter with flat wooden slightly grooved pallets they would deftly knock portions into perfect oblong shapes and set them on their ceramic scales. It was amazing how often they judged each weight correctly. Cheeses would be cut through by pulling on stainless steel wires and yet again be within a fraction of the desired weight.

The first task of us errand boys would be to grab buckets of hot water and bars of Sunlight soap, and kneeling in my precious long grey flannels, start scrubbing the tiled floor between counters. Starting at 8 am we had until 8.45 am to make it glisten. In the meantime all serving boys and girls had been making up boxes of goods for delivery by us two scrubbers.

At 9 am the store opened and we'd start loading our carrier bikes. Big cumbersome things that could hold about five or six boxes in the large deep sided, solidly built front basket.

If everybody had done his or her job right, we had our first and nearest delivery on top then the next and so on. Fortunately for us, the terrain wasn't too hilly and a lot of well to do people resided in the area. All the avenues were lined with flowering cherry trees and used to look a picture in early spring.

I loved the job and each time you offloaded a box of goods so you could go faster and faster. We would weave round the avenues chatting amiably to all our customers, who quite often invited us in for tea and cakes. Back at the store of course we had all those pretty girls to look after us, and each time boys and girls met in the back storeroom our poor forlorn manager had his work cut out to keep discipline.

THE WAY WE WERE

Considering the employment Jack had selected for me paid ten shillings a week, I reckoned I had done quite well because I was now earning fifteen.

Not far from the store I discovered a bakery and most days I'd pop in there and buy three hot bread rolls, straight from the oven. I'd scoff these while they were still lovely and warm and moist, just as they were, no butter or other spread and then wash them down with half a pint of tea straight from a used milk bottle. All this for tuppence. They considered you shouldn't eat rolls straight from the oven, all I can say is I never suffered any funny symptoms and with the energy I must have been consuming they probably shot straight through me at an alarming rate.

A joyous perk was going swimming with one of the girls, I guess I was looked upon as just a kid really, but she was certainly a cracker, and knew it. She had long light brown hair that used to catch the wind and an hourglass figure you could die for. Her warm, soft face and gentle voice welcomed all those who glanced her way. As we pedalled towards the pool she would allow her full skirts to billow above her knees displaying what I can only describe as a gorgeous pair of thighs.

Opposite the store stood a small jeweller's and one day she confided to me that she was going to marry the guy who ran it. Whether she ever did or not I do not know but I was jealous as hell at the time. Once again I thought why am I always too young! Funny that I should remember her attributes so vividly, but not her name, although on reflection, it could have been Ivy, but who cares I remembered the most important things!

Out of my hard-earned fifteen shillings I would give Ciss ten towards my keep, and felt quite the grown up, in doing so. On the only ground-war front we had, North Africa, we were doing extremely well. By January 1941 we had wrested Tobruk from the Italians and entered Libya. However ominous signs were afoot when on February 14th Germany's Afrika Korps under the command of Erwin Rommel landed at Tripoli, although by this time Field Marshal Wavell's British troops had gone on to capture Benghazi.

Any of our troops left helping Greece finally surrendered when Athens fell and the German swastika flew over the Acropolis.

After completing his EFTS Len had signalled that when his next leave was over he would be sailing for Canada, where he would continue his training on North American Harvard aircraft under the Empire Training Scheme. Concerned for his welfare Ciss had made him promise to send a telegram the moment he arrived. So many ships were now being sunk in the

Atlantic you dreaded the thought of any loved one's having to sail across it.

Already Jack's second youngest brother, Jim, had succumbed to Hitler's U-boats. Entering the army he had embarked for overseas only to be lost before reaching his destination. We finally heard that where he had been sleeping above deck only a gaping hole could be found after the attack. But it wasn't U-boats that bothered Len during that particular leave, but Goering's bombers, making him fume and jumping mad, because he still wasn't able to confront the buggers.

Having already endured nine months of virtual continuous bombardment, 550 planes indiscriminately dropped hundreds of high explosive bombs, including over 100,000 incendiaries, on London during the night of May 11th.

The chamber of the House of Commons was reduced to rubble, Big Ben, although scarred, kept its clock working, St Paul's Cathedral and the British Museum suffered severe damage, the roof of Westminster Hall was set ablaze and the square tower of Westminster Abbey collapsed. Not one of the four main line stations escaped the bombing and casualties reached over 1400 dead.

Other news equally as bad was when we heard that the 42,000-ton HMS *Hood*, pride of Britain's fleet, had been destroyed and sunk by the German Pocket Battleship *Bismarck*: entering one of *Hood*'s magazines, an unlucky shell had ripped our beloved ship apart. Desperately needing some encouraging news for his beleaguered public, Churchill ordered all stops be pulled to get the *Bismarck*. On May 27th our Navy produced the goods, after giving chase for 1750 miles; Hitler's pride was struck trying to reach the port of Brest. Caught by aircraft from the *Ark Royal*, she was then shelled by two of our battleships, *Rodney* and *King George V*, before finally being torpedoed by aircraft from the carrier, HMS *Victorious*.

It is thought the loss of life on both the German and British sides exceeded 2,300 men.

As Len ran the Atlantic gauntlet, so I continued with my ATC studies. Dressed in full uniform, each Sunday we would march behind our drum and bugle band through the main streets of Romford. Stirring stuff with people lining the sidewalks. At headquarters, navigation and meteorology became the main subjects for discussion, coupled with logarithms, trigonometry and algebra. Without doubt, I was now learning faster and in greater depth far more than I had ever contemplated during my school years.

THE WAY WE WERE

Brother Len did make it to Canada, sending Ciss and the rest of us news of his safe arrival by the promised telegram, followed by a letter. In this, he joked about having been selected to box against the Navy for the honour of the RAF. "Boy!" he wrote, "was I in a mess," but then quickly adding. "But you should have seen the other guy!" After this he described his wonderful journey since arriving. "You should see the lights Cissy, after our blackout in Blighty, it's like a fairyland here, and the wonderful fruits you can buy, every kind imaginable. The trains are huge and it took two of them to pull our string of carriages for four days as we circumnavigated vast lakes.

"Our SFTS [Service Flying Training School] is at Moose Jaw in the centre of Saskatchewan, and the Kites are something to be believed, full of dials, knobs and switches, nothing like our simple little Tiger Moths. But navigation here will be piece of cake, because all roads run East, West, North and South and you can see Moose Jaw from fifty miles away."

In two months he would complete a course that before the war would have taken six and by early September be back amongst us again, the proud possessor of sergeant's stripes on his sleeves and pilot's wings on his chest. He had now passed the age of consent, twenty-one!

One of the coach drivers Jack had befriended went by the name of Eric Dubois (pronounced Du-bwaar). He also became a strong advocate of the motor car and favoured Lanchesters among other makes, but his biggest forte, like Jack's eldest brother, Ted, was wireless, or radio as it became more commonly termed. Towards the end of the war Eric would also begin dabbling more and more in television.

With the loss of manpower, transport operators looked more and more towards the employment of women, and most conductors were now conductresses, one of whom on Jack and Eric's route went by the pretty name of Bonnie! Although in all honesty it was actually Maud. But like Ciss and her dislike of Harriet so it was with Bonnie and Maud! This particular lady took Eric's fancy even though he was already married and gradually one of those wartime romances blossomed. At the time of writing Bonnie, who eventually married Eric after his divorce and became a longstanding friend of Mary and me, is ninety-one and living in a care-home. She is in complete command of all her faculties and if I was to ask any questions of her life I am sure she could recall them with greater accuracy than I can recall mine.

Eric owned one of the new pre-war development houses like Ciss and Jack and Brother John. But after things grew serious between him and Bonnie he would need to part with this home and acquire a bungalow residence instead. This current house at 11 Kimberly Avenue in Jack's home town would eventually be bought by him and in turn rented to Sister Irene after her marriage to John McCarthy.

Before Len had even accomplished his first solo on the Harvard, Herr Hitler had made his monumental blunder.

Tearing up all existing treaties, precisely as he'd always done, he swept with the aid of Finns and Rumanians along an 1800-mile front into Russia.

About four weeks earlier, his deputy, Rudolf Hess, in a bizarre incident, had parachuted from a crashing Messerschmitt into the Scottish estate of a past acquaintance, the Duke of Hamilton. No one seemed to know why he'd carried out this strange act, although it was rumoured he was acting as Hitler's peace envoy. However, our British government scotched that idea immediately, by affirming there could be no negotiations with Nazis. After a twenty-four-hour silence German radio announcers declared their deputy, had been suffering from hallucinations.

Although we were still fighting completely alone the American President Roosevelt had requested Churchill to meet him, and unbeknown to the world, both men did enjoy one another's company, supposedly on a British battle cruiser somewhere off the coast of New England. The outcome showed promise in the form of help and aid that Roosevelt was prepared to grant, which meant the lifting of a great weight from our Prime Minister's shoulders.

Great Britain lay like a massive aircraft carrier on the edge of Europe: lose her and you would have destroyed all possibility of ever reclaiming that continent. We alone had turned Hitler from invasion and pushed his sights towards Russia. That was our contribution to history! And now because of it, I would one day witness the greatest influx of American servicemen and equipment into our little island you could have ever imagined.

Before her fiancé could be shipped abroad Rene decided to get married; it would of necessity have to be short and sweet with John acquiring a forty-eight hour pass for both ceremony and honeymoon. At twenty-four years old she felt such time had come, and John's absence may be prolonged, surely it would be far better for him to know he had a loyal and faithful wife to return to.

When I opened the door I couldn't quite believe my eyes, standing there grinning like a Cheshire cat in flying boots and Irvine flying jacket was my fighter pilot brother. "Hi Billy," he chuckled. "Is my number one girl at home?" She sure was and couldn't brush past me quickly enough. Apparently he'd been on a training exercise in his Spitfire and had developed a glycol leak (loss of anti-freeze).

"Had to put down at North Weald," he grinned; "thought while I'm waiting for them to fix my kite, might as well look you up, and perhaps see if my popsie is free this weekend." Always he had a popsie somewhere. Sometimes he'd bring them home, but seldom was it the same girl twice.

Nothing could stop the German onslaught; I dread to think what we could have done against such might on our shores. By only the twentieth of October four German panzer armies, each one consisting of 5,000 tanks, stood at the gates of Moscow. So desperate was Hitler to take the city, he had robbed forces from other areas to do so. His concern was understandable: already the severe Russian winter had started to show its ugly head, and this was precisely the point where Napoleon found he had to retreat in 1812. But this time fighting had not abated. "Grit your teeth," was the cry heard in Moscow, "Squeeze the enemy's throat."

More bad news in November: our aircraft carrier *Ark Royal* had been hit by an Italian submarine. Listing badly she sank while under tow to Gibraltar.

Relations between the USA and Japan were deteriorating.

A telegram from Len on November 27th left Ciss puzzled. She looked at Jack and I completely nonplussed. Then read his words. It says, "Please tell Dad to keep Mum." I must admit we were now all bemused. "Only one thing you can do," said Jack, practical as ever. "Ring your dad at the lido near Littlehampton, perhaps he will understand what it means."

Dad groaned. "I know what it's all about," he said. "Two Spitfires flew low over the lido this morning and one of them has hit our flagpole on top of the building, and not just that, about eight feet of it has crashed through a glass section of the roof." He continued: "Len obviously doesn't want anybody to know his dad works here, but it's too late for that because I have already suggested to people that I bet my son was flying one of the Spits!"

Yes! It was definitely too late. Many months later Len confided to me: "When I jumped from my cockpit, Billy, you could have knocked me over with a feather, there was this erk, AC2 ground staff, peering into a hole in the root of my port wing, and poking about and suddenly spurting out for all and sundry to hear. 'Hey Sarge! I think you've got the top knob of a flagpole in 'ere!'"

To get there of course meant it must have synchronised with the aircraft propeller in order to miss it, and to make things even more extraordinary, Len never experienced a thing. In fact it wasn't until shooting up a train afterwards, when he and the other pilot flew low along each side of it, that he thought he detected an unusual wing movement.

Even all these months later he was still excited about it, and was at pains to describe how they had both flown in off the sea at wave-top height, having to hedge hop over tank traps set in the sand, before zooming up over the lido.

Disaster followed disaster when the first thing to happen was both our sisters Irene and Ciss deciding, in order to save their vulnerable favourite brother from a fate worse than death, i.e. being forever grounded, they would have to speak with his commanding officer. Which they actually did, but although sympathetic the squadron leader could do little. Such an approach sent Len into, to quote RAF language, rolls off the top.

Then, not only to have the humiliation of his own father giving evidence for the prosecution, but after the court martial for Dad to get given the verdict awarded the other pilot, a severe reprimand, which Dad naturally thought lenient. The outcome of which caused him to send a congratulatory telegram that had to be read to Len by a provost corporal on the parade ground of Chatham Detention Barracks, where Len had been incarcerated for two weeks.

The mitigation forwarded by his defending officer tried to prove that as both pilots had been carrying out air to sea firing exercises off the coast at Selsey Bill they had of necessity been banking round close to shore. On this occasion when Sergeant Smith pulled from his dive he'd momentarily blacked out, finding himself to be much lower and closer to land than before, forcing him to take swift evasive action.

It made him sound like a hero really, but the air force was having none of it. Six months' grounding, three months' loss of rank, and two weeks in Chatham Detention Barracks was their answer, but at least he could return to flying if he kept his nose clean. They do say that if he'd been an officer, he would have been stripped of rank and never flown again, which apparently happened on more than one occasion.

Falling foul of the RAF very often meant committing a "black" against your character, these could be minor or major depending on the nature of the offence. In either case it usually meant furtherance of your military career was at a standstill.

THE WAY WE WERE

Without doubt Len's brush with officialdom had been major; life could be difficult from now on. But like the proverbial rubber ball my brother not only bounced, but fought back.

That Christmas of 1941, Len wouldn't come home. Confined to his air force station until his court martial early in the New Year he bided his time whittling wood for another model, and busying himself sketching his surroundings.

Lots of other people found themselves unable to enjoy this year's festivity too, because on December 7th the Imperial Japanese bombed without warning the American fleet at anchor in Pearl Harbour.

Secretly launching 360 aircraft from six aircraft carriers they successfully sank or severely damaged five battleships, fourteen smaller ships and destroyed 200 aircraft. Two thousand four hundred people lost their lives in this dastardly attack, but it signalled a change in America's outlook not only to the Far East, but towards Europe too.

In attempting to expand her nation, Japan declared war, not just on the USA, but on Britain as well. In reply the American Congress voted for all-out hostilities towards Japan and Germany, including any of their Nazi allies.

War had become global, with hardly a neutral bystander left.

Our government had ordered all unmarried women between the ages of twenty and thirty to report for military service, so acute had the manpower situation become, even women up to the age of forty must register. This meant approximately 1,700,000 were involved in the new conscription plan.

Hong Kong fell to Japanese forces on Christmas day, but the day following, Churchill delivered a powerful speech to Congress, receiving tumultuous applause.

Still the Germans had failed to capture Moscow, and amazingly Russian forces were not only stemming the advance but driving panzer armies back, showing remarkable tenacity in the fifty degrees below zero temperatures. By the middle of December 30,000 Germans had been killed and 700 tanks captured or destroyed.

By the end of January 1942 victory for us seemed beyond our grasp. Having failed to stem Japanese advances in Malaya, our 8th Army now began losing ground in North Africa. German panzer divisions deployed by Rommel had given his Afrika Korps an opportunity to create a tactical surprise.

In the same month as the government announced that the maximum price of a new suit must not exceed four pounds eighteen shillings and eight pence, so Singapore fell.

William S. Smith

All through the summer and autumn months I had gaily pedalled my trusty steed piled high with boxes of goodies. I very often used to sing at the top of my voice as I swept up and down pavements full of youthful energy. Returning to the International Store empty, I could even outrun some of the elderly motorists so exuberant and intoxicated had I become with the freedom and lightness of my load.

But ugh! The winter foretold a different story. Now with boxes covered with tarpaulin and me wearing a sou'wester and cape to keep out rain and cold I needed to struggle to prop up the bike and deliver my goods in decent order. I'd pray each time I rang the bell that our customer would answer the door, otherwise where do I leave his or her perishable goods? Many are the times an irate person has rung the store to berate our poor long suffering manager. I decided there and then that before enduring another winter of tortuous toil I would look around for something different. In any case quite a few of the boys and girls I had come to know and like were lining up to leave, prior to entering His Majesty's service.

I suppose it must have been about a year since becoming an errand boy that I entered Meakers, a men's clothing shop in Romford High Street, in answer to their ad.

Here another small, slightly built individual met me. Mr Dean wore glasses and had very high colour in his cheekbones, obviously he had been declared unfit for call up so had carved out a career for himself in men's retail clothing. Two other sales persons worked under him, a rather large, big bosomed, fresh faced, dark haired lady, called Miss Banister, who I soon discovered hovered indiscreetly towards our manager, and a Mr Ogilvy, a tallish, rather foppish gentleman, trying to get accepted for military service, but so far failing.

The order of sales I was told depended on the number of customers entering the shop at any one time.

The first person became the target for our manager, Mr Dean. Should a second enter then up stepped Madam Bosom! If we should be lucky enough to have a rush and a third person walked in before the first and second had been satisfactorily served, then Mr Ogilvy could win himself some commission.

You can see from all this, that apart from dusting everything that didn't move, and being shown how to dress the window, my experiences were of necessity going to be limited. I must pack and unpack boxes, make the tea and generally act as gofor. Any chance of serving a customer and thereby increasing my earnings was going to be minimal.

THE WAY WE WERE

Despite all these drawbacks however, I longed to wear the new adult suit Ciss had bought me, and at least I could keep cosy in the winter.

Pay had also been a big incentive, rising to twenty-five shillings, of which I could now give Ciss fifteen, this also left me better off. Not counting of course, any commission I may glean! This invariably fell upon a Saturday, when we remained open all day, early closing being on the Wednesday. So gradually I learnt how to display a tie properly against a shirt, by creating a false knot, and generally chatting to mostly women shoppers buying for their husbands, steering them cannily into what I considered the right lines. We used to stock military shirts, khaki as well as blue, which were similar to officers' material, so often servicemen would buy these to supplement their coarse other ranks issue, whilst they were on leave, to wear such clothing on return to duty could land you in trouble. Having said that I must admit that during my stint in the services, I did quite often wear these softer, kindlier to the skin garments. One of my worst jobs was when they needed me to travel to the big London store for out of stock items. Coach travel for some reason made me feel sick. I quickly learnt that I always needed to be in charge. So being a pilot, driver, or steering the boat suited me fine.

***

Bomber Command, under the guidance of Air Marshal Sir Arthur Harris since February, began to attack German cities with new four-engine bombers. Many years after the war and long after Harris had passed on, critics would condemn his decision to embark on saturation bombing of the Third Reich, I say let these people relive their lives as we did, before they cast brickbats in hindsight.

United States troops had secretly landed within the first month of this New Year in Northern Ireland, and already there was talk of bringing across the Atlantic the big new four-engine Boeing B-17 Flying Fortress bombers, so named because of the number of gun turrets they carried. Twin-finned four-engine Liberator bombers would also be used, and between them form a highly dangerous (from the crews' viewpoint) daytime bombing force, whilst the British Lancasters, Stirlings and Halifaxes would continue their nightly raids.

Production lines became so vast in America that before long Detroit factories could churn out one four engine bomber every two hours, and one prefabricated merchantman, of the type designated Liberty ships, launched every four days.

To prepare for the aircraft influx, huge swathes of land would be commandeered, and many miles of concrete runway constructed. This latter could be achieved by using American know-how on the ground, and British contractors utilising their own lorries to supply the vast quantities of ballast that was going to be needed.

Getting wind of this possible scenario, Jack wasted little time in checking out government bureaucracy to learn just what he might have to do to get involved. Obviously it was going to be important war work, and secondly he felt sure petrol rationing would be waived for those accepted.

The whole concept constituted a big gamble for him, not only relinquishing his employment with Green Line Coaches, but finding and laying out capital sums not that easily come by. Without hesitation he told us, he was taking the car to Norfolk where government offices had been set up. "I must see the lay of the land," he told a worried Ciss, "and just what sort of equipment I will need, including the type of returns I can expect." In the meantime he'd keep his current job until ready to give the new idea a go.

With barely less than one month remaining as a second class erk sporting RAF wings, Len crept home during the hours of darkness for a much sought after leave. Before anything else his first pleading request to our sister was to re-sew the stripes on his tunic sleeves, so he might win over the popsies and enjoy his nights out. With genuine shock and horror, Ciss would have none of it. "You must be crazy," she exhorted. "What if you're caught? Why! you might be banned from ever flying again."

To be fair, this was quite true and she naturally felt unable to be party to such an outcome. But she had reckoned without the boyish, teasing, utterly charismatic ways of her young brother, so in the end she gave in and having cast past traumas aside, Len thoroughly soaked in the first leave he'd experienced in five or six months.

Managing to keep himself pretty busy since his stint in detention, which incidentally he laughed off as a place, where, in his circumstances, one kept very much to oneself. He'd produced some more paintings for the station CO, and succeeded also in carving a beautiful wooden miniature of a Spitfire, which he now offered to Ciss.

Only about three and half inches in span he had mounted it on a brass base carved into an arrow, representing prison. Above the arrow, set in Perspex within a circular brass ring, to denote his accusers, he had set a RAF badge. Centrally welded beyond this, stood a single rod, portraying the flagpole. On top of which, carefully inserted into a tiny hole on the underside of its wing, nestled the little Spitfire.

It was truly exquisite and told the story perfectly of how his plane had hit the pole, and the discipline of the RAF had sent him to gaol.

This model I have today, carefully enclosed in a glazed corner unit alongside other models created by my talented brother.

For Ciss it would take pride of place in her home until the day she died.

Thankfully removing his forbidden stripes before his return to Aston Down, Ciss and I bid him farewell and good luck. Imparting a cheeky grin as he waved goodbye, lithely he sped towards the corner of our avenue, his broad back, straight as a ramrod.

Barely two weeks from this departure, his sergeant rank would be reinstated, and for the following twelve would subject his mind to concentrating on bags of duty piloting and, albeit on the ground, as many hours as he could muster on the Link trainer.

On June 6th about the time United States Navy ships were routing the Japanese at the battle of Midway, Polish underground sources were declaring one million Jews had so far been exterminated by the Nazis. Then, as Len clawed his way back into the air, it was announced that Erwin Rommel had driven the British almost to the gates of Cairo. Quickly re-establishing his boyish confidence, in less than two hours' flying on a Miles Master, he found himself amply rewarded on June 8th 1942. Grasping the controls of the one aircraft he truly loved beyond all others, he cavorted across the sky, at peace with himself in his long-lost Spitfire.

Having held the German offensive throughout a horrendous subzero winter, Russian forces were now struggling to contain their enemies new summer onslaught. By July 1st the great port of Sebastopol had fallen, and alongside Kharkov and Kerch, meant they had endured three defeats in a row.

In one disturbing report it was suggested their fighting men had to wear gas masks, because of the appalling stench created by the unburied. Meanwhile struggling to get badly needed supplies to Russian allies, our Arctic convoys were being severely mauled, with one in particular, codenamed PQ17, destined to lose twenty-nine ships out of a total of thirty-three.

So bad had news reports become that Churchill had to survive a vote of censure! This he did in triumph with only twenty-five votes against his conduct of the war. Even so, something had to give, and the great man decided that a change of leadership in the field should take precedence. He chose

William S. Smith

"the commander who had distinguished himself at Dunkirk and was known to operate an aggressive type of soldiering". Montgomery! He would be the new general to lead the 8th Army against the man who had become known as Germany's Desert Fox, Rommel!

Staring at us from ATC bulletin boards, notices declared that RAF aircrew selection officers would be visiting our headquarters at the end of September. All cadets over the age of sixteen would be subject to interview and medical examinations. Any exam reports must be available. All those seeking aircrew status were advised to collect appropriate forms and hand them in to the Admin Office; I thought long and hard about this, here I was more than six months from my sixteenth birthday, hell! What should I do! I studied the form and as I suspected date of birth was required, but no mention of birth certificate so taking the bull by the horns I entered "Born 18th September 1926", and after completing the remaining questions, duly returned the paper to my Administration Officer.

My medical was straightforward except when the doctor said eyes, hazel! So het up had I become about getting through the selection, I thought he said hazy, and immediately wanted to know why! He turned to me dumbfounded, putting my mind at ease in a curt sarcastic manner. Hazel, laddie, hazel, how's your hearing!

Standing to attention before three seated senior air force officers, I could feel my hands going clammy, and body starting to tremble. I was so nervous I couldn't totally recall the questions they had put to me. I know one referred to algebra, and another to do with true North as opposed to magnetic, and oh yes, why did I want to fly! I'm afraid I shamelessly answered flying was in the family, with my brother already piloting Spitfires. I hoped and prayed that they might reason there was every chance a younger brother would probably emulate him and any expensive training should not therefore be wasted.

Some three weeks later a list of successful applicants was posted, and to my relief I had been selected in the category of PNB. This stood for Pilot/Navigator/Bombardier: the broad reference didn't worry me, as it was merely the new type of terminology now used by the RAF in their selection process. What did concern me was the inference that a further interrogation needed to be endured at the age of seventeen. I would now study even harder!

My first reward from this appraisal was to be granted along with about five other lads a chance to fly in a Tiger Moth. Taking a form of air experience the Air Ministry liked to encourage, and to make sure we had the stomach for it.

THE WAY WE WERE

Hornchurch was our local field, and they used to get off-duty Spitfire pilots to take turns in looking after us.

The memory of my flight has never left me; unfortunately it was the first and only time I ever flew in a Tiger Moth.

After being helped into parachute and harness I waddled over to the aircraft and was helped aboard the wing and into the cockpit by one of the fitters. This same fitter after receiving suck-in fuel and contact signals from my pilot, then brought the prop to compression, and in one heave stepped smartly aside as the engine burst into life. Instantly prop wash tugged at my hair and I could feel the rumble of undercarriage wheels beneath my seat. In no time at all this sensation ceased and we were airborne, watching the land drop away through the spinning propeller.

For about twenty minutes we twisted this way and that, doing fairly steep turns but no aerobatics as such, or inverted manoeuvres, but when we came in for a landing my pilot gave a closed throttle silent side-slip, from about one thousand feet. Looking straight down towards the tip of the lower port wing all I could see was the approaching ground, and all I could hear was the whistling wind as it strummed the rigging wires. The effect on a young lad, who until that time, had never sat in an aircraft was absolutely thrilling.

On the eve of my fictitious birthday the battle for Stalingrad was at its height. The whole of the free world held its breath as gallant Russian fighters strove to keep the Germans at bay. Twenty-two crack German divisions were being contained in the Verdun on the Volga.

Sea war had also never ceased by this September, when a German U-boat sank the British transport ship *Laconia*, little did its commander realise that on board, as prisoners of war, jostled 3,000 Italians. Appreciating his mistake too late, before a rescue could be mounted a fight ensued between his U-boat and the US Navy. As the battle escalated so the *Laconia* sank, taking most of its human cargo with it.

As a measure of the success of Hitler's underwater war it had been announced that the shipping tonnage lost this year had been five million, and in June alone one ship was going down every four hours. To add to this terrible statistic, it was now estimated that soon a further 400 submarines would be put into the German U-boat service.

Jack had been calculating hard. After returning from further visits to the north, he'd decided to buy a tipping lorry, and try to operate from a local farm, central to where most of the American runways were to be built. Fortunately at the outbreak of war he'd managed to acquire his plot of land at Stone. This would make a good jumping off point, for storing a vehicle and anything else that he might need for the new venture. Tipping lorries were not going to be easy to come by, especially in times of war. Hydraulic tippers particularly were scarce and expensive, but he did manage to buy a hand tipper.

I had the misfortune to help in the operation of this monstrosity a few times, pulling on the winding handle, while Jack, his hand firmly over mine, pushed from the opposite side. I couldn't have escaped if I'd wanted too, and believe me it was no joke trying to gradually wind up the worm type wheel as you turned the threaded shaft, with three ton of wet ballast to lift.

This experience would come later, after he'd settled into his routine near the town of Thetford, in Norfolk, and deep inside fen country. The remuneration couldn't have been better, providing you could withstand the hard graft. Six pounds a load from pit-site to airfield, before expenses.

Jack had it all worked out: if you arose at 5 am, in time for a hearty farmers breakfast, warmed the Wagon and arrived at the pit by 6.30 am, with a bit of luck you could be the first in the queue.

Each crane driver usually started at 7 am, dredging up bucket's full of soaking wet ballast to drop unceremoniously into your tip-up. Good driving was essential too, not just to drag your vehicle away from sodden rutted ground bearing a heavy load without getting stuck, but to negotiate the hairpin bends on the narrow roads we had to navigate. Many are the times I have seen a vehicle, still fully laden, at the bottom of a steep gully just after a hairpin bend. Arriving at the airfield, a black American sentry (they were usually black) would wave a greeting of "Hi youall" and hand you a docket gesturing where to tip your load. Then it was a case of wind like mad till your muscles ached, leap back into the cab and drive hell for leather for the pit.

If the Lord was with you, most of the queue would have subsided and you were catching the crane driver's eye before he stopped for his morning break. Then with grunting gears and screaming Bedford engine, we'd be off again, chewing sandwiches on the way. Before your crane driver decided to pack up for the day, with any luck you may have scraped in four or five loads, with bad timing only three.

When Jack started operating with a hydraulic tipper he could actually achieve six loads a day. With each load worth a week's driving on a Green Line Coach, you can see how hard graft and ingenuity helped Jack enormously, and in turn, to a partial degree, pave the way for all of us.

THE WAY WE WERE

We were now approaching the end of 1942, and apart from changing Hitler's mind about invading our shores, very little had been achieved by Britain and her allies. The Germans virtually controlled the whole of Europe. In Russia, enemy troops had taken two thirds of devastated Stalingrad and were poised to enslave the Russian people. In North Africa we had only just managed to hold our line outside Cairo at El Alamein, and in the Far East, Japanese forces were within striking distance of Australia.

This was the type of daily news I learnt to absorb as slowly I approached my true sixteenth birthday. It is little wonder that the thoughts and aspirations I experienced during this period were of how quickly I could get involved to help my country.

I should like to think that if I was a young lad today, and Britain found herself in similar circumstances, my reaction would be the same. Unfortunately, so changed has my country become, with pride constantly eroded so as to almost equate to a dirty word, with our Royal Family so often castigated, which in my view means a denigration of my country. Family values undermined, law and order becoming a standing joke, and honest citizens liable to suffer more at the hands of our judiciary than criminal elements. I am afraid that I would have to think twice before subjecting my person to any form of danger, to protect these kinds of values. Naturally I still love my country and would hate to see it overrun by tyrants.

To look down on English countryside as I have done, from the open framework of my own Microlight aircraft. To see patchwork fields, stately homes and medieval castles whilst I circled at only 500 feet, is enough to make your heart miss a beat. But I am scared that all this is under threat, because of political correctness, poor government, and bad immigration laws. You may recall earlier in my writings that our population stood at approximately forty-four million, whereas today it is over sixty million. Our lovely country is too small, too delicate, too desirable, to be overrun by any greater numbers. My great-grandchildren will inherit a Britain by the year 2100 composed of even more people, fifty per cent of whom probably originating from beyond our islands.

I hope and pray they will find ample space, tranquillity and happiness, for it is not what I, as a young lad, or as a great-grandfather that I have just become with the birth of Nathan would have wished.

At long last Len wrote to say he now flew with a Spitfire squadron. On October 20th he joined 165 Ceylon Squadron on a sector reconnaissance from Gravesend.

William S. Smith

The omen looked promising, for only ten days later, after building up massive reinforcements at El Alamein, Montgomery decided to make a frontal assault. There was no other route. To the left of our armies lay the soft sands of the Qattara Depression, and to the right, the sea. The only way was forward, through five miles of minefield laid down by Rommel.

The island of Malta recently awarded the George Cross for its gallant stand against continuous heavy bombing since the outbreak of war, now provided large aerial support for our advance. At one and the same time other aircraft flying from her precious airstrips made all out attack upon Rommel's ships trying desperately to reinforce his Afrika Korps.

They do say that upwards of forty percent of all shipping trying to reach the Axis forces are being taken out, and fuel supplies in particular are being severely hit.

Within one month with the Russian winter once more assisting their rescue, huge Russian forces started to counterattack around Stalingrad, converging in two sweeps each side of the city to gradually surround General von Paulus's 6th Army.

At home, church bells that had been forced to remain silent and only to be rung in the event of invasion, suddenly burst into peals of ringing, heralding the news of great advances in North Africa.

At last Hitler's onward march had been halted, and from this moment on, only final defeat would stare him in the face.

With all this good news swimming in my head, I couldn't have been more excited when Brother Len informed me, as he prepared for his return from a forty-eight hour pass, that he wanted me to accompany him to his new station. "Billy," he said, "don that ATC uniform of yours, I am taking you to Tangmere to sit you in my Spitty." Enthusiastically he pointed out the various controls as I soaked in the atmosphere from my privileged position inside the cockpit of an active service Spitfire. I even loved all the smells as they invaded my nostrils, the mixture of benzene and alcohol, burnt exhaust, alloy, rubber, perspex. It had it all!

"See! The control column breaks for left and right aileron, look how easily the rudder pedals move, this is the gunsight and here's the firing button. These are the instruments: turn and bank indicator, artificial horizon and altimeter." On and on Len went, trying hard to inject me with the will to succeed, so that maybe, one day, he could, just like him, claim his kid brother was a Spitty pilot too.

THE WAY WE WERE

A day I shall never forget. How could I? There I was, alone, out on the edge of a grass field with my hero, being shown the secrets of his true love, describing like an overexcited schoolboy all the gadgetry of his latest toy. Only one word can describe it. Magic!

Deciding there was only one thing to do, Jack informed my sister he was taking his tipping lorry to Norfolk, and would work up there all through the winter. He would return by train to collect his car so that he could commute back and forth whenever possible.

Poor Ciss, now she too would suffer separation because of war, and Rene, recently married, was the next one to say goodbye to her husband, although in truth she had seen little of him throughout this past year. Taking a final embarkation leave, Rene's Johnny, like so many others, sailed for destinations and time-scales unknown.

News began filtering through that a big armada of ships had anchored off North Africa's coast, and allied troops were pouring ashore at the port of Oran in Algeria. This was Vichy-French-held territory, and it was the first big American contingent to assist us in the region. The American commander, Dwight Eisenhower, let it be known he had no wish to fight the French and was there only to repulse the cruel invader, who had snatched away their liberty.

This landing, called Operation Torch was designed to drive towards Tunisia and catch Rommel in a pincer movement. Surely and steadfastly, Germany's Desert Fox found himself pushed ever backwards by our now exuberant Desert Rats!

For a few days over Christmas we were able to enjoy a decent family gathering. As usual 86 was headquarters, and Ciss busied herself fussing over everybody. Brother John had managed home, and with Ivy bringing her sisters Maude, Maisie and Vera ostensibly to keep Len supplied with girls, we all ended up having a gay old time.

Dad was there, and the whole gang of us joined in a good singsong round Ciss at the piano accompanied by John on his saxophone.

Quite easily we could have talked of so many things that had happened to us since the outbreak of war, but such topics would be hardly entered into. Instead everyone would curl up in hysterics as time after time Len would cajole us into attempting some bizarre game or other that he and his fellow flyers had conjured up during inebriated nights in the mess.

Collecting two bottles of beer, wine or milk, whichever happened to be handy, he would stand with both feet firmly together on a marked line. Then stooping low, place each bottle upright on the floor before proceeding to walk forward using them as support, until stretched to almost the horizontal, yet without trace of any part of his body actually touching the ground apart from the very tip of his toes.

At this point he would reach as far forward as possible with his left hand and place the bottle held using a slight flick to leave it standing in an upright position.

Finally, with rippling, quivering muscles, due to the effort required, placing both hands firmly on the remaining bottle, he would force his body upwards in a hands press movement and ease back, dragging the remaining bottle with him until he'd reached an upright position again.

We were left admiring the discarded bottle, stretching some seven to eight feet from his toe line, which was promptly noted as a target to be beaten.

"Right," he'd say, "who's next?" Looking straight at Vera, the prettiest and youngest!

Unfortunately also the most delicate, so the challenge would be short-lived.

Jack would try, but built like a hefty navvy, without the right knack his effort had little chance of success. Brother John would cope, but although taller than Len's five feet nine and a half inches found it too unbalancing to out distance his younger brother. Pop was the only one who could outdo his devil-may-care giggling son. He was slim built and very athletic, at the age of sixty I saw Dad hold his body horizontally rigid on a parallel bar, using only one arm slightly bent and tucked well into his side. My early bottle game attempts would be abysmal, although later in life I did master the technique.

Although none of us knew at the time, this Christmas celebration would be the last most of us would hold together for at least five years.

Early in the New Year Len was again by our side, although I say that advisedly, for he hardly remained still for any length of time. When he did however, if it be whilst drawing something or modelling, he could do so with the utmost of patience. He would concentrate for hours on end to achieve perfection, portraying one of his personal habits, and a definite trademark. Always you would see the tip of his tongue protruding ever so slightly from between pursed lips. One can almost imagine just before the enemy met their fate, Len hunched and deadly behind his controls, finger poised, tip of tongue locked in anticipation.

We would go to the cinema, where in those days each performance ended with "God Save the King". His manner and bearing could only be described as

THE WAY WE WERE

exemplary, and woe betides the guy who didn't show honour and respect. As I have indicated before, this wasn't just for royalty! They were the figureheads for Britain. Len stood like an unmoving statue because of pride in his country, and anyone who didn't was letting the side down.

Despite the trendy media of this new millennium, he, like I, would still feel such attitude should apply. If not, why do we go berserk over a national football match, or if any British athlete should win, is this not national pride? If this is undesirable, then I say do away with all competition and flags and act like grey dull people.

He was not averse to chastising me, his baby brother! Two things stand out in my mind at this juncture. Once when he had occasion to correct my posture as we traversed Norwood Avenue. "Pull your shoulders back Billy," he'd rebuke; "for a young man you are too round shouldered." Even today I still self-consciously attempt to create the right image.

Another time as we walked, or should say marched (although he always seemed to do it with a springy bounce) he'd glance up, spying a formation of Spitfires. The three V's of aircraft looked perfect apart from one slight straggler. Len was furious. "For god's sake man," he yelled, as though the poor chap could hear him. "Tuck your ruddy wing in!" Then, as though to justify his outburst he turned to me. "If it's close formation, Billy, then its close formation." It was blatantly obvious Len would never accept anything shoddy, in himself or anyone else.

Von Paulus surrendered his 6th Army, despite Hitler's orders to the contrary; there was little else the German could have done, even though at the last moment his marshal status was upgraded to field marshal. It was reliably stated that the battle for Stalingrad had cost the lives of 200,000 Germans either through the fighting or extreme weather conditions.

Watching a recent televised programme it was claimed that out of 95,000 German prisoners taken at Stalingrad; only 5000 would ever see Germany again.

We weren't aware of it at the time, but after Len returned from that last leave, he had sailed for foreign shores. Throughout the latter part of February and the first week of March he had been searching for his new squadron. Just before my true sixteenth birthday he caught up with 152 Squadron in the Tunisian Desert at a place called Souk-el-Khemis.

Just prior to his arrival German armour had made a dramatic incursion into the Kasserine Pass, which fortunately had been effectively repulsed. Len had arrived just in time to deliver the coup-de-grâce. He was also just in time to discover his Spitfire would be asked to carry bombs, along with the rest of the squadron, something he did not initially relish. These were Spitfire Vs and superior to the Mark IIs he'd been flying at Tangmere, being armed with two cannon and four machine guns, as opposed to the previous eight machine guns.

Practice flying still needed to be carried out and there were many airstrips hastily carved from the desert, each one being given the name of a British railway station. My brother would fly from Paddington.

Action increased and ten days after Len reached the age of twenty-three, he scored his first aerial victory, a Messerschmitt 109G, which he later described in his diary as a hairy do. He hoped he would never have to ask his Spit to perform such aerobatics ever again.

The day following, heavy flak (anti-aircraft fire) struck his oil tank, forcing him to pancake from 8,000 feet. He landed with wheels up on our side of the lines.

It reminded me of the Messerschmitt I saw on the way to Stone.

All resistance ceased in Tunisia by May 12th, Rommel having high-tailed it back to Germany, and Von Arnim, left in charge, had been captured along with 110,000 Germans and 40,000 Italians.

Len claimed two more as probable including a direct hit on a multi-engined transport sitting on the deck, with one of his two 250-pound bombs.

I had been right about my boss Mr Dean and his large lady love, Miss Banister, they each confided to Ogilvy and me, that they were going to be married. I was too young to know much about love, all I could envisage was this ultra big, heavy bosomed, soft voiced, round faced female, crushing the life out of our tiny fragile manager. Anyway Mr Ogilvy had finally managed to get accepted into the Navy, time to move on I thought and began to scout around.

I think a fair description would be from the sublime to the ridiculous, but it was a move I never regretted. Not far along the road running from Romford towards London I'd spied a largish Timber Mills. Its address surprisingly enough being Alcoe's Timber Mills of London Road. What else?

This was owned and run by two brothers, Johnny and Eddie Alcoe. Mind you they didn't get their hands dirty all that much, particularly Eddie, who seemed more the studious type. He was quite a bit slimmer than Johnny, including thinner in the face. Johnny appeared very much like brother-in-law Jack, being bigger and burlier with rounded features looking quite flushed at times.

THE WAY WE WERE

I had been introduced to a small boned, pinched nose little man, who had two complete fingers and a half missing from his left hand and half of a finger missing from his right. He acted as foreman but was also Johnny and Eddie's saw doctor.

He would hold up both hands almost in pride. "Been saw doctoring for ten years," he boasted. "Comes as part of the territory."

I dread to think what would happen today, be a millionaire I shouldn't wonder!

He in turn lead me towards a saw-bench, where a huge mountain of a young man was busy forcing nine inch square timbers through a plate saw guided by a solid steel adjustable gate.

"This is Bill Russell," squeaked the foreman, his voice matching his physique. "Bill will look after you, just do as he says." Bill was about to finish cutting a nice one-inch slice from his nine by nine. "Get t'other end," he said, in a surprisingly soft voice. "Just pull on it gently, not too much now, let me do the pushing with this piece of wood." He'd picked up a fairly straight stout section from off-cuts spilled onto the sawdust-covered floor. Fine chippings were flying towards Bill as deftly he steered the remainder through the gate. Then stooping slightly he threw a switch. But as the plate-saw only gradually slowed, he took another off-cut, offering it to the teeth to bring the blade to an abrupt halt.

"Lesson one," he grinned, "never leave a saw spinning, did you notice Harry our foreman?"

"Yes," I said. "How awful to lose fingers like that."

"It always happens when you least expect it," said Bill. "Usually when a saw is just spinning freely and you let down your guard. C'mon, it's time for tea; I'll introduce you to the others."

So that's how I started my first day at Alcoe's and met the man who would become my greatest friend. The gentle giant I called him, whose one-line cryptic humour turned many a dull day into a hilarious one.

Invariably working together in pairs, Bill and I built up rapport. Sometimes journeying to nearby forests to fell timber, having to use hand-held cross cut saws where each one pulls in turn in opposite direction, so you must act in complete harmony.

At the mills, with everything in those early days worked by hand, pulling and heaving on Block and Tackle to raise swinging trees suspended by grab claws, high into the air. Lifting thirty-feet-long planks of sawn timber to stack them one above the other using evenly spread slivers of wood to keep them apart and permit the newly sawn timbers to breath for months on end.

If I had little muscle when I started, Bill was certainly building me into a Hercules as I strove to keep on a par with him.

Across the way stood our mealtime café, where we would collect in the back room and be waited on by sisters, Irene and Connie Coffee.

In turn I took both of them to the pictures, Connie was the prettiest, a slim blonde, although I suspect it was from a bottle, because Irene had dark hair, she was definitely more portly and cuddly. But when something funny showed up on screen and Connie began to laugh I could easily have run a mile, as it was all I could do was bury myself in the cinema seat as her hee-hawing cackle reminded me of an ass in full cry.

Big oval faced beaming Bill only had eyes for one woman; she would step daintily past Alcoe's every morning and evening. All whistles wound in her direction each time her chest hove into view. Sheila it had to be said looked like the epitome of the Promised Land, although not overly tall, she carried herself with such bearing and poise. You could tell she was a man's woman, and in all probability it would take a man of Bill's stature to care for her. With dark tumbling hair, twinkling eyes and creamy white skin, Bill was a goner right from the start.

I can't say I was ever actually jealous of Bill, but that's probably because I wouldn't have stood much chance anyway, but all through our lives, I like to think, Sheila always had a soft spot for me.

We had two methods for slicing up trees: one way was to clamp the trunk firmly to the base of a cross-cut machine. A twelve-foot long cross-cut saw would be bolted flat-wise into a sliding frame and set at the required height against the end of the captured tree. The whole thing would then be started up by our thirty something operative, who, if I remember correctly, was named Alec. Each time the saw traversed back and forth so the platform on which the tree lay would be ratcheted forward a notch. This way just over two-inch slices would be cut from the trunk complete with bark attached. An ongoing job for Alec would be to make sure his horizontal blade did not become over-tight in the cut, having to continuously drive in wedges from both sides as gradually the tree moved forward.

The other method, far more dangerous and one which I often assisted in, was to place the complete trunk on a moving bench whose backward and forward movement was controlled by a four-foot upright lever. The cutting

THE WAY WE WERE

part was performed by a thirty-six-inch plate saw fitted with separate teeth. Only the upper eighteen inches of the saw was visible with the bottom half below bench level. Behind the saw a flat steel bed remained fixed to which an adjustable gate could determine your depth of cut.

The idea was you wedged your tree complete with bark against the gate so as it passed through the blade, about three inches would be cut off, leaving a nice flat section that you could now turn your tree onto.

The problem with this method was three operatives were needed. One to hold the back end of the tree firmly towards the gate by using a crowbar, another to make sure wedges placed to the sides of the tree didn't vibrate loose, and the third to operate the lever to control the speed and direction of the platform. This last task invariably performed by our fingerless foreman: my unenviable job was usually to make sure the wedges stayed put, meaning a hair-raising ride on a moving platform of unknown speed, past a whirling screaming disc less than two feet distant.

I recall quite distinctly the dicey occasion, when a whistling sound followed by a bang, indicated that one of our saw doctors supposedly secure cutting teeth had dislodged itself: thrust from the spinning plate it shot unimpeded through the corrugated tin roof, twenty feet above us.

Another slight problem sometimes encountered, used to send our forlorn foreman apoplectic. This was when through no fault of our own we struck iron! Such phenomenon arose if some ancient farmer from the past had decided to drive heavy nails or suchlike into a young tree that then proceeded to continue to grow, thus obliterating the offending material. A high pitched scream from our cutter usually accompanied the re-finding of these culprits, which resulted in everything being shut down a trifle too late!

You could only feel sorrow for Harry, because a thirty-six-inch diameter saw measured in circumference equated to approximately 100-plus teeth, now all thoroughly blunted.

Something I always found incomprehensible was the fact that one of our fellow employees was epileptic. I appreciate he wouldn't of necessity be allowed too close to machinery, but to be permitted within working distance seemed highly dangerous to me. Two episodes spring to mind concerning this particular individual. Once was when we were all having lunch in the back room of the café, when quite suddenly his eyes rolled up exposing just the whites and one or two of us had to quickly settle him in an armchair to enable him to ride out the fit.

William S. Smith

The other happened whilst we were on tea break in our little office, fortunately on ground level. At the time, one of our endearing old characters, complete with cloth cap and home rolled cigarettes, who was teaching me everything I needed to know about cribbage, had me engaged in precisely that, when without warning there was an almighty crash.

Poised with cards held tight to our chest, in startled disbelief we turned to see our poor epileptic friend writhing full length beyond what was once the office window. The distraught man was covered in shattered glass and bleeding profusely. After he returned to normal, he assured us he had not known or felt a thing. I remember thinking that in all honesty it was we spectators that seemed to be affected the most.

Jerry still flew over most nights, there seemed hardly a time that the inky sky wouldn't be criss-crossed with stabbing searchlight beams. Heavy bombing of London had become second nature to us. Hardly anybody ever bothered to visit an air-raid shelter, unless you were in a particularly hazardous spot. Timber mills could fall within this category, a portent that had not escaped the notice of Johnny Alcoe, so he asked Bill and me if we would do fire watch some nights to help him and Eddie out and a few of the others. We wouldn't have to stay all night, just until Jerry decided to go home, and it meant more money.

On this score my remuneration had now climbed to the dizzy heights of two pounds ten shillings, plus a likely chance of some production bonus. Output volumes were arrived at by relying heavily on Eddie's book keeping: It was he who was responsible for noting how many and what type of trees passed through the Mill each month. If after consultation with Johnny they decided between them we were deserving of something, then so be it. Hardly a bonus, more a thank-you if their mood passed muster.

Neither Bill nor I ever experienced having to smother with our buckets of sand actual phosphorous incendiary devises, or extinguishing any fires caused by them. However we were often grateful for the tin roof covering the mills when on many nights shell fragments from our own anti-aircraft fire came rattling down.

May 17th would go down in history as the night of the Dambuster raid, it was truly a remarkable achievement and one we were hoping would make the Germans stop and think and maybe shorten the war. Alas that was not to be, but at the time it boosted everybody's morale and the following weekend we held a special ATC parade through Romford.

THE WAY WE WERE

ATC studies were taking up a lot of my spare time, but I was determined to keep at it. How amazing life can be, when, with so much packed into each day, as I now realise, yet still I could not grow up fast enough. Even with my false age I would still not reach seventeen until September, and Brother Len had written to say he was now in Malta.

Trying to make sure he didn't upset his number one girl he wrote to say he'd been involved in a slight accident, but not to worry, just a scratch to his leg. But he committed to his diary that the vehicle he'd been travelling in across Tunisia had caught another head-on and three of his fellow pilots had been killed in the horrendous pile-up. His so-called scratch was an eight-inch gash requiring many stitches.

When Jack came home in June it was to let Ciss know he had managed to acquire a hydraulic tipper, and on top of that set up his own caravan in the farmer's yard so that she could join him. It meant giving up her part time job as cinema usher, which, with Jack away had lead to her relying on buses.

As it happened any reservations were dispelled the following morning as I lay cosily wrapped between the sheets. I can only describe the sound as an express train running from the door and across the room. In a trice I bounded, to stare agitatedly from my bedroom window, and there across the far side of my old playground, flame and smoke spewed from one of the gasometers.

Later we learnt it had been a Focke-Wulf 190 that had attacked, one of the Luftwaffe's latest fighter-bombers carrying out a hit and run raid from across the channel, and sweeping at nought feet above number 86 to do it.

Bill Russell must have been a good seven months older than me, which meant he wasn't far off seventeen in June that year, a point worth remembering. Already I had introduced him to Ciss, who now referred to us as her William pair.

This month also saw our father tie the knot, after a lapse of sixteen years. A cook of many years' standing, including working as one of those downstairs ladies in a big house, tall, upright, kindly, middle-aged Mary Gardner, had won the heart of Dad. When he heard the news Len wrote quite a concerned letter, somehow he felt he should have been given an opportunity to vet the lady. Had he forgotten there was a conflict being enacted, of which he was a part of some hundreds of miles distant!

The tide of war began more swiftly to turn in the Allies' favour. One of the greatest tank battles in history was now under way around Moscow: having failed to take Stalingrad, Hitler had declared that this battle with the new Tiger and Panther tanks would prove to the world that the German armies were invincible.

He had reckoned without the new Russian anti-tank gun, called the Conquering Beast, a 152 mm howitzer produced in factories set deep in Siberia, and capable of a nine-mile range. Such a battle would end in a rout of the Germans and cause Hitler to declare a cease-fire to the attack.

In the Atlantic too, Nazi U-boats were starting to achieve less success, with tonnage sunk down from a high of 650,000 a month, to just 18,000 tons. Couple this with increasing U-boat losses, as more and more sophisticated equipment was brought to bear, and it looked as though we were gaining the upper hand.

From Malta Len had destroyed Italian Reggio 2000s in air battles, and was on the verge of assisting in the invasion of Sicily.

Just like Battle of Britain year, this summer seemed to have been a good one. Most of the time Bill and I were working stripped to the waist. Being young and easy going it didn't seem to bother us that, soaked in sweat with matted hair, and covered from head to foot in sawdust, we must often resemble a couple of wild men from Borneo.

The standing tap beyond our wooden staff shack, known affectionately as the office, was in continuous use. We filled up old lemonade bottles to keep nearby as we worked the saw-benches, or operated lifting tackle. Within no time at all, half was swallowed, with the remainder ending up over our heads.

Thank goodness Connie and Rene's mum taught her daughters to be such good cooks. Without the consumption of this family's home cooked pies, copious vegetables and delicious rice puddings, I fail to see how Alcoes could have survived.

Behind their homely cafe lay a piece of wasteland quickly adapted by Johnny and Eddy to house all their newly cut timber. Stacked in similar fashion to the tree itself, these two-inch plus planks, had now been reconstructed with one-inch spacers between each layer. Using steel dies of Roman numerals each one would receive at its base four crosses and three ones, denoting laid down in 1943. Most would lay there for four years at least, by which time, the ash, oak, elm, beech, or any other species bought by the brothers, would be nicely seasoned.

Bill knew all about the various trees, something I often wished I had studied, but at least he had been involved since leaving school.

Because of people's demand for daily news and entertainment the radio

THE WAY WE WERE

began to play a more important part in everyday life. Even as a gangling youth I appreciated this, because I used to listen avidly to the Tommy Handley comedy shows of ITMA, and most wartime factories had loudspeakers fitted in their canteens so that workers could hear our stars of the day like Gracie Fields and Vera Lynn.

But if your home radio gave up the ghost it wasn't easy to find someone knowledgeable enough to delve into its mysterious workings. Radios, or wirelesses as they were commonly referred to, were full of large valves, condensers and conductors, reliant upon umpteen bits of coloured wire running everywhere.

This is where Eric Dubois came in, being a bit of a radio buff as people were disposed to refer to them, he found he was having to devote a large slice of his off duty time helping folk sort out their problems.

Divorced from his first wife he had reached a crossroads as most of us do in life, I personally recall at least three or four. He would chat to Jack about his ideas, aware at least that here was someone not averse to taking a risk, a friend he could confide in.

Jack was for it, especially when it meant Eric giving up his house in Kimberly Avenue, which incidentally ran not far from the Alcoe mills. Eric needed a buyer, and with the fine rewards reaped from hard work further north, Jack was prepared to be the purchaser.

Everything was soon arranged; Eric left the Green Line Coaches, married his Bonnie, bought himself a bungalow and rented a small shop in North Street running from Romford High Street.

I cannot recall the name of Eric's shop but am quite certain that if so inclined to pester Bonnie, she would remember it in the twinkling of an eye.

Having gathered the news, sister Irene would jump at the chance of renting Jack's second property, keeping up payments, so that when her Johnny came marching home, he would have one, ready made to fall into.

Whether this heralded the final abandonment of 62 Usher Road I do not know, but certainly Dad never went back to live there, neither to my knowledge did Elsie, which would leave our First World War home empty. In this year of 2004 I can record that my surviving sister Irene is currently cared for in a nursing home, having been taken there by her daughters after losing her Johnny. They took her from the very house she first rented from Jack in Kimberly Avenue, yet in her now sometimes confused mind she is still back at 62 Usher Road.

William S. Smith

For some obscure reason Bill and my employers actually agreed to releasing the both of us from duty at the same time, and at Ciss and Jack's suggestion it was arranged that we would all journey to Norfolk for the week.

Excited at the prospect of Bill's pending seventeenth birthday, Jack cast an eye over my friend's physique and questioned him as to the possibility of coming to work for him as he now seriously considered acquiring another tipper.

Sometimes when we worked in the forests felling and removing trees, Bill and I would operate one of the brothers' tractors. Although this was off road experience, at least it gave us the basic knowledge, I don't think there was a farmer's son in those days who wasn't driving a tractor by the time he was twelve, and would go straight onto road transport on his seventeenth birthday.

Apart from rising early some mornings to shoot rabbits with our landlord farmer and generally enjoy rustic countryside, Jack had now concluded, under age or not, that he would get each of us driving his newly acquired hydraulic five-ton tipper.

Initially, Bill would be the more adept as opposed to me; obviously he had far greater usage of the forest tractors and certainly impressed Jack sufficiently to encourage him to pursue his idea.

Never one to be patient, I shall never forget my initiation given by Jack.

Having guided me firmly into the driving seat, he first taught how to double-declutch both up and down the gears. "You will find it much easier to engage smoothly," he'd bellowed. "Right, away you go, keep her moving! If you had a load on she would have stalled by now."

He would continue in this vein until safely installed on the highway, then, "Okay, open her up, more power, come on, more power!" I could see a bend in the distance, just as he reached across to plonk his right foot firmly over the top of mine, which hovered hesitatingly above the throttle. All I could do was concentrate on the steering, hoping to god he would relax his foot before the bend became too close. He never did, so I negotiated it as best I could, then to my horror having reached the curves apex he pushed down harder. "The way to take a bend," he cajoled, "is to give her a bit more gas at the halfway point, that'll push her round, see, makes the job easier!" Then he'd grin. "Don't worry Billy; we'll make a tipper driver of you yet"

In fairness I was only sixteen and my introduction started on a massive Dodge lorry driven on narrow Norfolk lanes. Our visit to the American bomber airfields was another piece of history I will never forget. Even after all these months they were still building more runways and taxi tracks, plus lots of hard standing for the big four-engine planes scattered all around the perimeter.

You couldn't get too near the aircraft but I do remember seeing quite clearly bombers that had been damaged during operations. I saw a Liberator with one section of its twin tail looking virtually like a colander, and that was from a distance. Another was a B-17 Flying Fortress with definite damage along one side, plus groups of American airmen huddled everywhere.

In fact the whole of Norfolk was one big vast Yankee encampment, with most of the narrow lanes constantly filled with American army trucks, toing and froing, a factor that much later brought disaster to Jack's ideas.

Not far from the farm flowed a section of river that could possibly have been the Little Ouse. One particularly hot day, having found an isolated spot, we decided to have a picnic and perhaps enjoy a swim. Being a bit of an adventurous idiot, I foolishly decided to throw a rope across a substantial overhanging branch reaching from a bank-side tree, this way you could launch yourself towards mid-stream before letting go. As luck would have it, Jack thought to bring one of his inflated inner tubes, for playing about with.

The stage was set and we lazed and swam and wallowed in the warmth of the sun, with all thoughts of war a million miles away. Finally I decided to give my Tarzan act a go, scrambling part way up the tree to catch hold of the rope. It wasn't going to get me far, but then the river at this point was only about twenty feet wide so I reckoned the swing should get me somewhere towards the middle.

I gave a short run, rendering my call of the wild as I went, and flopped with a great splash. The water couldn't have been much more than seven foot at its deepest and Bill and I had already enjoyed swimming from the bank without any problem. By the time I resurfaced and pushed the hair from my eyes, Bill was in the throes of preparing to launch, and the next thing I remember was he hit the river almost alongside me.

I trod water waiting for him to pop up like the big seal he was, but he didn't, and for a moment I couldn't understand why! There he was right at my elbow, arms floundering just beneath the surface, yet the only part of him that rose above was his hair. I yelled to Jack, "Jack! Bill's in trouble! He can't get his head above water," then immediately dived beneath him. All I could think of was somehow I needed to push him up, but instead Bill now grasped me so tight I couldn't do anything. He began pushing hard on my shoulders, but all this did was to force me to the bottom while still not raising his head above water.

I soon realised things were becoming desperate, and not just for him, but me also, and the irony was, it was all taking place within six or seven feet of the bank, in water only twelve inches deeper than either of us.

Then, thank god, he suddenly relinquished his stranglehold on both my head and shoulders, and I managed to surface, spluttering and totally exhausted. Quickly sizing up the problem, dear Jack had acted with speed and foresight, by throwing the inflated tube towards our life struggle, before diving in.

Somehow he managed to grab Bill by the hair and yank his head onto the tube, it was a few moments after this, while still retaining some semblance of thought that Bill decided to let go of me and reach for the inflatable instead.

Between us, Jack and I brought the rubber ring, with Bill attached, to the bank, whilst my sister, hands clasped in consternation, watched from the sidelines. With one last effort we managed to heave him onto safe ground, where we all collapsed about his prostrate figure.

Fortunately he was still breathing, but only just, and I'd never seen such a glazed expression on anybody. It took some minutes before Bill really rejoined the land of the living, when immediately we wanted to know what the hell had gone wrong!

They say it's the simple things that occur that catch you out, and so it appeared in this instance. Being able to walk into water and start swimming, Bill never gave a second's thought that it wouldn't be the same if he jumped in. But because he had no experience of diving or jumping and having to resurface from below water, his body never reacted correctly, he just had no idea how to get his head above the surface.

For years afterwards I wondered what I would have done if Jack had not been there, and even to this day I am unsure whether perhaps we would not have both drowned.

Fighting had progressed in Sicily after the invasion and when we returned from Norfolk it was announced that Messina, the coastal town facing Italy across the Messina Straits, had fallen and that the island was firmly in our hands. The Fascist dictator, Mussolini, had been deposed, and the ex-King of Italy, King Victor Emmanuel, had assumed command. It was now widely predicted that Italy would soon surrender.

Brother Len played no small part in this victory, although we wouldn't get to hear for some time, when another 109 fell to his guns trying to make it across the Straits.

One day prior to my fictitious seventeenth birthday Len wrote in his diary.

THE WAY WE WERE

"We have landed in Italy, which I myself think is a trifle too soon, for our Battleships are still firing inland with every so often a dirty great shell tearing across our Strip to explode on the hills beyond. On the approach to our Strip a big Tank battle is in progress with explosions going on all night. In fact as I came in to land the guns went off making my aircraft jump a little. The following morning we were having to shelter in a ditch while Focke Wolf 190's dive- bombed the place. A little later we did manage to get airborne, I being in one of two Spitty Mark IX's giving cover to the Mark V's below."

Coming along the Beachhead for the second time, I spied bombs going off in the water but fortunately missing our ships. All this time of course Jonesy and I were going down vertical after these buggers, I getting onto the tail of one, right on the deck. We passed over our Drome doing 460mph with our gunners opening up on this Hun, but missing him and coming damn close to me. Flying inland I managed to close to within 400yds as we came to some hills, instead of going round them the silly tit tried to get over the top enabling me to give him everything I'd got.

He didn't get over the top, instead he hit it, pieces going for miles.

No Italians were to be seen because nine days previously Italy had surrendered to the Allies, so even though we were on Italian soil only Germans were our enemy. Mussolini however has been spirited away by German parachutists in a daring escapade.

The following day, September 18th 1943, I began to wonder when the RAF might want me to attend my second selection board. *Hell!* I thought, *if I don't hurry up things could soon be over.*

By the time I received my letter, Italy had changed sides and declared war on their old ally, and the Russians had broken through on the 1300-mile German defence line along the Dnieper River.

Len's 152 Hyderabad Squadron now rested at Gioia-del-Colle in southern Italy, from where he wrote: "Wow Cissy! What a smashing country, and the girls, Boy! Are they beautiful? I think I could quite easily stay here and get married."

This time I would need to journey to London: I have an idea I had been asked to attend Ad Astra House and would be required to sit written exams as well as stand before the usual selection board. There was no denying that entry into aircrew training had become more and more difficult as each year progressed. So many eager young men had volunteered for this branch of the services it was becoming almost embarrassing for the RAF, with many other parts of the military crying out for recruits.

Already there was considerable talk and newspaper inches being devoted to the possibility of a Second Front in Europe, meaning the deployment of huge extra land forces. It wouldn't be long before Roosevelt announced the appointment of General Dwight D. Eisenhower as its supremo, with our own General Montgomery his field commander.

It left me with a feeling of trepidation, trying to pit myself against what were obviously many graduate schoolboys and brighter young men than me: so I breathed more easily when before Christmas a letter arrived telling me I had passed selection and was now regarded as an RAF reservist.

Another reason for congratulating myself happened when an idea announced by Lord Bevin stated that from now on one in ten men eligible for service, would be switched into the coal mines. I would have hated to become what was later known as a Bevin Boy.

By the years end many of my contemporaries had donned uniforms, Jack's brother Bob, responsible for my back-slang name of Libby had joined REME (Royal Electrical and Mechanical Engineers). His youngest brother Frank whom I'd shared a couple of my earlier years with and who outranked me by at least twelve months had been drafted into the army. During the D-Day landings, Frank would be in charge of an amphibious vehicle responsible for ship to shore transportation, known as a DUKW, and suffer the indignity of receiving shrapnel wounds from one of our own naval shells.

Whilst undergoing hospitalisation he and his nurse, Yvonne, would fall in love and later tie the knot.

My Morse code comrade Bob Underwood looked dapper in his Merchant Navy artificer's uniform, and one of two brothers I'd played with called Derek, who lived opposite number 86, had returned on leave sporting bell-bottoms and the jaunty round hat of the Royal Navy. Much later, after the advent of the second front, he would describe to me how he acted as gunner on one of the rocket-firing ships in the battle for Walcheren Island off the Netherlands coast.

Everybody, it seemed, wore uniform, which I managed to simulate whenever I attended my Air Training Corps sessions.

Awful stories were coming out of Far Eastern news services, telling of 1800 allied prisoners left beneath battened down hatches after a Japanese ship had been torpedoed. How, having escaped, three American officers retold their terrible story, of thousands of fellow prisoners captured at the fall of Bataan and Corregidor suffering forced marches, torture, starvation and murder at the hands of their captors.

These stories were all the more upsetting because brother Len had now written to say he had flown with his squadron to India. Although he couldn't be precise, we knew it meant they were going to fight the Japanese, plus having gone further afield to plunge into that forgotten conflict, there was no knowing when we might ever see him again. It is highly probable that this particular squadron had been selected owing to His Exalted Highness the Nizam of Hyderabad, one of the richest Indian Princes of the time, funding its original eighteen Spitfires.

They had flown in thirteen hops to reach the far side of India near Calcutta, a flight, Len said, that had created history, and on the way landed at a desert outpost called H3, a remote depot that just happened to be the exact spot Rene's Johnny was stationed, busily refuelling the many varied aircraft that dropped in. Neither would know of the other's presence, otherwise I am sure Len would have found time to exchange gossip with his brother-in-law.

We heard that the *Scharnhorst*, Hitler's last big battleship, had been caught after making a wrong move trying to track one of our Arctic convoys. The mistake, probably due to poor light at this time of year off the Norwegian coast, allowed undetected British battleships with their fourteen-inch guns to get within range and sink her. With the previous sinking of the *Tirpitz* and *Bismarck* our large ships were now free to fight in other seas.

One of the model aircraft I had decided to build was a complicated American Grumman naval dive-bomber. Being a twenty-four-inch span biplane, the aesthetics were very good, and the undercarriage could be made to retract into the sides of the fuselage. During the winter months, apart from study and the occasional flicks (cinema), I engrossed myself in this model, having to develop sliding alloy tubes and rods for the retraction.

One day, a while hence, I broke open some live .303 cartridge cases from ammunition I had won, extracting the matchstick-like cordite, to lay criss-cross fashion down Ciss's garden path, setting the final charge beneath my handiwork. It had become one of those white elephants that Ciss had long since wearied of dusting, so needing to remove this piece of nostalgia, I wished to recall a fitting end. If only I had any one of a number of cameras I have since owned, but alas I did not. So bending low without a tear in my eye, I set a match to my fuse, watching the little flame travel slowly towards the plane until in one woof, it exploded in realistic style, leaving only a pile of ash.

William S. Smith

By March 18th, my true seventeenth birthday, the Americans were trying to break out of their new bridgehead behind the German lines at Anzio. The British were busy dropping glider-borne troops two hundred miles behind the Japanese lines in Burma, and Russia had destroyed ten divisions of the German 8th Army at Kiev.

Another winter of humping tons of ballast for the Americans had brought Jack just rewards, income that he would now turn to good use by investing in a second tipper. But like scarce pilots to fly fighters in 1940, so the right personnel to drive tippers were hard to come by.

A conference held at 86 determined that my six-foot-one-inch heavily built friend, Bill Russell, and I would both give up our employment at the timber mills and move to Norfolk with Ciss and Jack. The decision needed to be reached quickly because Bill had barely three months left before call-up. In any case having reached the critical age myself, with added tuition I could succeed Bill if and when he left us. Jack naturally felt that time was fast running out on any further developments to the airfields, and quite easily this could be his last chance to make hay.

So while Rommel began strengthening the defensive wall of Europe against the massive forces of Eisenhower rehearsing throughout the whole of southern England, Ciss, Jack, Bill and I left for flying fields in Norfolk.

With two trucks to maintain life was never going to be easy or straightforward.

Bill had started well and soon found his way round the narrow lanes and tortuous twists of fen countryside. Busy coursing from pit to airfield and back to pit, he had departed extra early one morning, leaving Jack to attempt a repair on his lorries fuel tank. Helping with the initial removal I had since joined Ciss in the caravan, preparatory to driving her into Thetford for a few badly needed rations.

Outside, Jack studied the removed tank, where he now ascertained the offending leaks lay buried along one seam, only molten metal applied here, could produce a permanent repair.

In this situation it is a well known fact, that you either fill the tank with water, which Jack was loath to do, or pump it full of exhaust gas to drive out the fumes left after removing the petrol, a much better and less troublesome method!

Our runabout was a Lanchester saloon, a second-hand vehicle acquired by Jack with a clutch system of semi-automatic design. You selected your

THE WAY WE WERE

gear first, and then depressed the clutch afterwards. It took a little getting used to, but basically he had bought it to encourage Ciss to drive and give her something easier to handle. There was no such thing as learner plates, or driving instructors, except in the services. You acquired a licence then drove with somebody experienced until you and they felt you were competent. My presence enabled Jack to keep his freedom without worrying too much about my sister's road use, so far she would only drive with me at her side.

Running a piece of flexible tubing from the Lanchester's exhaust, Jack duly pushed this into his petrol tank filler pipe and allowed it to chug away for some minutes before effecting the repair.

As Ciss and I consulted on our shopping spree, there was suddenly a terrific bang and we both leapt from the caravan to ascertain its source, to find Jack staggering around arms outstretched and both eyes tightly shut. Hastily we guided him into the caravan, sat him down and nervously inspected his face. Bits of white metal were adhering to his skin and each set of eyelashes appeared to be soldered to his cheeks. Being a tough character he was instantly at pains to reassure us that he was okay, and that all we had to do was remove the hard solder so he could open his eyes.

Agitatedly, Ciss stared at me. "What can I use?" she quailed. "It's stuck fast." I have to admit, I was at a loss, after all the, only thing I knew to dissolve solder was heat.

But fortunately my sister was wiser, and began bathing Jack's eyelashes and face with Vaseline. Thank goodness it was a commodity always kept to hand!

After persevering with this treatment for some time, gradually the solder began to fall away. Poor Jack, for a big guy, he could so often look sheepish, especially when he'd done wrong, or come to grief through his own actions. Grinning and apologising like an errant schoolboy!

We discovered after investigation, that there had obviously been a pocket of fumes left between baffles set inside the tank to overcome movement of the fuel during travel. Using a paraffin blowgun to melt the solder, Jack had inadvertently overheated and highly pressurised the interior before finally igniting the pocket. The resultant explosion had sent not only the end section of the tank shooting across the nearby farmer's field, but two of the internal baffles as well. Meanwhile the offending seam had ripped asunder, throwing the molten solder straight up, into Jack's face. There were so many ifs and buts in this accident it didn't bear contemplation. How lucky the leak had been side on, it could so easily have been at the receiving end of the full blast, or what if Jack's reaction had not been quick enough to stop hot metal entering his eyes. But the gods were kind, and all that had to be accomplished was the acquisition of a second-hand fuel tank.

For a short while after this traumatic experience life continued fairly straightforwardly, with Jack allowing me to drive his wagon many times to the pit and airfields. One pertinent point I learnt, was how much lighter the steering became when we were fully laden, you could feel the wheels virtually bounce on the road, as the soaking wet ballast weighed heavily towards the rear.

Then one dull damp morning, Bill's lorry failed to start. Although only half-light Jack seemed anxious to reach the pit site with both tippers before others beat him to it. "Grab the tow-rope!" he hollered to me, then to big Bill, "I'll give you a tug, keep the clutch out in second and wait for my thumbs up before letting her in."

We were off with Bill trying hard not to let the rope go slack and me alongside Jack ready to do his bidding. From the corner of his mouth he spat my cryptic instructions, "As soon as we've cleared this bend I'll give her the gun and signal Bill, if she starts I want you out and unhitching pronto. With any luck we can still reach the pit before the others!"

Throughout my life with Jack I experienced many situations involving being towed, one of which I shall enter at depth a little later, but two things he taught me specifically. One was, never to allow a tow to go slack, and two, always trail the towing vehicle precisely, and I do not exaggerate when I say I have had to accomplish both these edicts with Jack pulling me in excess of fifty mph.

The first he would demonstrate by insisting the vehicle being towed did all the braking this in turn guarantees keeping the tow taut. To achieve this, his procedure called for hand signals from the person in front. Raise one arm and display a flat palm for gentle braking for greater pressure shake the hand slightly, and for hard braking show a clenched fist. The second Jack Rouse law meant keeping your vehicle inside the offside boundary of the vehicle doing the towing. There was nothing worse than a wagon so close up your backside, sticking out to obstruct your wing mirror vision or upset traffic coming towards you.

Halfway round the bend we spied a shape, a big Yankee army truck with the unmistakable white star spread across its bonnet. In the half-light it looked huge and bearing down quite strongly.

Its sight never deterred Jack, there was room on this narrow country lane for his old Green Line Coach to pass let alone a Dodge tipper, so he continued unabated, anyway there was little point in slowing and making life difficult for Bill to keep a taut tow. But Bill was fighting to keep in line with only a nine-foot gap between him and the backside of his towing mate.

As Jack negotiated the bend, Bill's cab swung slightly wide, just at the inopportune moment. The bump was quite substantial, at least for Bill. A solid bulwark running vertical on the American truck had slammed into the vulnerable corner of the Dodge that gave support to the driver's door and windscreen surround.

Everything came to an abrupt halt, with two coloured Americans giving close inspection to their vehicle, while Bill struggled over gear levers and handbrake to clamber down the near side, his driver's door being completely solid.

All I could hear was the bated breath passing between Jack's lips, as he climbed from on high to size up the mishap. My thoughts at this moment were with Bill, I couldn't help thinking, there but for the grace of God go I.

At least the two burly Yanks seemed unruffled by the collision, after all their truck built like a tank had only suffered paint damage, whereas Jack's second Dodge looked decidedly the worse for wear. The impact had not only distorted the corner pillar so that the door had jammed, but the windscreen stuck grotesquely halfway from its recess.

"I couldn't see round the bend," groaned Bill, which only made matters worse as far as Jack was concerned. "I'm the only one needing to see where we're going," he snorted, "all you had to concentrate on was watching my backside."

Giving a sympathetic wave the Yanks parted company, they weren't bothered about taking matters further, if anything it meant far less trouble for them to hush the whole thing up.

We couldn't turn round because Bill's vehicle still hadn't got going, so Jack decided to take the long way home to the farm, making Bill stay on tow without any screen for protection, but at least we travelled fairly slowly. I could sense the day was not going to be very promising.

Never one to cry over spilt milk, in no time, Jack had ratchet operated body spreaders in place and was busy enticing the cab back into shape. He managed to get the door to open and close after a fashion, but the windscreen required a more precise piece of engineering.

Diving into the caravan, he brusquely brushed past a rather harassed, sad looking Ciss, to retrieve a pair of motorbike goggles, thrusting them into Bill's hand. "You'll have to use these," he said. "Let's try again to get you started, then you can follow us to the pit!"

This time all went well, and before long we were in the squelching queue for the drag crane driver. As we ground our way, heavily loaded, over deep ruts, towards the exit and current airfield, we spotted Bill's wagon in the front line, just about to receive buckets of wet concrete-making material.

This particular field must have been about ten miles distant, so by the time we arrived and tipped our load, we reckoned we should catch sight of Bill within one or two miles of our return journey, he being only about ten minutes behind us.

After three miles we expressed anxiety: "Don't tell me he's taken a wrong turn," queried Jack; "he should know this route off by heart now." It certainly seemed odd, what else could possibly go wrong! Over halfway back, a good six miles from the field, and only four from the pit we suddenly came across him, or I should say his tipper. It lay drunkenly on its left-hand side, with both front and rear, near side wheels in a ditch, accept that the front axle nestled against the rear. Buried into the back of the driving seat, the steering wheel showed vividly the velocity of the impact, and three ton of wet ballast had been deposited forward, covering the driver's cab completely.

With a screech of brakes Jack leapt from our truck, searching desperately for signs of Bill, who, nowhere could be found! We called whilst pacing up and down, but to no avail, so Jack decided to pay some near-by homes a visit and it was here, we learnt from one occupant, that Bill had phoned the farm and they think he'd got a lift to it. What a day, what a mess! We finally caught up with him in the comforting company of Ciss, and I can't say I blamed him. Listening to his story, I couldn't help watching Jack's face. I am sure he would not have extended insurance and with a missing windscreen there was no way he could recoup any losses, everything had now turned to scrap, plus he would be held responsible for clearing up the monumental mess.

Inclined to mist over so making it difficult for Bill to see clearly, he had mistakenly pushed the goggles to the top of his head. Why they should do so, to this day I do not know, for motorcyclists and pilots wore them all the time. The next thing to befall him was an insect hitting one eye, causing a hastily raised arm to rub the offending irritation. This in turn affected his control of

THE WAY WE WERE

the steering and allowed the near side front wheel to catch the grass verge and thereby drag the vehicle further towards the ditch. The final debacle came when, seeing the drainage culvert heading towards him, without further ado Bill, lithely leapt from his seat and vacated the lorry. Which judging by the position of the steering wheel was just as well!

The solid brick culvert carrying a drainage pipe inside the ditch had been the last straw for Jack's added venture, when cleanly it removed the front axle to place it firmly alongside the rear.

We all studied one-another, breathing a sigh of relief, that once again Bill had escaped certain death. "That's it," summed up Jack. "We shall clear everything and make tracks for Romford and a well earned rest."

The last thing I remember about Norfolk is having to help heave tons of sopping wet sand and stone from a toppled tipper, high over my head, to reach the bed of an upright one.

Although it wouldn't be long before Bill entered the army, at least Sheila was pleased to see him return in one piece, they were courting quite strongly now and marriage appeared very much on the cards.

That was fine for Bill, but I needed to find gainful employment. Jack had decided to give Norfolk one more go and this time Ciss would stay with him, so after a chat with Rene it had been agreed I would live with her at number eleven Kimberly Avenue, not far from the timber mills.

Work was always plentiful, provided you didn't mind what you did, and of course I seldom did.

This time I joined company with a small jobbing builder, attending to first-aid repairs on damaged property. The remuneration looked good, six pounds per week for the usual five and half days.

The timing couldn't have been more opportune, it was true that German bombing raids had all but ceased, in fact it was the Allies that sent one thousand planes at a time to destroy our enemy, but the first of Hitler's secret weapons, the flying bomb had reached our shores.

As Bill entered the services the announcements of the day were of landings on the Normandy beaches. D-Day had begun and the beginning of the end had surely arrived.

Allied forces swept defiantly past Monte Cassino and Rome fell two days before the invasion of France. In the Far East, Americans had retaken the island of Guam and were striking at the Japanese held islands of Marianas.

Meanwhile my brother's squadron had been moved up to inside the Imphal

Box. Here, British and Indian troops had been surrounded when Japanese forces cut our supply route from Kohima, forcing hard pressed Allies to have valuable supplies needed to conduct adequate defence air-lifted by hundreds of Dakota transports and Mitchell bombers. For two months life would become desperate.

Life at home was not all a bed of roses either, as droves of the new weapon designated V-1 and nicknamed by us as buzz bombs, or doodlebugs sped inland from the coast at low altitude and 400 mph. The fierce red and orange flame spurting from its tailpipe was almost as long as its entire body. Fuelled by petrol and compressed air and steered by gyroscope, the one ton high explosive lethal weapon carrier quickly fell from the sky as soon as its throbbing engine stopped for lack of propellant.

I have stood, fascinated, to watch as many as six in line abreast, flying at no more than 1000 feet and one mile apart sweeping towards me. Many is the time I ducked low as if that foolish act could have helped me when I suddenly realised there had been a flame out, mesmerised as its nose tilted towards the ground.

Government directives were at pains to explain, that when you heard an engine cut there was only fifteen seconds to take cover, which cryptic statement assured one, you needed to be standing virtually alongside a shelter to enjoy any margin of safety. Few of us really bothered, as there was faint warning of their arrival, which could be anytime of the day or night.

I can recall quite vividly lying half asleep in the back bedroom of Rene's house whilst she remained on shift duty at her fire station, listening to these doodlebugs going over and holding my breath when one of the engine notes died. At night they seemed to come over singly about two or three minutes apart, I suppose the idea was it would upset the sleeping arrangements of the whole capital. The only time I really became agitated was when I could tell the ominous unmistakable sound was coming towards the house and about to pass very close. Then you would grit your teeth and pray the damn thing would have enough fuel to keep going, and breathe a sigh of relief when it did.

Looking back on these occasions now I find it hard to believe how nonchalant we all were.

But one thing it did do was to keep us first-aid house repairers gainfully occupied.

My job entailed boarding up broken windows and re-establishing collapsed ceilings, the latter of which had me constantly working with my hands above my head fixing new plaster boarding, before stirring large quantities of Seraphite with added water, for my more experienced plasterer and boss to administer.

Poland had once more become the battleground as Russian forces swept the remnants of German armour from their land, and Churchill has declared that over a million children are being evacuated yet again from Greater London because of the threat posed by Hitler's new terror weapon.

Still I had a month to go for my unofficial eighteenth birthday to arrive, and already, French tanks had led the way into a liberated Paris. Over on the occupied Channel Islands, Germans began leaving as the strategic loss of Brittany to the American army meant there was little point in their remaining.

With advancing Allied armies sweeping towards Germany, many of the V-1 launch sites began to be overrun, but the Führer had one last card to play, the forerunner of the space rocket, his sadistic long range fifteen ton V-2, carrying a one ton warhead.

Returning from Norfolk to take up permanent residence at 86, Jack declared that work on the American bases had come to an end. Consequently he needed everything south and would utilise Stone as a holding station. Could I return with him to drive the Lanchester while he towed the caravan behind the Dodge!

We were establishing these effects at our riverside home, when hearing heavy aircraft engines my instinctive habit led me to glance up. There, stretching across the sky, as far as the eye could see was the most amazing armada I had ever witnessed. Many times from way on high, I'd observed dozens of Flying Fortresses with their vapour trails streaming in parallel vortex's, looking majestic and awesome, but never anything like this.

Wave upon wave of low flying Dakota aircraft, many of them towing gliders, were quite literally flying above our heads, they seemed to go on forever, heading slowly in the general direction of the Channel and towards the Netherlands.

The following day all would be revealed. Operation Market Garden had begun and a bridge too far was about to be born. It was the terrible attrition of Arnhem.

Excited eyes had followed 10,000 of our finest men being transported beyond enemy lines, of which only 2,500 would return.

Whilst waiting patiently for my reserve papers, I continued at the task of restoring people's homes to a liveable standard. At the same time, looking for suitable premises, Jack had reached the conclusion there was no way he was going to work for someone else again. Ideally his best outlook lay in setting up his own motor workshop.

To this end he construed a hiring opportunity may exist, as vehicles for private use were far and few between and initially acquiring a second car could be a good way forward.

Some two or three weeks after the Stone episode I arrived as usual by cycle for work. Each day or week may take us to a new district, depending on where rockets had fallen. They were terrible missiles; one never heard a thing until they exploded on the ground.

You could be happily attending your business when without warning, Wham! And if the impact were not too far away a pall of smoke and flame would shoot into the air.

The first thing my boss said to me was, "We've gotta go to Kimberly Avenue."

I looked stunned "Hell, why?" I said, dreading the worst.

"'Cos a V-2 dropped behind there last night," he answered, nonchalantly, unknowing of the reason for my concern. "Right on the railway line, how lucky can you get considering these bloody things are indiscriminate."

I thought hard, if I wasn't mistaken sister Irene was on duty last night, I hope to God she was. Whilst I of course had also been lucky, having so recently decided to move back into 86.

Peddling as fast as my two wheels could carry me, I arrived to find Rene's lovely home in an utter mess. Bricks and mortar had struggled to hang together, but anything remotely movable had split asunder. By now I had encountered most devastation, but this was the nearest to a total write off I'd come across, without actually being so.

Properties adjacent the railway line crater, were completely unrecognisable, as were those immediately behind Kimberly, about five displaying nothing but rubble with three or four either side requiring drastic surgery. Loss of life remained unknown, I hoped like Rene people had been absent from home, but that wish could not be upheld.

To give some idea of the chaos, I needed to step over the front door and every other door leading off Rene's hall, to reach her half-demolished kitchen, where doors and frames leading to the garden had actually been blown halfway across it. After scrambling over dirt and debris to reach upstairs, the first thing that struck me was how each bedroom ceiling nicely covered the bed, because without prior knowledge you wouldn't know a bed had existed. Obviously the Lord had decided it wasn't time for my sister or me.

Naturally not a window remained and every roof-tile to the back of the house had followed the pattern of the blast, sweeping upwards to leave the lower battens, bare, as they tumbled in haste over each other to reach the ridge.

At the earliest opportunity I contacted Ciss so that she may pass on the dreadful news to her husband and our sister.

Dear Rene's home lay beyond small repairers' capabilities; it would take much bigger and better contractors than ours to correct such destruction. We would attend to less serious damage, further from the blast.

Apart from hearing distant rumbles that these weapons caused, the only other time I lived through a close presence was when I happened to be traversing across Romford's main marketplace late one evening, with everything wrapped in total darkness. Without warning buildings and square alike became bathed in brilliant white light, iridescence that lasted for about one and half seconds. Instinctively I crouched, waiting for the almighty bang! But it never came; all was eerily silent, as I froze, hunched over, glaring at the cobbles, feeling like an idiot. Later that evening I exploited my theory that it must have been a V-2 prematurely exploding in the stratosphere. Although I searched and listened for news of the phenomenon, I never did see or hear any corroborating evidence, but to this day I am positive that my conclusion was the only answer.

As an indication of Germany's air efforts above Great Britain, V-2s apart, the government has announced in this October 1944 a partial relaxation of blackout laws. Youngsters under five are able to see shop and street lighting for the very first time.

Complete with familiar sunglasses and battered hat, General Douglas MacArthur waded ashore at the island of Leyte on the twenty-first, to keep his promise to the Philippines that he would return.

Erwin Rommel, scourge of the British Eighth Army had committed suicide.

The British had re-landed in Greece and marched into Athens three and half years after being driven out.

Shortly after Hitler announced the formation of a German Home Guard, so the British government declared ours were to hang up their weapons.

German troops are now on the run right across Europe, everywhere through every city liberated people had been pouring onto the streets. Sights and sounds in all probability never to be repeated on such a scale ever again.

William S. Smith

Almost the whole of Europe, apart from Germany, was rejoicing.

Even brother Len had written to say that after a spell of leave, trekking through Himalayan Mountains, he was delighted to inform us he was now commissioned and something else had happened that would make his sisters proud to walk out with their kid brother. That something we would one day discover was the award of the DFM (Distinguished Flying Medal),'a recognition that can only be won whilst flying as a NCO 'Non Commissioned Officer'. A much rarer commodity! Now in this politically correct world, removed from RAF awards, so that Officers and NCO alike receive the same recognition in the form of the DFC, the Distinguished Flying Cross.

But yours truly would not be able to share in all this euphoria, because just over one month after my unofficial birth date, hanging on every post to receive my final induction into the RAF, I received instead a very informative letter, telling me I am to journey to the county of Devon using the enclosed warrant. One saving grace had emerged: they actually referred to me as AC2 Smith No. 3003030.

Torquay would be my venue for five days, where I would be subjected to every type of test, mathematical, meteorological, navigational, aircraft recognition, air gunnery, bomb aiming, Morse speeds, aptitude tests, and even personal x-rays. All to determine my fitness or otherwise for entry into RAF aircrew training. The reasoning, I was told, was to weed out further, those selected, due to over large numbers awaiting service with the RAF, now no longer required, whereas forces to complete the ground war in Europe were in urgent demand. My gut feeling told me the whole exercise smelt of a gentle letdown. To be able to determine who was better than whom from such a complicated process would be nigh impossible.

So it was with a heavy heart and much disbelief that I set out to do the round of Torquay's hotels to find which one housed Len's paintings.

There must have been hundreds of us hopefuls passing through every week, being shepherded from one set of buildings to another. I recall having to sit in something like a Link trainer with a moving light shining centrally before me, which would suddenly move to one side and you had to realign it with a control column. Whilst you were concentrating on this, a red or green lamp would flash at your side, which you extinguished by moving a second lever forward or back, depending on which colour illuminated.

When being tested for bomb aiming they used simulators for the process. You took up a prone position on a high plateau, peering through a window in the floor at a three-dimensional map below, representing a night raid. You were required to operate in almost total darkness. A red spot directed onto the map had to be guided towards a given point, where, after allowing for aircraft speed and wind velocity you selected the right moment to release your bombs, which would show up as flashes as you depressed a button under your right thumb.

I wrote to Ciss telling her despondently that they were unhappy with the keenness of my eyesight. Okay for aircrew but they were doubtful of recommending me as a pilot. Also I had been unable to locate any murals of aircraft bearing Len's signature, although of course he did many.

Whilst I awaited the predictable results from this third attempt, Jack let it be known that his hire car had broken down, in of all places, Devon! His customer had telephoned rather irately to declare a big end had gone and he was leaving the vehicle where it had come to rest and was catching the next train home. This occurrence on early vehicles was actually not uncommon, and the cheapest way out for Jack, would be to tow the broken car home. Provided you had someone willing to follow that close for the best part of 200 miles. "Come on Libby," he said, "I'll make it worth your while."

The month had reached November, cold and raw, no luxury car heaters just blankets wrapped round your knees. "We won't use a rope," he smiled. "I'll take this steel tube and bolt it to each bumper with a swivel, so they'll be no worry about keeping a taut tow."

A novelty indeed, entering a steep hill somewhere on the return journey, Jack gave the customary hand upright signal for brake, then he waggled his hand and I braked harder, finally he was displaying a clenched fist, and I was standing on the confounded pedal. To no avail, my vehicle was still attempting to overtake him, but such a move was impossible because we were held together by steel, so it began to push me sideways, which I endeavoured to counteract, so it shoved me in the opposite direction. Then an almighty crunch developed, and I found myself staring back up the hill from whence I'd come as I travelled at a rate of knots backwards, minus my front bumper! Meanwhile, having to contend with a weight pushing him faster than he desired to negotiate the approaching bottom bend, Jack suddenly found himself sliding sideways towards an ugly looking ditch.

We did eventually sort the whole mess out, and fortunately no other traffic came near us, in fact you could travel miles on country roads without seeing an opposing vehicle. Of necessity our route wound straight through the centre of London, and what should we encounter but one of its famous pea-soupers.

It may seem hard to believe today, but this fog was so dense you could hardly see anything beyond the bonnet. "I'll watch the front," called Jack; "you stick your head out of the near-side door and yell if I stray from the kerb."

We were actually making steady progress like this, with me yelling instructions, every time I noticed the gutter receding, when for no particular reason I happened to glance through the windscreen. At first I did not appreciate the significance of what I saw, a wheel rolling beside me and then on past Jack. Instantly Jack stopped, leapt from his car, and stuck his head through my open driver's window.

"You lost a back wheel?" he enquired, rather aggressively.

"I don't think so," I answered; "at least I haven't felt anything."

Unable to even see the rear of my car he left to check for himself, returning in next to no time, declaring, "The damned offside rear has come off; you're riding on the brake drum." I could only think that leaning far out to the left as I concentrated hard on the edge of the highway had somehow distracted me from any alteration in the car's stability.

Whether the nuts had been working loose ever since the hill mishap we couldn't know, but certainly all the necessary fittings were now missing. Not to be outdone we removed one nut from each of the three remaining wheels, having first rescued the runaway, and re-establishing this truant quickly continued the adventurous journey home.

At Stratford the fog began to lift and thereafter all would be well.

I have been towed many times throughout my association with Jack, but none do I remember quite like that one.

Fog could play a big part in life in those days, with all the coal fires adding to the general confusion and disgusting air quality. Some years later when conducting my own taxi service, paying passengers have stepped from my vehicle to walk in front and kindly guide me through the smog.

About the time of our tow experience, Len became only the second RAF pilot to down all three of our enemies, German, Italian and Japanese. Being the first squadron to re-enter Burma, it seemed rather opportune that 152 now carried the image of a large black panther leaping over the fuselage port roundel, of its Spitfires. The emblem had been derived from a painting submitted by Len to his commanding officer, the idea originating from a fellow conspirator, a certain Sergeant Duval who had spotted a much smaller design on the nose cone of a Dakota.

In any event the notoriety had quickly caused them to become known as

THE WAY WE WERE

the Black Panthers of Burma, a development Len proudly enhanced, when in a skirmish at first light on November 5th, he destroyed one Zero and damaged another.

December arrived with my last communication from the RAF, a printed circular signed by Sir Archibald Sinclair, the then Minister for Air. There was no surprises, just confirmation that he was very sorry to inform me that with immediate effect I was being transferred from RAF Reserve to army duties, and was expected to report to army barracks in Alexandria. My disappointment had been so complete I failed to read the remainder, and for a moment expected to be dispatched to Egypt. However, reading on, I soon realised this particular Alexandria lay in Dumbartonshire, Scotland.

To this day I have no idea what my results were from five days of rigorous testing, whether I came last out of umpteen thousand or perhaps halfway, or who knows maybe nobody got through and the whole exercise had been a sham.

It didn't matter, my future had been decided, although given the choice I think I would have plumped for the Navy. Nobody could say I hadn't tried, and now I must report to the frozen north on December 7th for subjection to army training at the tender age of seventeen years, eight months and three weeks.

As I travelled to the banks of Loch Lomond, news of the day declared that twenty million German people were now homeless due to allied bombing. With statistics like that it was little wonder trainees for aircrew were a low priority, unlike four years earlier Britain and her allies now enjoyed mastery of the air throughout Europe.

Before I had hardly settled in however Hitler made one last attempt to turn the tide. Taking advantage of poor flying conditions, Field Marshal von Rundstedt mustered twenty-four divisions, ten of which were armoured, to thrust forward through the Ardennes forest.

This was the exact same route as taken in 1940 that had achieved such devastating effect. But this time the tactic to reach Antwerp and thereby cut vital Allied supplies could only slightly prolong hostilities. All we had to do was contain the breakout until the weather cleared. By January 9th 1945 the Battle of the Bulge, as it became known, had virtually petered out and all along the front Allied troops began advancing once more.

On December 8th I had written Ciss, requesting a tin of sorts to house shaving gear as I was unable to purchase anything suitable, and currently rummaged deep inside my issued kit-bag for small vital necessities. I also intimated completion of clothing supplied by the army, and would be forwarding my discarded civvies, home to 86. I didn't bother to describe the itchy nature of my new attire or the weight of hobnailed boots attached to my feet. I did wish everyone well including Teddy and Monty. I have omitted to mention these two additions to our family. Teddy was an auburn haired chow, a lovely looking dog, not unlike a husky, and a great pal of mine. Monty was our tortoiseshell cat, who, similar to most cats, only made a purring fuss if food looked likely.

Routine at Dalmanarch Barracks, Bonhill, near Alexandria, consisted of physical training before breakfast, when we ate porridge at 7.30 am, with the remainder of the day taken up by lectures, parades, and instruction on handling and firing various weapons, including the Lee Enfield rifle, as used in the First World War; the Bren gun, the British standard light machine gun; and tossing grenades. These last little gems needed the extraction of a retaining pin to release a spring-loaded handle, which you were instructed to keep a tight hold of, before lobbing cricket-ball fashion, high and as far forward as possible beyond your dugout. After release you had four seconds before they went off, during which time you were expected to observe where it had landed and only then duck your head below the parapet.

In one letter to Ciss, I explain how a particular guy let go the sprung handle as he pulled the pin, on which occasion little effort was made to observe the point of impact before throwing himself prostrate towards the trench floor.

Very often we would be running alongside the loch in semi-darkness, wearing nothing but a woollen pullover, shorts and plimsolls. Soaking in the winter scene of snow-covered mountains majestically tumbling towards the opposing bank, in temperatures well below zero.

This initiation covered six weeks that took in the Christmas and New Year festivities. I take my hat off to our welcoming hosts. Local ladies circles catered admirably for us conscripts, organising parties and dances wherever and whenever they could. Each time extensive efforts produced girls galore, so that no squaddie went unaccompanied. I recall one rather buxom lass after trying to teach me to dance, not an easy task, dragging me outside the hall and attempting to work her wicked ways. Unfortunately I was an innocent shy fool when it came to girls, so I'm afraid I made rather a hash of things, finding a lame excuse to return to barracks. Poor kid, I bet she cursed her luck getting stuck with such a timid ignorant English boy.

Towards the end of our introduction a list of army trades and regiments spread across the bulletin boards for all to study and subscribe to.

Looking down the columns I fancied nothing, despite there being everything you could think of: tanks, artillery, REME, dispatch riders, different infantry regiments. Then I spied "Parachute Regiment". Ah! I thought, why not, at least that way I can become airborne. Several other guys fancied this too, I don't suppose for one moment anyone of us stopped to think, "Oh my God, I wonder what its like to step out of an aeroplane."

At last I began to feel happy again, cosseted by friends, some of whom had experienced similar disappointments, all anxious to get away from this early induction and get involved in something more meaty.

With one week to go I fell ill, it was all this pesky jumping up and down in the gym. I'd caught a cold and then it went to my chest, but I couldn't get rid of the congestion that followed, it kept welling up inside me every-time our instructor insisted we follow his antics.

Unable to rid myself of the mucous, I gradually grew worse, until the time came to depart. Volunteers for the Parachute Regiment would entrain for Southampton, camp overnight in transit and catch the ferry to the Isle of Wight the following morning.

Somehow I had to reach the island, there was no way, having come this far, that I was going to lose friends newly made, by missing my ITC (Initial Training Course).

Travelling by train usually meant standing in the corridor, which I did for nigh on 600 miles, accept at odd times I sat on the floor and slept with my head on the kit bag, a head that wouldn't stop throbbing with features bathed in sweat.

At Southampton a few of the guys carried my kit to enable me to reach the camp, where I promptly lay down and died, well it felt like it, and stayed unconscious until the early hours. By morning it was obvious to all concerned I was in no fit state to travel and a medic was brought. He scratched his head, gave me some tablets, and suggested if I could make it to the ferry, I could be cared for much better on the island.

Yet again mates came to my aid, helping me dress and shave to look partially presentable, and taking command of all my gear. Fortunately the ferry journey is fairly short, but in my state of mind, time seemed meaningless.

Lining up on the quayside we were informed that a march to Albany Barracks, Parkhurst, was the order of the day, I cannot remember exactly but I think this meant a gruelling four miles. Adding insult to injury, just prior to entry through the gates, a command rang out for shoulder arms and march to attention.

Full of apology, friends strapped me into pouches and backpack, and finally re-established my rifle onto my left shoulder, as smartly we swung into the barracks in full military style. Once shown to our quarters, I collapsed onto the nearest bunk, virtually oblivious to all. Within minutes the camp doctor was at my bedside taking pulse and temperature, he studied the glass. "Hum!" he grimaced. "Hospital for you me lad, its reading 104 degrees."

Totland Bay on the west side of the island overlooked a mainland area not far from where I would eventually reside. At this point, lying only some six miles distant, the beautiful southern seaside resort was unknown to me. Yet within a few short years and henceforth for the following fifty plus, Christchurch would become mine, my children's, and my grandchildren's home.

Standing proud near the cliff edge rose a lovely minaret style building, which must surely have been a magnificent hotel in pre-war days. The weather too seemed to be shining pleasantly for late January it's a pity I couldn't appreciate all these aspects, as my khaki coloured ambulance pulled up at the door.

On February 2nd I wrote Ciss from what had become Totland Bay's military hospital. I explained that although not yet allowed out of bed the pain I had endured had become less of late, that when the day came to dress and journey outside I would have to wear a red tie, white shirt and blue trousers and jacket. Perhaps, I jokingly suggested, I should also carry a Union Jack.

Describing the view overlooking the English Channel as really smashing, I refer to lying snow beginning to fast disappear, but high winds making the sea extremely turbulent. Each day we watched the hospital ships going backwards and forwards to Cherbourg ferrying wounded.

I was concerned for her safety as I heard quite a lot of V-2 rockets had been landing nearby, but with the way the Russians were advancing Jerry must be nearly finished. But most of all I was desperate for mail and enquiring about a missing parcel.

Still refused permission to vacate my bed, even for visits to the toilet, I constantly bemoan my lot in a further communication four days later. I was definitely suffering from pleurisy, which is fluid on the lung, and everyone was being cautious, although I was hopeful I could get round my lovely angelic nurse, but my company had started training and the delay was making me mad! Finally I received the missing parcel, but unfortunately the apple pie had gone bad, the mints turned to crumble, and acid-drops gelled to a solid mass, which hastily I added, would still nevertheless get eaten.

Although previously I have been at pains to defend our saturation bombing of the Third Reich, I must admit that as I lay gathering my strength to join the fray, I was unhappy when news was relayed of Dresden's demise. As a young soldier my extreme ignorance of such matters would need much education. At the time arguments for and against centred around Dresden being utilised as staging for onward German reinforcements to the Russian Front and an important industrialised area.

But Germany was in the last throes of a lost war, and over the past decades I have come to the firm opinion that my young gut sentiment was the correct one. By sending 800 Lancasters on the night of February 14th, followed by 400 Fortresses next day, we were not trying to win a war but wreaking revenge on a defeated enemy.

The fact that horrible atrocities had been uncovered at Auschwitz and Hitler seemed hell-bent on fighting to the last man, may have contributed to our thinking, but such an excuse is still not sufficient.

After an escapade beyond hospital confines, where Jock and I found ourselves cut off by rising tidal waters and outcrops of rock, we finally crept back to Ward 3 in time to hide our pitiful state in the bathroom. Writing home I confessed having to wash not just me, but my filthy clay covered clothes in the bath water to prevent an irate sister from chastising the pair of us.

But the adventure had proved conclusive, in that both my Scottish friend and I felt fit enough, and able enough, to rejoin our units.

The doc gave us a thorough going over, we knew it had to be A1; anything less, because A2 was also an army category, would mean an immediate discharge from the Parachute Regiment. Thankfully we passed okay, so my next port of call was a formal request to my commanding officer to allow me to rejoin my pals and try to catch up on their training. This turned out to be a dead duck. "Sorry my lad," he said, although to be honest he well understood and gave sympathy. "It would be too difficult to accomplish and totally unfair to you, so I am putting you on light duties and sending you on early leave. On your return the next intake will have arrived."

It would become ironic, for I had constantly emphasised to Ciss that India in all probability looked like my port of call once training finished, giving me a chance to catch up on brother Len. This is exactly where my original pals sailed, but my illness and subsequent delay cast me towards different shores.

April 1945 went down in the annals of history as one of the most momentous months on record.

On the 1st United States troops landed on Okinawa, by the 4th Allied forces had entered Osnabrück, on the 7th Japan lost its biggest battleship, the *Yamamoto*.

Franklin Delano Roosevelt, destined never to see the end of the war, now only weeks away, died on the 12th, at the young age of sixty-three.

Notorious concentration camps were overrun, Belsen on the 15th and Buchenwald on the 17th.

The RAF sank Germany's last pocket battleship, the *Lützow*, on the 16th.

In San Francisco, Roosevelt's successor, Harry Truman, received forty-six delegates on the 25th to form the basis of a new United Nations.

Partisans shot Mussolini and his mistress Clara Petacci on the 28th, stringing them up by their feet from the façade of a petrol station in Milan's Piazzale Loreto.

And on the last day of the month, the man responsible in one form or another for the death of over thirty million people, Adolf Hitler, architect of the Third Reich that was to last for a thousand years, killed himself, together with his mistress whom he'd married twenty-four hours earlier before she succumbed to poison. He'd retreated deep inside his Berlin bunker. There, sitting bolt upright on his one sofa, he shot himself, straight through the mouth.

Someone said it still called for an epitaph. Churchill had already declared it, way back in 1940 when Britain stood in lonely defiance.

"Hitler," he said, "is a bloodthirsty guttersnipe!"

Somehow I'd managed to spend my proper birthday on leave; this was something I had to constantly hide from my superiors, so never discussed the anniversary with roommates. I can verify the timing when investigating a letter to Ciss dated 24th March. This tells of arriving at camp without problem after leaving Waterloo Station the previous day.

I knew now that training would begin in earnest at the start of April and was cock-a-hoop to learn we were allowed to wear ties when off duty. This latter became a strong crusade of mine as I always felt the stiff collar done up to the neck looked degrading.

Although I wrote many letters to all my sisters, and to Pop and Len, seldom did I seem to receive replies as constantly I badgered Ciss to chastise them for their recalcitrance!

THE WAY WE WERE

Albany Barracks, Parkhurst, I believe eventually became part of HM Prisons, but I doubt any inmates of that fraternity ever suffered the disciplines or austerity that young conscripts training to reach parachuting maturity had to endure. By the middle of the month I was at pains to pass on our daily routines of assault courses, rope climbing, leaping across water obstacles, and reaching up to clamber over nine foot walls. The rush to indoctrinate us never seemed to abate as day after day we were subjected to increasing muscle torture. What, I wondered, were we being trained for, as they sent us hell for leather thrusting bayonets into dummy targets, fifteen times within 200 yards, and back again in case we hadn't plunged deep enough the first time.

It's true that Japanese forces were known to never give in, and rumours were rife that a sea invasion of Singapore was on the cards, where paratroops would be expected to hold up any enemy reinforcements approaching along the peninsula.

I was obviously learning to become more aggressive: I even acknowledged to my gentle sister that her young William fought it out with his fourteen-stone corporal, and won, thereby winning respect, not just from him, but the rest of the squad.

I'd heard that Len had finally left 152 Squadron after serving with them for two years, going from sergeant with a blemished record, to decorated flying ace with the rank of flying officer. And now he is attending a fighter leaders' course at Armada Road near Calcutta, before returning to Peshawar near the Himalayas to take up test pilot duties, which in all probability meant not catching the boat home for at least another eighteen months.

He'd written some months back to describe a trek undertaken through the Himalayan Mountains, when recovering whilst on sick leave from a bout of malaria. Journeying along one edge of a sheer drop he romanced over the beautiful scene looking down into the valley of the Sind River and what a lovely place it was for anyone to come to die after a long and fruitful life.

Len had also been writing to a little blonde bombshell called Alex, introduced to him by sister Irene, and he wanted his kid brother to meet this femme fatale, expecting me to pass on any positive thoughts or otherwise. He was obviously smitten, leaving his mind doing rolls off the top in anticipation. So far I'm afraid to say all I had managed to accomplish was a written word or two.

Another bit of news falling into my lap showed an imminent return of Rene's Johnny and I couldn't have been more pleased for her.

William S. Smith

But anxiously I kept pressing for news of my old friend Bill Russell; it was the devils own job to keep track of friends who were constantly moving from place to place, for as fast as one got settled the other was sure to be re-billeted.

War in Europe was fast coming to an end, but before it did they wanted me to step in the boxing ring. Two rounds of only one minute each doesn't sound much, against an opponent you had never met. The corporal said make sure you keep moving, so I did. No! I didn't run the other way, I just tore into the poor sod and within twenty seconds his face was a mass of blood, but he had what the army wanted, guts! During the second round he fell down twice but still he recovered to fight on, by this time I was so tired I felt like collapsing myself, and only just made the corner when the bell sounded. Then the ref went over and congratulated him on a magnificent stand, before turning and saying I'd won. I had the distinct feeling he was unhappy to admit it!

I swore I would never go in a ring again; I just hate to hit a guy if he's losing, until some bright spark caught my collar and said, "Having won, you will be expected to fight again next week." "Don't worry," I wrote my sister, "I think it will be my turn to take a beating, because if I win again I shall be expected to Box in the semi-finals, and can you imagine how tough that could be!"

Two days later at precisely 2.41 am on May 7th the war ended, at last I could stop worrying about all the family. The commanding officer was opening up our barracks to the whole of the island, we were to be given the Tuesday and Wednesday off to celebrate and start home leave at twelve noon on Saturday. All we wanted now was to find 3,000 girls to comfort us 3,000 guys, with time on our hands.

It was approaching the end of May and training had been stepped up in earnest, apart from firing Sten guns and mortars we were now exercising with the PIAT gun. This stands for Projector Infantry, Anti-Tank. The kick from its recoil was like a mule, and you could follow the hourglass shell it fired quite easily. The nose tapered almost to a point, the idea being that provided you had aimed it correctly, as it struck the tank, preferably at a weak spot; the explosive was concentrated in this narrow portion. This then punched a small hole through the armour plate, before expanding its pent up energy inside the vehicle.

Our instructor assured us it worked, and so efficiently that you could take out the crew inside without actually destroying the tank.

It has been reliably suggested, a truth I have recently had confirmed in this

THE WAY WE WERE

year of 2004, that one of the Arnhem paratroopers managed to take out three tanks, firing this weapon from the hip.

Should it not be held firmly enough the spigot would fail to re-cock itself, meaning you either had to stand with both feet straddling the shoulder holster, as you strained like mad to pull the body upwards against a tremendously strong spring, or you lay down to keep yourself out of trouble and carried out the procedure in the prone position facing upwards.

Field training could be hectic at the best of times: one day we were told to give a pint of blood before setting off on a five mile trek in full kit and carry out a complete rifle attack as soon as we arrived. I was pleased to report no ill effects.

At last I had caught up with news of Bill and it was not good, the poor guy had been in hospital too, and just recovered from a two-day sleep. That sounded pretty ominous to me!

A couple of times I had held out hopes of promotion, but on each occasion sod's law had kicked in and moved me across to another unit. Apparently I did wear a Pegasus flying horse on my sleeve with crossed swords beneath, denoting a crack shot, which is something to shoot a line about when I next wrote my ace brother. Then in a letter dated June 3rd I once more infer the possibility of reaching the dizzy heights of lance corporal. "I've been recommended by my section Commander, and suggest that it may be due to being both the fastest and most accurate with the Bren gun." It was nearly the end of Parkhurst training, only one week to passing out parade, my old C Company who left six weeks ago had already reached India.

My next port of call would be up in Chesterfield, at a place called Hardwick Hall, I think it must be some Lord's residence, but I doubted that we would see the inside. This was where you would make or break trying to complete a commando course.

Before this however, they placed me in charge of a section of ten men and lost me somewhere out in the country, supplying me with a map and orders to attack certain targets that could be anywhere on the island.

The exercise was to last four days, and on the first we had to make our way towards remote positions, and use ideal strategy and camouflage in the approach. We covered twenty-four miles and only got lost once, but earned good marks for the attacks. That night was spent sleeping on a disused hotel floor. By early the following morning we were travelling again, criss-crossing the island all through the day and most of the night, getting very little sleep.

All the time we were expected to keep up an average of five miles per hour, which I comment is pretty good going, especially when you are not only loaded down with equipment, but are having to find your way.

By day three we passed three other sections that left before us, each one starting out fifteen minutes after the other. This put us a good hour ahead of everyone else. That night we spent without rest, having to carry out patrols, attacks, and goodness knows what! We were firing parachute flares, mortars and blanks all over the place. We also had to dig our own slit trenches, but never actually got the chance to lay in them.

Oh! By the way, in case you wondered, I never did have to enter the boxing ring again although scheduled to do so. As it happened, the particular evening they wanted me I had been appointed to fire picket duty, so they scratched my name off completely. The funny thing was instead of being glad, I showed annoyance; I would so much rather have gone down fighting and thought the decision most unfair.

One of the chaps in our dormitory, called Holmes, slept alongside me, I am afraid I cannot recall his features, but I wrote very highly of him, explaining, he used to entertain us with his guitar playing. I enquired of Ciss if she saw his name in the *Sunday People*, because he was apparently killed when one of our blast walls collapsed on him.

The first correspondence from Hardwick begged forgiveness for poor writing. "You see Cissy," I confess, "before I left Parkhurst my mates and I got rather squiffy, in other words, the worse for drink, and I am still suffering from being light-headed ... Trouble was the following morning reveille sounded at 4 am, so you can imagine how we all felt, but when you wave goodbye to the RSM [Regimental Sergeant Major] you have to celebrate somehow."

By the end of the first week I knew what commando training really meant! "So far," I wrote, "they have been preparing us for the tests we will have to undertake. Each morning begins with a two-mile run, followed by one hour of physical exercise, then its over to the assault courses.

'These include scaling cliffs and descending, swinging across deep pits by rope and crossing large lakes by varying method. Firstly, standing on a cable, you hang onto a rope; gradually sidling you're way across, demanding great effort from arms and upper body. Then to grasp either side of a pulley wheel and be whisked at alarming speed above the water along a cable strung to a far tree. A tree fortunately wrapped with mattresses to cushion the blow. I might add that none of these daring do's entailed the wearing of helmets or safety

THE WAY WE WERE

harness, just the red beret, of which we were all proud.

Another tortuous piece of fun was when they shoved you down a hole and expected you to crawl on your belly, because it only measured eighteen inches or forty-six centimetres high, in complete and utter darkness inviting you to find your way out the other end! What they didn't tell you was, halfway through, after slithering over mud and puddles of deep water, that they had created a many-tunnelled outlet at a spot every humorist in the camp called Piccadilly Circus. This circular area rose to a generous three feet or approximately one metre of height at its centre, where partial daylight had been allowed to filter into the dome like cavern.

In the eyrie gloom one studied the various options before journeying on. To suffer a wrong choice meant a twenty-minute claustrophobic crawl along winding passages, only to end up back at Piccadilly!

Being six feet tall gave an advantage in some directions and distinct disadvantage in others, the previous exercise became more difficult the taller you were, but one I enjoyed was clambering up high wooden scaffolding whose rungs were spaced seven feet apart. Decidedly not easy for the little guy!

The second and final week at Hardwick confirmed our previous tortures had been just child's play. This time, if you showed signs of flagging, the Parachute Regiment really didn't want or need you.

There would be no let up on previous training, just additions to it, as if that were possible. Now after our two-mile run and one hour's PT, we climbed into full battle gear and assaulted a three-mile hill. At other times we were expected to continue whilst heavily laden and complete two miles in eighteen minutes, and run 200 yards in one minute forty seconds, carrying a second individual, also fully weighted down, and bolster his rifle too.

One of the final tests had us all doing a quick march for 100 yards, then at the double for the next 100, until we had completed ten miles in two hours, all fully equipped with heavy water bottle, ammunition, and slung rifle.

I recall standing to attention on the parade ground at the completion of this marathon, watching fascinated as various types literally fainted, falling hard forward onto their faces, until realising the problem stemmed from the excessively hot day, the order to dismiss was quickly given.

Before those that survived two weeks of agonising endurance could congratulate themselves, one last hurdle was thrown at us. I remember being quite appalled at this inquisition when they announced those remaining must undergo a psychiatric examination.

It seemed awful to suggest that after all our dedication we could still be found wanting, but apparently these mind doctors could have the final say on whether you went on to Manchester and parachute jumping or not. I tried to explain to people back home the weird and silly things they were asking of us, but decided in the end the exercise wasn't worth it. "You'll just have to keep your fingers crossed for me Cissy, and hope these guys know what they're about!"

I'd heard Jack had started up in business, and wondered how he was progressing. Running down the side of Romford's gasworks curved a road called Crow Lane. It followed almost identically the direction of the V-2 bombed railway line as it headed towards London. At its beginning, and railed off for some distance along its left-hand side, lay the large acreage of our local community burial ground, Romford Cemetery. Further, as the lane ran on, it meandered through open fields to its left and gave access to single-storey government-sponsored dwellings opposite. These establishments were smallholdings, set aside after WWI, to assist ex-servicemen start a new life. Behind a few of these holdings, not far beyond the cemetery, stood a section of unused ground running parallel with the rail line.

Able to acquire a sizeable chunk of this, with good access between smallholdings, Jack began to expand on his new venture. Utilising his five-ton Dodge, he had won for himself a fairly large second-hand building, constructed of steel girders and corrugated iron sheeting. Proceeding to dismantle and remove it with the tipper, he was soon erecting this on a concrete plinth he'd previously prepared on his newly rented plot.

With the addition of water and electricity, nothing could stop him now, only a lick of paint and handmade sign were needed, to give birth to Norwood Motors.

As Britain began to prepare itself for a general election, the conquering powers had agreed to carve up the defeated German nation.

Russia would annex something over half, leaving Berlin deep inside its controlled territory.

In the end Germany's capital city would be ruled by the British, French and Americans, as well as the Russians, where in time a wall separating them from the rest would be constructed. All due to the desperate measures taken by Germans trying to flee into the hands of Western Allies.

Many other important things happened this July, apart from the first general

THE WAY WE WERE

election since 1935, to be held on the 15th. In this Churchill would suffer a shock defeat, as our war weary populace turned towards Labour to provide post-war prosperity. German civilians would be forced to visit Nazi death camps, to see for themselves the hideous evidence of mass extermination that most had refused to believe.

Suffering eighty-three days of the bloodiest fighting in the Pacific, Okinawa finally fell. Its defending commander, Lieutenant-General Mitsuri Ushijima, vacating his cave bunker, immediately committed hara-kiri in front of all his staff officers.

After more than 2,000 nights of almost total darkness, Great Britain rejoiced on July 15th in the full glow of total illumination, everything now switched on, never to be extinguished again!

In America, on the 16th, the first atom bomb test heralded a new age for the whole world.

It had taken over 100,000 workers, housed in three new cities, working in vast factories, throughout the New Mexico desert, many years to complete the Manhattan Project.

Yet in essence all but a few had any idea what they were actually working on.

One of the principal cities had been Los Alamos, which grew until it had 70,000 inhabitants.

The secret lay in dividing out the one percent of uranium 235, from natural uranium, only this fraction would accept complete fission, splitting itself into two parts and thereby forming a chain reaction. Such a phenomenon had been discovered, unbelievably, by the German scientist Otto Hahn, before the start of the Second World War. Minds can only speculate on the horrendous potential if Hitler had been able to develop this lead before being brought to defeat.

This fact alone almost condones the awful sacrifices made during five years of fighting.

Strangely my young mind did not dwell on these often remote happenings, for I remained firmly focused on the task in hand, how to stay cool, calm, and collected, as I learnt to step out of an aircraft!

171 Course, at the obscure address of Box 200 Manchester, had embarked upon its run down towards this walk into nothingness. Writing profusely I was delighted to inform my number one girl that her baby brother, having passed his mind tests, had reached his final goal at Ringway Airport, and would soon be flying high. To be honest not so high, because we had been told that

jumping heights would extend to no more than 700 feet, allowing one all of thirty seconds to prepare for the meeting with terra firma!

I was at pains to describe our practice leaps from thirty-foot towers attached to a harness, that in turn hung by a cable wrapped around a drum, turning a tiny fan!

> *'It doesn't look a very substantial fan, Cissy! And it seems a long way down when you first step off, but after the initial go and discovering the bump is not too severe, we can't get enough of it'.*
> *'They concentrate on getting you to roll correctly on landing, feet and knees together, pull your head well down towards the chest, tuck the arms in as you grasp the harness above, and always hit the ground sideways on'.*
> *'Never backwards, striking heels, bum, and back of head! And certainly not forward with toes, knees and nose.'*

There was no such thing as wing parachutes in those days, that you could steer and flare just before landing, the best we could do was pull on front lift webs, to reduce a backwards thrust, or back lift webs if the ground came fast towards you. There was an element of side control exercised by the same webs, pulling on one front or back, but at all times the body must be aligned to collapse in a sideways motion.

Oscillation of the canopy always had to be borne in mind, you may be descending in forward flight, only to swing past the approaching ground and come in backwards. And wind levels could be a devil, for not only did you hit at virtually the same speed but could also quite easily find yourself careering across the terrain at ten or fifteen miles per hour as the chute billowed and acted like a sail, before you could release yourself. In this event we were taught how to roll onto our backs, twist and bang the harness central release, hard, so that the crotch webbing could be freed. Then over onto your stomach as quickly as possible, slide one arm from beneath shoulder webbing and allow chute and harness to drift harmlessly away! All this of course as you hurtled over ruts and boulders, or anything else that happened to be strewn across the drop zone.

Some bright spark had spread the word that parachute landing was likened to leaping off the top of a double-decker bus, going at the same speed as the wind. It sounds horrendous, but we were undaunted!

Satisfied that they had inculcated enough common sense into us, I was busily telling Ciss that after being kitted out with parachute pack and rubber helmet, they carted us off to Tatton Park to introduce us to Betsy and Bessy. These two ladies were our ex-barrage training balloons, although as it happened this was to be the third attempt at trying to acquaint us with them, having held reveille over the previous two mornings at 04.30 am. It is a well known fact that on most early mornings, wind levels are at their lowest, except for yours truly, hence the three day delay.

Seven up and five down, called the instructor, meaning five of us would now clamber into the wicker and wire basket slung beneath Betsey, and the winch-man must let out 700 feet of cable.

Order of descent was already designated, so I had little choice but to hang back when informed, "You, Smith, will be number five!"

At least I was required to enter our temporary home first, which resembled a cage, with a strong fixture to hook your static line to. This line would pull your canopy out of its pack as quick release fasteners undid themselves. At the apex of the canopy was a thin nylon tie attached to the static line, the theory went that this tie should hold until all the chute and rigging lines were drawn out of the parachute pack, leaving you dangling on the end. Only then would the tie break, freeing you from your nest.

I expressed my feeling to Ciss as a somewhat nervous tummy, as slowly Betsey took us to our ceiling. Clinging to the cage I watched fascinated, noticing how everyone left on the ground had grown so small I could no longer distinguish who was who, until without warning Betsey gave a little bounce and stopped rising. Most of us had never experienced looking down on earth surrounded by pure space, at least I had flown in a Tiger Moth, but that time we had side-slipped back to the field. Certainly we appeared to be quite a way up.

Another gem of information they had gleefully imparted was that the Americans jumped from 1,100 feet, because they had a reserve chute, but the British chute they assured us was so good we didn't need a spare! Thank goodness they were now mostly made of nylon, because we had heard that some guys who had been issued with silk ones actually caught fire owing to the friction created on the silk. The term Roman Candle was used to express the resulting stream of flame.

Fortunately when you collected your pack, the WAAFs (Women's Auxiliary Air Force) were benevolent enough not to tell you what type they were handing you and we never asked!

Attached to a strong point above the cage opening were five straps of about fifteen inches in length, at the end of which sprouted stout, spring-loaded clips. To these had been fastened the opposing clips of our static lines that in turn protruded from bulky parachute packs by about eighteen inches. Securing pins would now be inserted to alleviate any undue parting of the ways. With all five firmly hooked, it was left to our dispatcher to carry out the execution.

As I peered beyond the perimeter of our abode towards ground level, these thoughts were suddenly interrupted, when I spied a green light, appearing to shine directly at us. "Time to go," quipped our dispatcher. "First man take position." Dutifully, my colleague shuffled forward, placing both hands beyond the aperture pressing backwards on the side supports, left foot firmly on the rim of the cage floor, staring straight to his front. "Go!" came the command, coupled with a hefty tap on the back.

There was a snap and rustling noise as he fell away, then a crack as his chute deployed, and he was free and on his way. Nothing to it, piece of cake! Next!

Before I realised, I too now stood poised at the gate, my compatriots all gone, the only other human, our dispatcher, now studying my expression with a wry smile. "Feeling lonely old chap?" he said. I half turned, diverting a fixed gaze from a distant fluffy white cloud. Was he joking, I wondered! Then, as nonchalantly as I could, "I don't mind," I answered, reverting once more to the cloud. I felt a firm pat on my back. "Go!" he yelled, and I was on my way, but my stomach didn't jump with me!

The fall from a balloon is straight down, no slipstream, as you would get from an aircraft. The two or three seconds it took for my chute to deploy were the longest on record; it would take all of one for internal organs to catch up. Mesmerised, I stared at both feet, as ever so slowly they rose higher and higher until well past shoulder level, then, with a loud crack, I hung stationary in the air.

It takes a drop of about 150 feet for this to happen, and then nothing, I felt suspended on a string.

First I looked up, checking my canopy, then down at the ground to check my drift angle, everything was going well, but instructions were being yelled at me through loud hailers from mother earth, that strangely, still seemed hardly any closer. "Pull on back lift webs," they were demanding. I could just make out a faint shortening of my horizon, meaning a frontal approach, so reaching above my head, I yanked hard on the rear webbing, bringing braided canvas to shoulder blades, trying desperately to brake and at the same time turn both feet for a side impact.

THE WAY WE WERE

Suddenly everything was rushing towards me at a colossal pace, when, in that instant, my chute turned, sending me sideways into the perfect position and a copybook roll. Feet and knees together, elbows tucked well in and head buried towards my chest. As I collapsed onto the ground, able to tumble correctly, the bulk of the shock was taken diagonally, right across my back.

The adrenaline was flowing through my body, "Wow!" I thought, "tomorrow I do this all again."

By July 24th I was writing my sister again: things had moved on in the world, with Labour now in power at home, and Churchill unhappy, with not just that, but his latest attempts alongside President Truman to reach a decent understanding with Stalin on the division of Germany. Already the Russians were showing intransigence, and making horrendous demands to give themselves massive control over the future of Europe, and Germany in particular. Churchill coined the never-to-be-forgotten phrase, Iron Curtain, which he declared would now fall across Europe, cutting it in two. I believe there were actually leaders at the time suggesting that while we still had vast numbers under arms that perhaps we should confront Russia, even if they became aggressive. Yet again the world had reached a crossroads, and it could jump either way.

As it transpired we did not pursue our requests of reasonable behaviour, instead we brokered a compromise, that would divide up the German capital between the conquerors, but leave it deep inside Russian-held territory. I think the greatest irony stemmed from Poland now being firmly under the control of the Bolsheviks, the very country we entered the war to save from slavery and dictatorship in the first place.

From that moment on the world became a dangerous place again, and at times stood on the brink of WWIII, that could so easily have annihilated us all, so perhaps the pundits who advocated striking while the iron was hot could so easily have been proved correct.

Personally I was of an age where I wasn't even allowed a vote, needing at the time to be a grown up, responsible twenty-one, so whatever the outcome I would be doing as I was told. All I needed to concentrate on was the completion of training to make me one of the British forces elite.

Apparently I had upset my sister by telling her I had put Len's girlfriend's name on my rubber jumping-hat. This article of headgear looked a bit like a round pork pie, with a cushion of two-inch rubber running round its rim to give added protection during training. I don't know why I put Alex's name on it, seeing as she wasn't my girl anyway, but I was insisting to my sister that she alone would always be my number one!

I now had only two jumps to complete before being granted parachute wings, which were worn on the upper sleeve of the right arm, because I was told the RAF objected to seeing them emblazoned on one's chest. How true the revelation is, I do not know, but such an imposition wouldn't have surprised me.

In this letter I emphasise that my remaining jumps were one by night from a balloon, and the other, a full stick of twenty men from a Dakota. So far I had left the aircraft in sticks of four and ten, with and without an eighty-pound kit bag, this latter temporarily attached to the right leg with its weight being firmly carried by the foot.

The idea associated with this bag, which carried all your equipment including firearm and ammunition and could be quickly opened down its length, was that after your chute had deployed you tugged on a small cord with the left hand, to release pins located through ties entwined round your leg. Then with a firm kick, cast it from the toe of your boot, to allow some eighteen feet of attached line folded concertina fashion from the harness, to run through canvas sleeves held tight in the right hand.

We had been assured that line length had been scientifically arrived at. This, they categorically confirmed, would allow the eighty-pound weight to dangle and oscillate at sufficient distance below your feet, so that when final contact with mother earth was made, your canopy will have all of a split second to breathe a sigh of relief. Letting you down nice and gently!

I had met a sergeant in Totland Bay hospital who described how his bag release cord had broken during the drop on D-Day; he finished up with a busted tendon in his right foot after landing in a tree. Perhaps it was just as well; otherwise he might have smashed a leg. Incidentally, he reckoned colliding with a tree wasn't so bad after all!

Another sergeant, who seemed very reluctant to speak, finally owned up to capturing a village near Caen, with twelve men, after they had knocked out several German tanks. In the end only he and two others were left. Both received the MM and he received the DCM.

When dropping in sticks of four, the pilot had to circle the drop zone and come in at the right speed (which I informed Ciss was a mere 150 mph) and height for each group. On one occasion I happened to be number one, and after the red light came on, stood to the door, with left foot forward, ready to throw

THE WAY WE WERE

my right leg out and clasp both hands together as I grabbed my trembling thigh and swept beneath the tail, legs glued together. Standing there, I kept studying the lights above my head, waiting anxiously for the red to go out and green to come on. For at least two minutes I held station, waiting and waiting, wishing to hell the pilot would get on with it. Obviously somewhere down the line he must have miscalculated, until eventually almost like a curtain up on stage where you are anxious not to freeze, I began to think for too long. Fortunately our dispatcher standing close to my side also showed concern, but it was all right for him because he would be landing with the aircraft.

When it came, the thump to my back seemed extra heavy, I guess its enforcer had appreciated what a long delay could mean, I caught the word Go! as I tumbled down the side of the fuselage, once more hurtling through turbulent slipstream. Two further pieces of instruction were expected to be absorbed, one of which concerned entry into trees (just mentioned) should you experience that misfortune, and the other, dropping into water.

There wasn't an awful lot one could do about a tree, if you had already tried avoiding it and lost, the advice extended, included crunching yourself up like a tenpin bowling ball and seeing how many skittle-like branches you could knock aside without actually damaging yourself. When heading towards water, whether salt or fresh, orders stipulated that you needed to slide swiftly out of your harness and quite literally hang by strong fingertips from the lift webbing, until both feet touched the briny. Only then should you let go (which comment seemed obvious to us) thus giving your parachute a chance to drift harmlessly away. Otherwise, they emphasised, you could find yourself smothered in nylon as you fought to keep your head above very often ice-cold water.

In later correspondence I refer to acting as number nine in a stick of ten, a position I was quite happy about, as we stood ready hooked up to the overhead cable. At this point every man had had his security pin checked by the chap behind (which goes to show what a close-knit fraternity paratroopers are). Patiently we waited for the green and our signal to shuffle conga-like towards the rear of the aircraft and our removed port side door aperture.

This snaking movement of left foot forward followed by a dragging motion of the right continues right up to the exit, while the left hand, held high, pushes Static lines along the cable above our heads. Even from my rearward position I could clearly see the green come on and the first man disappear as we all immediately began shunting into one-another. I failed to comprehend our sudden collisions until I spied number two stuck stubbornly at the doorway. There seemed to be some discourse taking place with an animated dispatcher, that after what seemed an eternity, but in truth, lasted probably no more than a minute, ended with the guy dropping out of sight.

The trouble was that within that minute we should have all gone, whereas our transport had now over-flown some seventy percent of the drop zone, before the last man left the aircraft.

My usual placid disposition had become agitated and annoyed, resulting in a bad landing in which my right foot suffered excruciating pain. I had confirmed correctly that my fast drift was sideways to the right, only to be overruled by a cantankerous wind that swung me sharply backwards. With amazing presence of mind I managed to extricate body from parachute before being whisked along at a steady twelve mph. Which was probably just as well, because when I stood up on my one decent foot I couldn't help crossing myself in the Lord's mercy, for there, not five yards to my left, was a lake. Just to make me feel even happier, a couple of yards behind ran the start of a small copse of trees. After that the pain in my foot subsided quite quickly, as religiously I counted my blessings!

Before I leave my reminiscences of parachute training, one further doctrine became enshrined, associated with rigging lines and their tendency to misbehave. It doesn't stretch the imagination too far to appreciate that if you became over enthusiastic on throwing your right leg beyond the open doorway, you could cause the body to twist. Reflect then on the ensuing act as canopy and rigging lines are drawn from the pack with their owner spiralling beneath the tail of the aircraft, somewhat out of control.

To be fair the chute does all it can by continuing to open, albeit with rigging lines resembling a plaited rope, ending in a piece of nylon about two-thirds its normal size. Now with a fast descending umbrella, you must ascertain the direction of twist and kick wildly in the opposing direction, until with a relieving crack you witness a full envelope and neatly spread lines to bring you in at a realistic descent. My worst experience of this folly happened when I swung a right leg full of kit bag, too hard, and found at least half a dozen agonising twists, culminating in a drastically reduced sized canopy.

Whatever else happened my first priority must be to release the bag, which I fervently did, before swinging both legs wildly to remove the tangle, only to immediately realise I was making matters worse as fiercely I now kicked in the opposite direction. As the chute snapped to full envelope, granting me the

THE WAY WE WERE

chance to gaze earthwards, so my kit hit the ground, which I accompanied a mere spilt second later. All was well and another of life's experiences had been tucked into the recesses of the mind!

Before brother Len finally said farewell to 152 in March of '45, his Black Panthers were well within sight of Mandalay, and the Burma campaign began rushing towards its fruitful conclusion.

A particular task asked of the squadron was close ground strafing support, where one of their pilots, liaising with forward army positions, directed attacking Spitfires onto targets sometimes less than one hundred yards to their front.

Before monsoons broke, the longest pontoon bridge ever built enabled our Fourteenth Army to sweep across the Irrawaddy River and instantly strengthen their surge towards the strategic port of Rangoon.

At this point a small anecdote is worthy of the telling, one that I refer to in detail in my writings entitled *Birth of the Black Panthers*.

An American Harvard similar to the aircraft Len flew in Moose Jaw, Canada, was always allocated to British Spitfire squadrons as a general runabout, usually ferrying grog (gin) from Calcutta. Often Len and a friend of his, a certain John Willoughby Vickers, undertook this pleasant duty. However on this particular occasion, an RAF photographer, wishing to film the Irrawaddy crossing, requested an early morning flight for just this purpose. The trouble stemmed from the extreme likeness of the Harvard to some Japanese types, and a somewhat unauthorised mission. Operating nearby nestled No. 17 Squadron, who sent up a couple of Spits to make sure no intruders tried to spy on our boys, and in doing so spotted what they thought was a Japanese Oscar, with one of them taking a pop at it. Suddenly over the RT came the cry, "Bollocks! It's a Harvard!" But it was too late as the crippled aircraft plunged for the nearest paddy field.

The outcome was a court martial for the poor Spitty pilot, Flying Officer Rathwell, who later returned to his native Canada. Both pilot and photographer survived their ordeal, with the photographer actually taking a snapshot of FO Jackson, the Harvard pilot, standing by the wing of the downed plane. It was long after that I learnt the photographer was none other than Harry Ashley, chief photographer for the *Bournemouth Daily Echo*!

With the fall of Rangoon our forgotten Far Eastern army under the command of Louis Mountbatten (someone whom Len had actually met and conversed with, and in a later telegram to his CO, wrote asking for thanks to be conveyed to Flying Officer Smith and fellow pilots who flew with him) had completed the recapture of Burma.

To do so, they had, with the help of Indian and African troops, covered 1,000 miles of the worst terrain and weather conditions encountered in the world, destroying in the process 97,000 of the enemy and capturing 250,000.

The way now lay open for the invasion of Singapore and the next stage in the Far Eastern campaign.

Long before Burma had been completely retaken, plans had been drawn up for the follow-through to Malaya and Singapore. Designated Operation Zipper, it called for some 500 aircraft, with Spitfires and Seafires flying from aircraft carriers.

I came home on leave the proud possessor of brand new parachute wings, fully trained and itching to get into a battalion. Hardly had I been home for a week when news broke of the atomic raid on Hiroshima, to be followed three days later, after Japan's refusal to surrender, by another on the city of Nagasaki.

Posted to Knaresborough, I was quickly transferred to a reserve battalion at Beverley in Yorkshire, where we learnt of the Japanese surrender on the 14th August.

My long struggle to join the fray, firstly to emulate my brother, by studying hard and offering up a false age had ended as a fully trained and very fit peacetime paratrooper. What now, I wondered, would the powers that be, do with us?

I experienced no regret at the war's end, only a quiet acceptance of the way things had transpired. I could not in all honesty fail to be relieved that I would no longer have to worry about various members of my family. That Ciss and Jack had been able to relax from fear of those awful rockets, after the advent of VE day. And now Len could not be recalled from India to perform active service against the Japanese, that sister-in-law Ivy would soon be reunited with our brother John, and dear Rene able to settle down with her husband Johnny, after his return from the Middle East.

I had witnessed some of the most traumatic times ever to befall our beloved island, aerial dogfights from way on high, armadas of enemy aircraft darkening our skies, almost front line drama played out over the roofs of Romford. Watched helplessly as virtually one third of London suffered destruction. And I had been privileged to do my bit helping the American air force establish bases from which to strike our enemy, even the timber I helped to produce would one day go towards rebuilding Britain.

Since joining the ranks of His Majesty's services I had made many friends, whom I'd laughed, cursed and striven to achieve something worthwhile with.

THE WAY WE WERE

Five years had elapsed since helping Jack dig a hole for our shelter; five years in which I had grown from a boy into a man, these years they say can be the most informative and deeply ingrained, of one's whole life. Certainly I had encountered a strong feeling of our country pulling together, a spirit of great unselfishness that from that time forward would gradually be eroded as slowly but surely we became dragged into a faster and far more materialistic world.

By the middle of November 1945 promotion seemed on the cards and after attending umpteen courses and trying to get my soft voice to carry commands across the parade ground, I looked well and truly destined for the exalted rank of lance corporal, one of the lowest of the low! The boys had taken sympathy on my feeble efforts at vocal chord projection, desperately straining their ears to follow distant commands almost instantly lost on the slightest breeze.

The army had obviously been brought up by those who could shout the loudest, and didn't take kindly to weak ineffectual voices; one day in the future this attribute along with a rather gentle approach to my pals, still reclining in the "private ranks", would be my undoing!

Post-war prospects did not look good, Britain was bankrupt and the Labour Party was firmly in control. Rationing that had seemed pretty severe during hostilities showed signs of becoming even more stringent. Sure we'd won, now all we had to do was pick up the bill. Workers, who had previously put their backs into saving our country with little thought for themselves, began to make ever-greater demands. On 14th October 6,000 troops were needed to unload precious supplies when 43,000 dock-workers downed tools as a protest against the new government's refusal to meet their twenty-five shilling a day minimum wage request.

Something that would impinge on me happened when the newly formed United Nations were referred by Britain to the question of Jewish immigrants trying to enter the country of Palestine. Having suffered the Holocaust at the hands of Hitler and his Nazi henchmen, the Jews were desperate to found a land of their own, and who could blame them. They would use history going back to the Israelites of Biblical times to enforce their arguments, but what about the poor Palestinians. In this year of 2004, as I write, the problem has not been solved, plus, United Nations directives have never been implemented. A lot of terrible things have happened over the intervening nearly sixty years throughout the Middle East and elsewhere. I'm afraid I would have to attribute many of them, including the catastrophic crashing of jumbo jets into the Twin Towers of New York and onto the Pentagon building, to this lack of resolution.

Unfortunately it is a well known fact that the Jewish lobby in America is very strong and because of it I see faint opportunity of ever being able to resolve the issue that I was sent out to help my country contain all those years ago!

Many peoples under British protective rule, when most of the world map still remained coloured pink, as in my school days, now started to flex their muscles and shout for independence. India, Burma, Malaya, including Indochina wallowing under French colonial rule.

Trials began to take place of Nazi perpetrators and notorious camp guards, such as Josef Kramer, the "Butcher of Belsen".

Retribution against bad people would dominate the headlines for some time to come, with a few Nazis, like Goering, committing suicide and thereby saving us the trouble.

Our family entrepreneur, Jack, was encountering stiff opposition from Romford's local politicians as he fought to establish Norwood Motors. I would write from various locations as I travelled from training depot to training depot before reaching the bizarrely named village of Piddle-Hinton. "Poor Jack," I penned, "he works so tirelessly and deserves to be treated much better, I only hope I have his patience if ever suffering similar obstacles." An observation that did indeed ring true, many time's during the following fifty-plus years!

One thing we discovered during our movements was that when we came to require lift off for battalion jumping, they suddenly realised with wars end and withdrawal of American equipment, we didn't have a plane capable of dropping British parachutists. I found myself staring at a hastily carved hole in the bottom of a four-engine Halifax bomber. The makeshift transport became a poor substitute, being able to carry only eight chaps, and only two of them could carry kit-bags, as you were required to sit on the edge of the hole with both feet dangling, ready to push yourself into space. These two guys needed to ensconce themselves in the jump-off position before the aircraft left the ground. After they vacated the aircraft then two more would quickly slide into their empty positions, and follow them down through the hole and out under the twin tails, but there was no way they could do this with an eighty-pound kit-bag strapped to their leg!

Later I leapt from an experimental Stirling bomber, which had a bath shaped hole, and could carry twelve men, but neither plane was really suitable. I believe it was then decided to lease Dakotas to enable us to function more realistically.

No one could say the paratroops were resting on their laurels because the war had ended, if anything our training became even more rigorous, in one letter to Ciss, I tell of going further north and being expected to march back over 150 miles. In another I describe four-day exercises where it meant fording rivers with nothing but what we stood up in, wrapping all our kit and clothes, including firearms, in our ground sheet, and floating the makeshift bundle across each river, whilst we swam naked, pushing and clinging tentatively from behind. In this I was surprised to discover just how many types couldn't swim, and was placed in charge of a rescue team designed to help those who got into difficulties. Once more I had cause to congratulate Jack on his forthrightness!

Our new Labour government had clearly set its mind against private enterprise when it announced that all civil aviation would be controlled and run by the state. This was precisely the attitude that Jack found himself up against. Also in November '45 the Russians declared they were going to build their own atom bomb. Hardly had we laid down our arms when suddenly the world was looking a dangerous place again.

By the 7th a Gloster Meteor jet had achieved 606 mph as it flew across Herne Bay in Kent.

The 20th saw the first trials of Nuremberg begin, all the faces we had seen a thousand times before began lining up in front of us. Glued to local cinema newsreels, we watched fascinated as the Nazi tyrants were paraded one by one. Goering, Hess, Ribbentrop, Keitel, Dönitz, Streicher, von Papen, the guy who helped put Hitler in power, and Fritz Sauckel the slave labour overlord.

Within the following month the American General, George S. Patton, would die of chest wounds sustained in an automobile accident. Known as Blood and Guts for the way he led the American 7th Army throughout North Africa and Europe, he had raced Montgomery across Sicily to beat the 8th Army to the Straits of Messina.

January 1st saw the test trial of Britain's first civil aviation flight. Flown by British South American Airways to Montevideo, the converted bomber took off from a barren area with few facilities, comprising tents, huts, and some telephone boxes, known as Heath Row. Over twenty million pounds had been earmarked to develop the area, and already a 3,000-yard runway had been built. This would be, according to government spokesmen, the future terminus for long distance flights. How right they were!

Before I had a chance to arrive home on embarkation leave, Royal Indian Naval ratings were demonstrating in Bombay to oust the British. Similar protests, only more aggressively so, were being staged in Cairo, demanding our departure from Egypt. Slowly and assuredly the proud days of British

William S. Smith

Empire were beginning to unravel. And yet in all honesty we had not been terrible rulers and to be fair we had brought many advantages to the peoples we governed. Indian citizens are still plagued with status divisions, people still die overnight in their streets, and the railways introduced by us are still using the same rails and rolling stock we gave them.

I sailed on a Sunday, a few days after my nineteenth birthday, as a lance corporal of Number Six Platoon, B Company, of the 17th Parachute Battalion, part of the 6th Airborne Division. The same division that had been first to drop on D-Day in Normandy, and later, over the Rhine

We filled the SS *Orontes* from bow to stern as she steamed out of Southampton water and up past the Isle of Wight.

Our initiation into seamanship took place at lights out, when everybody had to grab a hammock. Each one of these encased a blanket, which you somehow had to fold round yourself. But having secured one from stowage, the most difficult task was acquiring two hooks to hang it from! The only method I could think of was wrapping a big toe round one, while I clung desperately onto another, seven feet away. Then gritting your teeth as you slid a ring smartly over this second support, you made a hasty dive for your toehold and congratulated yourself on a tortuous achievement!

Now came the tricky part, somehow you needed to hoist your body high enough and horizontally rigid enough, to ease both legs into the blanket, buried deep inside this curled up banana shaped piece of canvas! After several attempts, I decided the only sure way was to spread the blanket on the floor, roll myself up in it, and let a couple of the boys lift me in. Unfortunately that idea was received with catcalls and derision!

Sleep also became a problem, exacerbated by being seven decks down. Permeating through shafts from above, air culminated in swivel vents that each dozing paratrooper became obsessed to point in any direction but his own. We would take it in turn to extricate ourselves from our once cosy cocoon, and shove the damn thing away, but of course, the action, always meant some other poor devil ended up with a blast of cold air down the back of his neck. We finally each gave up, burying ourselves beneath our one, solitary, coarse coverlet instead.

Before sailing I had congratulated Rene on her forthcoming motherhood, due hopefully within three months, and Len had written to say he expected to be in Blighty before the end of the summer. He had expressed a love for a certain Alexandria nursing sister, by the name of June, after receiving a Goodbye

THE WAY WE WERE

Johnny letter from his English petite blonde, Alex. But he had decided instead that England was the place to wed, so the family would be welcoming him home after all, whilst his latest love became unable to avoid being posted to Japan. So despite all my efforts on Len's behalf, I had obviously been useless when it came to quelling Alex's desires over a certain distant cousin she had secretly been seeing, the amorous cause of her break with my brother! She came to visit Ciss, bringing with her, at her father's insistence, a beautiful gold bracelet set with seven opals, a token of Len's affection, that he had lovingly bought for her, via the courtesy of a clever Indian jeweller. To this day Mary treasures this emblem of Len's love. Also, Ciss was to expect a visit from one of his latest flying chums, a certain John Willoughby Vickers. A tall, slim, mustachioed, charismatic character, who had flown with Len's Black Panther 152 Squadron in Burma, Vicky had finally caught up with Len at Peshawar; he himself was already married to a lovely brunette called Bette, who maintained their family home at Southend.

One day under fraught circumstances I too would meet Vicky, whom just a few days ago I discovered had passed away at the young age of eighty-two. My letter of condolence to Bette was my first contact in over twenty years. It was in 1984 that I'd had occasion to gamble on an old phone number when wanting to ask Vicky some questions concerning my brother Len. He couldn't believe hearing my voice after so many years, and immediately felt transported back to the late forties. How true it is that the years flash past, and writing about them foreshortens time further still!

In spite of relatively choppy seas whilst negotiating the Bay of Biscay, I was happy to report, during writings home about life aboard, that I'd managed not to succumb to sea sickness, putting this down to peering beyond the bows to concentrate hard on steering the ship both in and out of the waves. For some reason I also wanted Ciss to insure Rene was made aware that the Bay water did appear jet black, a point of obvious dissent between my youngest sister and me.

By Friday 29th March I was able to post my scribbles, when for a few short hours we stopped at Malta, "a harbour at that time still full of British Man-o-War ships", before sailing on to disembark at Port Said, Egypt, on the morning of April 1st. I hoped it denoted good luck! Here, we encountered the usual outstretched pleading backshees (grovelling) arms of welcome, which to our young and inexperienced eyes seemed almost like another world. Everything and everyone displayed a poor and tatty existence, with natives clad in little else but rags, while beggars and vendors vied vehemently with each other to elicit our attention, and of course, our money. I describe how the lads discarded lumps of bread and gasped in amazement when these were quickly pounced upon, scraping them from the filthy sand to stuff them unceremoniously, without so much as a cursory wipe, into waiting, ravenous mouths. Not that we felt in the least bit rich, with such a lowly stipend awarded us, although in fairness, we did at least get a shilling a day extra for leaping from aircraft! But quite obviously, compared to our hosts, we were akin to Lord and Lady Muck.

Sanitation also showed signs of being non-existent, with street Arabs prepared to perfect their faecal functions just about round any available corner, and living quarters often extended to little more than excavated holes in the sides of cliffs.

In no time at all we were shepherded into what could easily be mistaken for a line of cattle trucks, and sent packing, at the prestigious pace of twenty mph, for a thirty-six hour desert journey.

After a couple of interesting stops, one at Ismailia, a much more civilised venue, built by the French, with wide tree-lined avenues and picturesque dwellings, all sparkling white. And another shrouded in desert dust known as El Kantara, we finally finished up at a remote tented encampment called Quassasin, where the CO promised us his first priority would be to sort out the grub situation, because it was b-awful!

Here, I was able to quickly jot another note home, for I had realised, in all probability, it would be a further week before such a chance presented itself again. One of my paragraphs inferred a sighting of future promotions, where I had witnessed my name recommended for full corporal.

If I had been just that little bit older to have entered the RAF and lucky enough to have qualified for any form of flying duty, I should automatically have been promoted to sergeant. Apart from this, I should not have had to bellow my way around a parade ground to have achieved it.

Many of my parachuting colleagues promoted alongside me would return home as sergeants, but alas, fate had a different twist in store for me!

Traversing onwards, we wound through desert sands by the darkness of night, each time now, that we stopped, so a cordon would be thrown around our train, just in case insurgents threatened to attack, until eventually we crossed into Palestine. Immediately we steamed further inland to reach alongside another tented encampment about ten miles from the azure blue of the Mediterranean.

From this unnamed piece of orange grove country, we would strike out at dusk, wherever patrols were required, to deter would-be Jewish infiltrators from establishing themselves as genuine residents. One of my first duties earmarked the defence of a coastguard station, from where we could sweep along the moonlit beach in search of unauthorised boat people trying to come ashore.

This was not war, but we could be shot at, only then, so orders went, were we allowed to protect ourselves, but with one proviso! You must wait till the officer said you could shoot back. Except of course you could only fire up in the air, or at least make certain it was over their heads. For this imperative piece of important policing I was instructed to bring up the rear of our squad, with nothing less than a Bren gun. However, having been told to lug this heavy automatic weapon over soft sand for umpteen miles, I was also instructed never to fire more than one round at a time! Another important point ingrained into us by the CO downwards, implied, any deviation from these directives leading to the loss of someone's life, even though, as they struggled ashore they might be firing at you from the hip, could end in one of us being tried for murder! It was a far cry from parachuting into enemy territory.

Our CSM (Company Sergeant Major) keeps cropping up in my correspondence, he was obviously somebody who didn't gel very well with me! These types can vary tremendously, sometimes acting like a mother hen although at the same time expecting everyone to toe the line, which is fair enough. Others though, can be like spit and polished little Hitler's, who love the sound of their own voice and can't throw their weight around enough.

Unfortunately C Company had one of the latter, a sharp faced evil looking type with a rather pronounced pockmarked reddish nose, so we have all christened him "Strawberry" and methinks both he and I are very much on a collision course. I write quite openly of preferring to empty my magazine into him as opposed to any illegal immigrant. It occurs to me that maybe he got sight of my letter and decided to seek revenge!

Back home in May 1946, a joint Anglo-American report had been published on the dire situation in Palestine. It recommended the continuing presence of Britain in acting as honest broker between the Jews and Arabs. It detailed the decision of allowing up to 100,000 Jewish refugees who had suffered from Nazi and Fascist persecution, to settle in Palestine over the coming year, compared to the 1500 per month that were currently being accepted. The fact that Arabs were also recognised as being part of the country did little to thwart their anger, and the Jews were still totally dissatisfied. Life did not bode well for the poor British squaddie stuck in the middle!

William S. Smith

Writings from Len expressed disaffection with the way his repatriation was progressing too. Having marched boldly from Norwood Avenue at the start of 1943, his absence from home now stood at three and half years, also he couldn't stop dwelling on his genuine concerns over the extremely high possibility of his imminent dispatch into Civvy Street. "Gee Billy," he would write, "I dread the thought of no more flying, and of course being a fighter pilot won't help get you into any private Airline jobs either. I know of many ex four-engine bomber types with thousands of hour's experience who are already applying for that very opportunity."

Corresponding with one or two of Len's flying pals over recent years, they always regarded their de-mob days as ones of trauma and cosmic change. To not only suddenly find yourself bereft of fond friendships, but having to provide everything for your livelihood, meaning, work, food, shelter, etc., plus applying the dreadful thought of never ever flying again, must have been like a bolt to the heart.

Letters from Ciss painted an austere picture of our once great nation, rationing had become much worse and as it transpired would continue for another eight years until 1954. For the first time since the outbreak of war the country was to be subjected to bread rationing.

And although it seems hard to believe today, they were actually suggesting that workers in heavier industries would get more than people doing clerical jobs. (Imagine such a scenario in today's world of June 2004.) She and Jack were talking openly now of emigrating to New Zealand. Jack had still not been able to start his own motor garage for the constant negative bureaucratic wall he kept coming up against.

All this plus the appalling weather they seemed to be experiencing drove Ciss to apologise for her downbeat entries. "I'm so sorry," she wrote, which was a shame, because her young brother was lapping up the gorgeous sunshine and warm seas, and as long as he received adequate communication from home whatever the content, remained over the moon.

Apparently Sister Elsie had given birth to another boy, which now made five boys! Derek, Ron, Brian, Robin and John: poor Elsie, she seemed destined never to have a companionable daughter.

The remainder of the family were all doing well and one by one, finding their feet as civilians.

Bill Russell had been another of Ciss's visitors, having returned on leave from Germany, and spoken warmly of his love for Sheila. They had decided at long last to tie the knot, as soon as he became demobbed. It was great hearing how fine Bill was and so full of life, it had certainly been impossible with so much travelling between us, to entertain the remotest chance of keeping in contact. His decision brought no surprise, although many a time he had fought shy of the commitment. He would confide these desires and doubts, but I always knew Sheila would capture him in the end and without question she would make a loving and devoted wife.

One of the arguments Len had been espousing revolved around his urging me to put in for an officer's course. These opportunities did exist but as I painstakingly pointed out to my promoted brother, the only possible way I could apply would be to sign on as a regular for twenty-one years. "Fine," I argued, "if one wanted to remain a parachutist in the army, but I only stepped out of aircraft so that I could fly in them in the first place." In fact I had now taken off in various aeroplanes at least fourteen times, and never ever landed in the damn things! Somehow, I insisted, I would achieve this goal back in civilian life. I was nothing if not determined, although probably a bit naïve.

There had been uproar in the Commons when premier Attlee declared he had decided to pull our troops out of Egypt. Churchill was aghast. "How," he asked, "can we defend our interest in the great British and French enterprise of the Suez Canal?" (One day in the not too distant future, this short cut across the world would be torn from us as assuredly as most other hard-won British achievements throughout our crumbling empire.)

We were constantly being sent on detachment to various outlying establishments that quite often took the form of a fort. They reminded me very much of a then popular film called *Beau Geste*.

This old black and white depicted characters like Wallace Beery Senior as part of a French Foreign Legion contingent, holed up in a fort complete with castellated battlements, set in a desert landscape of undulating sand. Here, with only a small volume of water between the garrison they would fight off marauding Bedouins to the last man. Our venues, established as control posts for the Palestine Police, who themselves wore those peaked hats with neck protectors, just like the Legionnaires, gave glamour to our duties. Even more so, when one day, a tribe of Bedouins happened by, complete with young barefoot dancing girls all dressed in black and covered in many necklaces and bracelets of brightly coloured beads. Then, as if to show off to the British Red Berets, a couple of their men-folk took off on what could only have been racing camels! If I had not witnessed such a sight with my own eyes, I never would have believed the speed these ships of the desert could achieve.

Returning to our tented encampment after one of these forays our company padre asked if there was anyone due leave that would like to accompany him on a pilgrimage to Galilee and Nazareth, so a few us, about twenty in all, stepped smartly forward.

The journey to reach the biblical area entailed clinging to an arduous, twisting, climbing highway, where sometimes hairpin bends became so sharp they literally doubled back on each other.

Each time this caused our sweltering driver, to grind to a halt and back up before propelling his four-ton troop carrier forward again. After an equally tortuous downhill run we suddenly swept into a broad plain, where the town of Nazareth lay sprawled across low hillocks before us.

It comprised lots of small white buildings, hovels almost when you got up close, which I am quite sure would have looked much better and more pristine during Christ's day! We entered a tiny Church purported to have been the very one in which our Lord preached, also shown a carpenters shop similar to one that he and his dad worked in. I'm afraid my impressions left a lot to be desired, telling Ciss in no uncertain terms, that the whole area seemed to be constructed of tin cans and mud and simply reeked of goats and urine!

Continuing our tour we dropped 700ft below sea level to arrive at Lake Tiberius. Here, in conditions on a par with the tropics, was the very spot that Jesus fished, in order to feed the five thousand, and walked majestically upon the water. Some of the boys and I ventured onto the lake in a rowing boat, but as I later explained to my No.1 girl when tentatively attempting the same trick, my tootsies went under, so presumed I was too much of a heathen to repeat that spiritual act. I did however purchase a Bible, only to discover I had committed the cardinal sin, being cheated out of my hard-earned Ackers, because it had been imported from America and was definitely not of local origin.

Having acted out my lowly rank for all of six months and with barely weeks remaining before promotion to full corporal, I reverted once more to private status. It wasn't cast upon me but self inflicted so it came as no surprise. You could say it was due to frustration, or a propensity not to suffer fools gladly, or more probably to do with the inheritance of some of my mother's Irish blood.

The whole sequence stemmed from an altercation with Strawberry,

THE WAY WE WERE

naturally! I had suffered this vicious, arrogant, imbecile long enough, but that was still no excuse for allowing him to get the better of me. Unfortunately company sergeant majors can be a law unto themselves, normally they are experts at reciting the King's Regulations backwards, and pride themselves on razor sharp creases in their trousers, mirror shine boots and dazzling brasses. In other words they can be full of bullshit but not always brains. Having said that, there were some, soldiers would follow to the ends of the earth, and trust implicitly in any kind of combat! But Strawberry definitely did not enter that category. The way his reasoning worked you would doubt any dubious command he ever needed to utter!

The situation had developed during one of the many detachments upon which we were constantly deployed, yours truly being entrusted with mounting the guard. As guard commander my nightly duties meant little sleep as every two hours I was responsible for awakening the next man for the watch. I had carried out this function on frequent occasions without any untoward interference, except this time Strawberry had chosen to accompany the detail.

Even so, I paid scant concern to his presence and calmly got on with the task in hand, dutifully awakening each of my colleagues as their turn came around to perform this military ritual. If I recall correctly it was the 5 am watch that I apologetically aroused Private Roberts to make preparation for. Five minutes later I retraced my steps to the billet, checking on his readiness, only to find my charge had fallen fast asleep again. "Robby," I hissed, so as not to disturb the others, gently shaking him by the shoulder. "Robby, show a leg, its time for your guard duty."

Of course it was sods law that Strawberry, unbeknown to me, had witnessed my tentative attempts at arousing Robby, glaring down his blotchy nose as he confronted me outside the Billet!

"Corporal Smith," he spat, gleefully, "when we return to camp I am placing you in front of the CO for acting in a manner likely to breach discipline and for being over friendly with the private ranks." For two pins I could have clocked him one, there and then, but my wiser head prevailed. "Sergeant Major," I said, as forcefully as I could without being insubordinate. "I can vouch that any man in my platoon will follow me whatever I ask of them and I do not consider I have breached any disciplinary code."

I would have loved to have added, that I could also assure him that were we ever to go into action, he could very easily be the first casualty, but I bit my tongue leaving my eyes to do the talking. So there you have it, sure enough Strawberry kept his word, and our poor commanding officer, had the onerous task of reprimanding one of his NCOs. The trouble was, even COs had minimal power when it came to company sergeant majors, they would confront the officer with *fait accompli* evidence, quoting King's Regulations, and almost daring their superior to deny its existence.

The CO stumbled over his words a little, saying my action could be construed as prejudicial to good order, and that I must refrain from being overtly friendly with those of private rank.

By this time I began to see red, squaring my shoulders and staring straight ahead, "Sir," I said in my strongest voice, "I cannot in all fairness be expected to forgo normal friendship with soldiers in my platoon who I have served alongside for almost twelve months now. I give you my word that any or all would do anything I ask of them that's how much respect they have for me!" I had the distinct feeling that my CO had been got at, and it was going to be a battle of wills between Strawberry and me as to who had the right attitudes and approach.

In today's army of course there would be little doubt that my reasonable but firm relationship would win the day, but in the aftermath of WWII in 1946 it was a different kettle of fish.

As the CO studied my face, he appeared almost resigned to an unhappy conclusion, trying hard not to notice the grim statue of his sergeant major hovering menacingly at my left shoulder.

He cleared his throat before speaking quietly and seriously, "It strikes me corporal," he offered, "that you value your platoon friends more than your rank, and perhaps you might prefer to relinquish it."

How could I back down now, somehow I abhorred the idea of returning to the lads and informing them I could no longer act as their friend. Had I had more time to reflect upon the situation, I might have construed that perhaps I could knuckle down for a while, and who knows maybe, just maybe, Strawberry would have been moved, even if only sideways to another company. It was highly possible even the CO would like to see the back of him.

But I needed to make my judgement there and then, besides which there was the distinct possibility that the CO might be forced to issue court martial proceedings. A resignation would avoid that. What I was unaware of at the time was the army attitude towards resignations, which they were loath to overlook when it came to new promotions.

THE WAY WE WERE

My sentiments may have been noble therefore, but my reasoning was stupid, so whether it was pride or anger or sheer cussedness, I do not know, but I declared quite firmly that I definitely valued my friends before any promotion the army had to offer.

After six years absence because of the war, the English Derby horse race was re-run again on the 5th June, and lots of my pals parents won good money, because out of sentiment to their offspring they backed Airborne, and it romped home!

In Rome, after royalist riots on the 7th, the Italian government declared a republic on the 10th, which King Umberto II refused to acknowledge, alleging poll irregularities. However by the 12th, Premier Alcide de Gasperi assumed the functions of head of state.

At the age of fifty-eight, John Logie Baird, the first person to send moving pictures over the airways, died at Bexhill-on-Sea on 14th June, and on the 15th sister Irene gave birth to her first child, a girl whom, her and husband John McCarthy would name Maureen.

By the 18th there was a full-blooded curfew in place in Palestine, after two British officers had been killed and three others kidnapped by Jewish terrorists. It didn't help when we heard that one of those kidnapped was our own quartermaster, a certain captain from B Company. Now my sisters really would be worried! Throughout June and July several things were to happen, including me being put in charge of the Platoon PIAT. I have described this thirty-eight-pound monstrosity before. I guess they felt that my height and bulk leant itself to the abominable kick it gave! The one good thing about it was, they took away your rifle and presented you with a revolver instead, also supplying you with a No. 2 who would carry six bombs for the PIAT, in two panniers of three.

After standing on the shoulder butt and heaving upward against a heavy spring to cock the thing, you would take up a prone firing position, and flick up a strip of metal with holes drilled in it to sight whatever close range you chose. Your No. 2 would then place one of his missiles in the front cradle.

To have any degree of accuracy the enemy tank or vehicle would need to be no further than 100 yards distant, at which point you squeezed the four inch trigger with two fingers, pulling the main body and butt hard into your right shoulder. The action released a long shaft like spigot held back by the spring, which in turn travelled up a hollow tube, attached to the nose of the bomb. This tube also supported a circular tail fin to assist in the bomb's forward flight. As the spigot slammed into the base of the missile, it struck a detonator, so that the resulting explosion sent the bomb winging towards its target and at the same time, providing you had the butt firmly jammed into your shoulder, allowed the reverse blast to re-cock the whole contraption!

Such was the slow speed of the bomb's flight, you were able quite easily to observe its spinning trajectory, and if mis-aimed also watch it skid harmlessly off the side or top of your target. Then of course one had to hope you had gripped tight enough to enable the heavy coil spring to do its job properly, so you could quickly re-aim and fire again.

A short time after this elevation to anti-tank gunner, the 17th Battalion and B Company in particular took part in an exercise some 120 miles inside Egypt at the location of the Sinai Desert. I remember watching fascinated at the many dust devils (small whirlwinds) spiralling upwards, as I lugged this most cumbersome piece of important parachutist equipment uphill and down in sweltering heat over many miles, whilst our artillery boys laid down a creeping barrage from their 25-pounders.

Forever keeping 300 yards to our front, they continued firing until they had expended 900 shells, by which time, despite my fitness, I was just about ready to collapse.

The other thing about this operation was the learning curve of all night desert bivouacking, trying to curl up in hastily dug slit trenches, and spreading a groundsheet over the top, to stop the amazing coldness and dampness from creeping in. Finding at dawn how everything was suddenly wringing wet, and then being confronted by swarms of flying beetles, four-inch wingspan bugs, buzzing us at no more than four or five feet above the ground. The boys had a field day with these things, haring around trying to swat them with anything they could lay their hands on. If only we'd had a movie camera available to catch half-naked troopers cavorting over arid desert, arms flailing, sporting nothing but pants and field-boots!

Before the end of June, leaders of the Jewish Irgun Zevai Leumi terrorist organisation were threatening to execute our kidnapped officers, unless two of their number held by the British authorities had their death sentences commuted. But as so often, in fact just like today in July 2004, nearly sixty years on, during the aftermath of our invasion of Iraq, where poor kidnapped innocent foreign workers have been threatened with and actually suffered execution by beheading. So those in charge were afraid if they capitulated to terrorist demands, it would only encourage others to follow suit.

THE WAY WE WERE

The King David Hotel in Jerusalem, headquarters of the Palestine Army, erupted on the 22nd July; one wing of the famous building was totally destroyed. Forty-two people were immediately pronounced dead with a further fifty-two missing and fifty-three injured. How ironic that today's Israel cannot understand the plight of the Palestinians and their resort to terror bombing, it's as if there was no acknowledgement to the learning process.

Hitler had terrorised and slaughtered the Jews, British forces had been in the forefront of their salvation, yet now, here we were, dying at the hands of those very people we'd helped to liberate.

Immediately a cordon was thrown around Tel-Aviv, and I would be in the thick of it.

Had this been the work of the illegal Jewish army, known as Haganah, everyone wondered, or was it more likely the hallmark of the Stern Gang, a notorious killer group, who one day would be responsible for stringing up two of our sergeants in an orange grove.

We dug in round the vast perimeter of Palestine's city, where by 04.30 we were in position and ready to move forward. A total curfew had been imposed and everyone was apprehensive.

Earlier, before receiving orders to move out of camp, we had witnessed the arrival of the entire King's Shropshire Light Infantry Division. Hell! For one minute we thought they had come to relieve us and rumours abounded that we were being shipped out to India or Ceylon, even Java or best of all Blighty. But no! All they were there for was to increase the numbers for the Tel-Aviv operation.

Most of our 1st Brigade would hold position, but at 5.15 am B Company was ordered into the city to start searching house by house, tenement by tenement. Nobody was allowed to leave their dwelling or even step on to their verandas.

Everybody between the ages of sixteen and forty-five had to be taken away for interrogation and fingerprinting.

For three days we kept this up, working fifteen hours a day. Yet I could only feel sorrow for the people. I would be stationed at strategic points, so that should it become necessary my lethal weapon could destroy part of a building if resistance was encountered. However after thirty-six hours of this and aware that women and children were beginning to starve owing to the intransigence of our authorities, I and others, against officers orders would vacate our positions and start to deliver bread and milk to people as best we could.

William S. Smith

When I eventually wrote home about these affairs I was at pains to make the family aware of the true nature of things. Explaining that at no time had it been necessary to fire a shot, yet we had heard many fired, but never by our brigade. "Besides," I went on, "you still required an officer's permission to fire, and then only in the air, yet despite this people were injured, possibly from ricocheting bullets, because they had ventured onto veranda's. I'm afraid, despite my now, lowly position, I castigated these officers for there ignorance and childishness, after-all, the last orders given, were that we were to act as Ambassadors for Great Britain. Even our own Platoon officer refused us permission when we wanted to help."

It was after this last straw that I instructed my number two to look after the PIAT while I visited various dwellings to ask if I could shop for them. This way I was actually able to trek backwards and forward delivering about a hundred loaves for the incarcerated populace.

Already there had been some rioting, and I considered our friendliness bore much fruit and saved many a similar reaction in our sector. "Frankly," I said, "I would not have put up with half what these poor devils had to endure. Imagine," I scribed, "half a dozen burly, armed to the teeth troopers, trampling all over your living rooms and bedrooms, whilst a further dozen or so lay siege to the outsides of your premises. Then to see your men-folk frog-marched away, not knowing where to or for how long."

Even without the enlightenment of another fifty-eight years, I thought the whole exercise over the top. "Why," I ventured, "a good ninety per cent of these terrified people were innocent anyway." I was fully aware everyone had to suffer with the guilty, but there were still reasonable ways to proceed.

One of our boys spied a chap from another battalion raise his rifle and aim at someone leaning over their veranda calling for help. We rushed forward ready to clobber the idiot when we spied his officer intervening, thank goodness.

On the Wednesday they decided to lift the curfew for two hours from 5 pm to 7 pm, but instead of having something organised, they expected the citizens to queue wherever they could. Consequently the lines were too few and many deep. We paratroopers were inundated with mothers carrying babies and old disabled folk pleading to be let to the front, sick people vacated their beds and came to us dressed in pyjama's to prove they were ill. Vainly we tried to pacify everyone but it was a thankless and impossible task, trying desperately to decide who was the most deserving. When the curfew

THE WAY WE WERE

finally ended, I suppose a good thirty per cent had not been catered for and would have to wait a further twenty-four hours.

In anger I penned my frustration, why in god's name didn't we supply wagons full of bread and milk to satisfy all these desperate souls? I hoped the family could understand now why we ignored our officers, and even escorted people to the shops against army orders.

Having vented my feelings, I then wryly stated that in all probability we ended up worse off, because we had been on our feet a good eighteen hours every day and our grub was wicked. I bet they didn't print that in the papers back home either, I joked!

Eventually we heard through the grapevine that some terrorists had been snared by this operation, so were optimistic that despite the resultant bad feeling created, that maybe somewhere down the line we had been responsible for the saving of a few British lives.

In the middle of all these happenings and just prior to the Tel-Aviv do, I did manage a spot of leave. The venue wasn't all that far from camp at a place called Nathanya. It felt like heaven, waited on hand and foot by ex-Italian prisoners of war still waiting to be repatriated home, and sleeping between sheets on sprung mattresses. Among my many leisure pursuits, were sailing and horse riding, with the latter becoming one of my favourites! Nearest thing to flying, I reckoned; during a fast gallop, I made a mental note to try and pursue this pastime if I ever got the opportunity. Girls were rather a non-starter for us British; the Jewish fair sex exuded great appeal, with their micro shorts and bronzed skin, but unfortunately because of our opposing political regimes remained constantly out of bounds. We would cheerily wave as they worked industriously in the orange groves, but rarely did they reciprocate.

On the other hand you hardly ever saw a Palestinian Arab woman, as they were conspicuously draped in long black robes and high yashmaks. I did tentatively visit a brothel once in the centre of Haifa. As opposed to Tel-Aviv which was virtually all Jewish, Haifa held a population heavily mixed, I never stopped wondering how it was that beside a smart pristine Jewish establishment you would find an Arab hovel. It was as if the Arabs had no intention of ever wanting to better themselves and were quite content to continue as they had for the past 2000 years, but who knows, when you survey the modern world today, perhaps they were right after-all.

As the lads I was with led me slightly inebriated into a down at heel two-storey building, I noticed at the top of the stairs, cavorting in their underwear, some very attractive giggling girls. I am quite certain they were all of Arabic descent and from what I could see for the very first time, very highly desirable ladies they were too! I kept thinking that maybe the time had arrived for me to dip my toe in the waters of the fair sex; certainly the temptation was there, as each girl in turn flaunted their curves seductively over the banister rail. Then a stern voice from deep within kept reminding me of our Padres lectures and his dire warnings of the consequences that could befall the weak willed. So reluctantly and somewhat out of character, plumping for a decision I'm sure my elder brother would have abhorred, I left the others to it, watching them bound up the staircase as I timorously backed out of the building.

August had arrived and mail seemed to be held up, I rather hoped the delay had accrued because of Len's return home. I couldn't have been more anxious, nearly four years now since I had seen my brother, and the way things were going looked very much like a further twelve months at least before we could shake one-another by the hand.

By the middle of August I was writing to him at number 86, congratulating him on meeting and talking to Lord Louis Mountbatten whilst in Burma, and fully appreciative of his disgust at the state of Britain. Rationing had become even worse, now they were suggesting there may not be sufficient coal to get through the winter, and the Labour government was intimating the nationalising of everything. And a further piece of earth-shattering news was that footballers were threatening to go on strike if they were not paid £7 per week. How the world does change!

The whole family are now talking quite openly of trying to get to New Zealand, especially as Len had been corresponding with one of his brother officers' sisters over there, and she painted a glowing picture. I had asked my pal Bob Underwood, my next door but one Morse-code compatriot, to obtain the necessary forms for both of us.

Another bit of jolly news filtered through, Great Britain had informed the United States it would not allow further illegal entry into Palestine. Somebody had to draw the line for the Palestinian Arabs, and I guess we were the fall guys!

On 11th August two more ships carrying 1500 refugees from Europe had joined a miserable flotilla anchored outside the port of Haifa because of a blockade by British warships. New arrivals were to be intercepted by British

THE WAY WE WERE

destroyers. Barbed wire had been strung along harbour walls to prevent escape, while onshore camps were already holding a further 3,000.

The distraught ships are becoming floating slums, and Britain now had to decide whether to increase tension by diverting the whole lot to the island of Cyprus.

One day it would be my painful duty to act as escort on board one of these ships as we sailed for this Greek Isle. Down in the holds hundreds of desperate Jews were confined behind cages of steel bars, where once again it would fall to me, alongside others, to try and help fetch food and water.

Other moves were afoot, without a genuine war the numbers of parachute battalions were to be reduced and our 17th would be amalgamated and become the 7th Light Infantry Battalion. Some chaps came over to us from Penang in the Far East, feeding us stories of how out there each of them had his own girl, and how they had enjoyed the life of Riley! I didn't like to disillusion them but it wasn't long before they bumped into Strawberry!

October 16th saw the hanging of ten Nazi war criminals. Just prior to his last walk, as I have already commented upon, Hermann Goering managed to cheat justice with a cyanide pill. When Field Marshal Wilhelm Keitel, who stated he'd only obeyed orders, stepped onto the scaffold, he uttered the immortal words, "More than two million German soldiers died for their Fatherland, now I join you my sons."

In America, President Truman was continuing his attack on Britain for not allowing more Jews into Palestine; he was demanding the 100,000 discussed earlier be granted access. Our Prime Minister, Clement Attlee, was furious. Already in delicate negotiations between Arabs and Jews alike over this very issue, he accused Harry Truman of trying to undermine his position at this critical stage. Arab leaders were incensed, threatening to withdraw all co-operation throughout the Middle East over oil concessions, including severance of diplomatic relations.

The parallels today, sixty years on, are enlightening!

One pleasant day this October 1946 we carried out a ten-mile route march at 6 am and leapt from a Halifax Mark IX at 6 pm. In this latter they actually deployed the converted bomber over the sea and surrounding area, including above Tel-Aviv for a good hour. For me the treat meant everything, although currently for most people, peering through a hole in the bottom of a converted bomber's fuselage would seem bizarre in this modern world of air travel. I explained how one of our number jibbed at stepping through the aperture, unable to summon the courage: "I never blamed the guy," I wrote Ciss, "sometimes it takes more guts to shy away from such action in front of the eyes of your mates, than to actually complete the jump." Being part of an operational battalion meant he must go before the mind doctor, if he agrees his nerves are shattered, then it's okay, but if not, it could mean 112 days in detention!

On this occasion I carried only a rifle, slung inverted diagonally across my chest. "Best landing I had ever done," I informed, "but you should have seen the barrel; somehow it must have embedded itself into the ground, in the process, becoming completely clogged." Good job I hadn't been on an operational drop because it took ages for me to dislodge the rammed-in dirt. Next time they promised, we would jump over Cyprus, where, carrying my PIAT in a kit bag, I would be first man through the floor!

At this stage the world was still in turmoil; when was it ever not!

Just before the surrender of Japan, Russia had rushed into China so she could acquire some say in the surrender terms. But soon after the Armistice she pulled back again, and with Japan also gone, Mao Tse-tung renewed his communist ambitions against Marshal Chiang Kai-shek and his nationalist regime. The suspended civil animosity that had brewed between these opposing forces for nearly twenty years before Japans invasion now erupted with a vengeance. With a million already under arms and twice as many guerrillas on his side throughout the vast country, Mao felt strong enough to declare outright war on the Nationalists. America relinquished all efforts in trying to broker a deal between the protagonists, and freely admitted she had achieved total failure!

Just as our company was assigned new billets high in the mountains on the borders of Syria and Lebanon at a place called Safad, so news came through that eight more of our compatriots had been blown up by Jewish terrorist organisations. These groups were also fighting between themselves, with Moshe Sneh the leader of Haganah, the self styled Jewish Defence Army, declaring whilst on a visit to Britain that they had destroyed arsenals held by Irgun and the Stern Gang.

This encampment would be our home for many months to come, although from time to time we would sally forth on various assignments. To be isolated in just company strength was so much more rewarding, we could organise our own inter-platoon competitions, with football and rounders being a couple of the favourites.

THE WAY WE WERE

Adjacent to the camp was a very enterprising Jewish family comprising father, mother, and one twenty-something son. They ran a sort of hotel retreat, and our arrival must have seemed like manna from heaven. I forget the number of wonderful evenings we all gathered around long trestle like tables outside their establishment, to drink and laugh and sing ribald songs, as we soaked in the exquisite air of the mountains. Now I come to think of it their eggs and chips were out of this world, and sometimes we would have, a couple of beautifully fried eggs placed inside an envelope of round freshly baked bread. There's a name for these, which I've forgotten!

By this time most of us had been thrown together for almost two years, and I am so pleased my dear sister saved my correspondence, for I wrote their names down to send her. "Each chap," I said, "has a tag." There was "Slim" Baird, "Slash" Rice, "Happy" Apps, "Scouse" Williams, "Jordy" Robson, "Taffy" Cotter, "Starry-night" Story, "Ginger" Brooks "Togo" Neal, "Puddled" Pallatina, "Cast-iron" Steele, "Simpo" Simpson, "Daddy" Sweetlove, "Rooter" Raeside, "Bill" Cody, "Mash" Marshall, "La" Parker, "Dave" Hart and me of course, "Smudger" Smith.

I explained how I could go on forever describing this really great bunch of guys, there were Taffies, Jordies, Jocks, Paddies, Brummies, Scousers and not forgetting the good old English Cockney. Not one I declared would I mistrust; every one of them a true and valued friend. Can you imagine sitting next to or opposite these types as you approached a drop zone, with Slash Rice cracking one of his disgusting jokes, only to be outdone by Togo Neal, or Ginger Brooks breaking out into a corny song and everybody telling him to put a sock in it!

I remember before we even set foot on Arabic soil, how Bill Cody and La Parker had visited the shipboard barber and had their heads shaved, prancing around like a couple of Tibetan monks.

I think it was Mash Marshall who was our pianist who did us proud over Christmas 1946 at Safad. I had a reasonable voice then, and two or three of us would give varying renditions of the current popular songs as Mash thumped the keys. Beer would flow and smoke filled the air and you couldn't see the top of the joanna for parachutists and pints.

Gradually as we got to know our hotel owners, I was invited to games of chess with the son or father, both of whose names escape me. Once again I had to thank Jack for my knowledge of this game, but furtherance of my education towards intricate moves must be down to these two gentlemen.

On occasion I did have the good fortune to beat the son as gradually my thought processes improved, but I'm afraid, I have to admit total defeat when it came to the old man himself. He would show me how important pawns were where, the loss of just one, could so easily transform a game.

Before that Christmas, one of our detachments centred on Lydda Airport, the main and I think only avenue of flight to and from Palestine. Here I enjoyed my first introduction to the American jeep; being permitted to drive one throughout the airport perimeter after dark. We would belt off in varying directions so as not to set up a sequence or timetable of where we might suddenly appear, and pierce the gloom with a well aimed high intensity spot light. But I have to admit that despite doing this for a couple of weeks before relieved by another squad, at no time did we interrupt anyone of a sinister nature.

Another sojourn developed when news was received via an Arab source that Jews had set up a roadblock in the middle of the night. Off we went winding down the mountains from Safad, the whole platoon jammed into the back of our four-tonner, me hugging my faithful PIAT, to finish up trudging about three miles through orange groves looking for possible intruders after failing to find the supposed barricade. The episode ended about four o'clock in the morning after it was discovered the Arab in question was some sort of propagandist, and a damn liar! Leaving me with a tortuous tum after eating unripe oranges to sustain a flagging strength as I humped my heavy bomb thrower from grove to grove.

Hard decisions were being made by a frustrated Britain fighting to stem the tide of terrible injustices about to be perpetrated. A course of history that was going to reverberate and remain unsolved for the following sixty years. We had reached January 1947 and our situation in Palestine had become so dire and untenable, it meant British women and children, including non-essential personnel, must now be evacuated home. Dearly, we wished to accommodate Jewish aspirations without upsetting the one million-majority Arabs who in turn were emphasising the 600,000 Jews must remain the minority in what they, the Arabs insisted was their country. Britain favoured a partition of land that would satisfy both parties, but Jews everywhere, nursing the scars of the Nazi holocaust, were being fired by the Zionist vision of a Jewish national home. Desperately we tried to pursue a policy of peace, only to have this cruelly side-tracked by the blowing up of a police station in Haifa, and Irgun had rejected Golda Meir and David Ben-Gurion's (two highly influential politicians) pleas for an end to terrorism.

THE WAY WE WERE

Meanwhile as all this was taking place in the moderate climes of the eastern Mediterranean, people back home were suffering from one of the worst winters on record. By the 6th March 300 roads were blocked by drifts of snow and fifteen towns completely cut off. In Norfolk, Lincolnshire and Yorkshire the RAF was, having to drop food to stranded villagers and their animals alike.

In London the government announced a ban on mid-week sport in an effort to increase production. At the same time MPs had agreed, after learning of the many violent attacks perpetrated by various factions, to go ahead with the idea of quitting India, and Prince Phillip of Greece, our future Consort, had become a naturalised Briton.

It was ages since I had had any leave, last June I think, and here we were in March 1947. Before coming out here, they (the army that is) had the audacity to suggest that leave abroad would be much more frequent than at home, which was usually every three months. So I had lost all faith in these profound statements made by tongue-in-cheek generals, and looked forward to the day they sent me to Port Said for shipment home!

By the beginning of April I was thanking Ciss for a cablegram received on my birthday; this was my true one on 18th March. I had now reached the distinguished age of twenty years, and to think I was only fifteen the last time I saw brother Len. Having been scheduled for duty that day I was busy informing my ever-worrying sister that I had not indeed been able to toast the occasion and remained perfectly sober throughout. "Which was just as well," I continued, "because only the day previous I had played a strenuous game of football and despite being as I thought the epitome of physical fitness, I feel stiff all over! But at least we won 5-1."

Funnily enough I think I must have inherited some of my sister's doom and gloom, because I was constantly harping on about my prospects or lack of them when I did hit Civvy Street. At my request Jack had sent me a book on the mechanics of internal combustion engines, and I told of plans to study this alongside such fundamentals as logarithms and quantum mechanics.

I guess after over a year out here I had seen virtually all there was to see, having travelled the length and breadth many times over. I had swum naked in the Mediterranean, camped on the summit of Mount Carmel, stood on the very spot where Jesus was crucified, now enshrined by a Sepulchre Arch, and even kept guard over a loony bin housed within the confines of Acre prison. It was while here, I watched fascinated as two inmates walked constantly in circles all day and every day. Each time the fellow in front stopped and stroked his hair or something, so the guy behind followed suit, it must have driven the leading loony even nuttier! Until one day as I watched, the first type, coming to a standstill, started to undress. Having removed his shirt and trousers he then proceeded to turn them inside out and thoroughly inspect them. Finally, placing them right side in again he redressed and continued his walk about as though nothing untoward had happened. All the while our second in line, having stood there patiently waiting for the whole sequence to run its course, trotted off obediently behind his leader with never a sound or word issued between them. I found the whole episode bizarre to say the least, but then again these two strange souls must have been locked into a happy world where nobody could touch them.

Then at last it happened, not only did Strawberry disappear, somebody said he'd been shipped home, thank god, but they sent me to Shangri-La. I described the venue in letters home as Palm Beach; somewhere I had never been but obviously had high visions of. It was a paradise leave centre just outside Ismailia: remember that clean crisp ex-French town I reported on when first arriving in Egypt? The camp was actually situated on the banks of Lake Timsah and it had everything a dusty dishevelled raring to go paratrooper dreams about. Lovely showers, soft sheets, oodles of ice-cold lemonade, melon chunks that washed both ears as you sank your teeth into the middle and Cairo within easy reach.

I told Ciss how she would love to shop here, in Ismailia's glittering stores, always as long as you could keep one step ahead of the touting Arabs. Laughing about one such outing, where within five minutes of entering an establishment, I had been accosted to buy a fifteen-jewelled, shockproof, waterproof, anti-magnetic, stainless-steel luminous watch for £3–10: three shoeshine's, a fly swatter, peanuts, sunglasses, a vest, and umpteen packets of cigarettes! And if you did take a fancy to anything, then bargaining became an art: if you were asked for four English pounds, you would study the item and suggest one! If he dropped to two, you would walk away. It was odds on that before you had covered three steps he was down to thirty bob; just keep walking and before you could get out of earshot he'd be calling you his best friend and as a special favour you could take it for a pound. Then it was up to you whether you wanted to clinch a deal or just be cussed and say, no thanks.

"It is truly amazing," I reiterated, "how they will reduce their demand by 75% in as many seconds!"

THE WAY WE WERE

They took all of us leave personnel to see a German prisoner-of-war orchestra. Yes! Believe it or not, two years since war's end in Europe and still many of the Fatherland's servicemen had not seen their homeland. But at least they eventually would, which is more than could be said for those poor devils captured by Uncle Joseph Stalin! Throughout my varied upbringing I had never seen a real live orchestra, and without a doubt the Germans did us proud. Their professionalism was a credit to their nation, the sight of hundreds of British servicemen listening and watching in total silence and giving rapturous applause at the end was something that I would never forget.

These poor devils never had any money so to help themselves; they would turn their hand to various forms of craft using any materials they could lay their hands on. It was not dissimilar to captured French sailors during the war with Napoleon, where they started to carve beautiful little galleons and somehow fit them into bottles. These particular Germans did all sorts of things with discarded aluminium mess-tins. I bought for a few precious Ackers a finely designed cigarette case. This had the outline of the Taj Mahal complete with filigree worked all around it. Open etched work was then fitted with precisely cut coloured celluloid. All parts of the case were engraved both inside and out, and the whole thing handsomely polished. Never in your widest dreams could you imagine this was once an ordinary alloy mess-tin. I still retain this emblem of hard work in a troubled time, where on their eventual return these men would find a divided and totally destroyed Germany.

Another purchase of mine whilst lazing in this particular paradise was a girls, baby, pink silk cape-like coat complete with head cover, just like Little Red Riding Hood, for my niece Maureen, now reaching just one year of age. Something my sister Irene was very thrilled to receive and cherish for many a year.

Len had been home almost twelve months now, enjoying much leave in the comfortable surroundings of 86, but writing little to his kid brother. I was disgusted, and forever badgering our big sister to place pen, paper and readily stamped envelope in his hot little hand, before reading him the riot act. He'd been sent to Chalgrove in Oxfordshire which housed No. 8 OTU (Operational Training Unit) and flew as the OC (Officer Commanding) the PRU (Photo-Reconnaissance-Unit) flight, starting from August 21st 1946, but by October had been made OC B Flight.

When I finally rejoined the lads at Safad it was to learn that we were scheduled for three jumps at a place called Aqir. The first was to be a stick of

William S. Smith

slow pairs, then a jump with kit bag, and the last a fast stick of eighteen where you literally leap onto the shoulders of the guy in front. "This is probably the last jumps I'll do," I told Cecilia, "Then the boys reckon some of us in our grouping will be selected for repatriation homeward, so keep the old fingers crossed!"

As the days passed I began to think of all the great times I had spent with my compatriots, days that were fast becoming fewer and fewer, it was a time difficult to put into words, so I wrote in rhyme instead and sent the result to Ciss!

They were honest and true, these lads that I knew.
With ne'r a frown, but always a smile.
That a guy could respect all the while.
They would see you by, these lads of the sky.
Often crazy, some perhaps, lazy.
But hearts remained good when heads became hazy.
They would never despair, these chaps of the air.
For laughing and joking, they couldn't be beat.
To live, work and play with these types was a treat.
So I thanked them all for such a swell time.
And to save any blushes I've put it in rhyme.
Cheery-bye fellers, we've come a long way.
Then a lump caught my throat, and that's all I could say.

"You wanna know something Ciss, I'm too sentimental and dramatic, but that's how I feel. Boy! When I roll up outside number 86 I bet the first thing I see is Jack bending over the bonnet of a car, or more probably just his feet sticking out from beneath the front bumper."

But was Britain a country worth going back to? Our government had just ordered a new economy drive, putting everyone in a worse position than during the war. Hugh Dalton, the Chancellor of the Exchequer, said there would be substantial reductions in petrol and tobacco, and newspapers must revert to the wartime size of just four pages. Already more than half of America's huge loan had been swallowed up, and the country was in desperate straits. With victory in Europe two years old, the queue in London for potatoes was a thousand people deep! The tinned meat ration had been cut to two-pence-worth a week, while ministers for comment were conspicuously absent with a sudden mysterious illness.

However, staying put had its drawbacks too! Just before I'd gone on leave the very prison where I'd observed the two loonies, Acre, suffered a surprise attack by Irgun guerrillas. Setting off diversionary explosives, machine gunners strafed the guard towers from attacking jeeps and 100 masked men broke in and succeeded in releasing 251 prisoners who were pre-warned of the attempt. Smoke bombs covered the escape, fourteen Jews were killed and several British soldiers injured. Adding further insult, the freed prisoners, both Jews and Arabs, were driven away in stolen British trucks.

As the saying goes, "there but for the grace of God"!

How about this statement for a sign of the times!

Church leaders were declaring that the romanticism of both cinema and radio was leading our youth into gambling and dishonesty, sexual permissiveness and drinking. I wonder what those same gentlemen would say of today's society!

By the middle of August the good ship Cheshire beckoned me from her anchorage at Port Said. With a couple of Number Six Platoon's members and 671 other paratroopers I waited patiently alongside a total of 3,000 for the call to embark. Residing for the best part of a week within sight of the dockside, longing for this ship's arrival, had not been an easy exercise. There were still many pitfalls to encompass before setting foot on her gangplank, not least the fact that she only carried 1,068, so somebody was going to be tearing their hair out.

But we did receive a bit of good cheer when one of the Draft sergeants assured all three of us, we would be waving farewell to the sand flies when she sailed on the 15th.

And as my flamboyant brother practised in his Spitfire XVI for the coming 1947 Battle of Britain Air Display, so I entered the nostalgic waters of the English Channel. Battered and bankrupt Britain may have been, but I was thankful and delighted to be coming home.

Within five weeks of my sailing, Britain declared, "in spite of American and United Nations objections", that she was going to leave Palestine. She was fed up with trying to broker a compromise between Jews and Arabs while everybody else sat on their backsides wringing their hands in consternation with never a thought of accepting some of the responsibility. Whilst all the while, good, honest British servicemen were being shot at or blown to pieces.

William S. Smith

Another milestone slipped past, as I draped myself over the starboard rail of the good ship *Cheshire*, mesmerised by Egypt's fading shoreline. British rule came to an end in India. Under the guidance of Lord Louis Mountbatten, this great British Far Eastern empire had been split into two dominions, Pakistan and India. Yet despite all the effort and goodwill poured into this agreement, war would still engulf both nations.

I arrived at 86 via the military town of Aldershot, the British home base of the Parachute Regiment. Life here, although fairly limited in duration, was going to be one round after the other of spit and polish and cause me to be even more desperate to reach the day of demobilisation. I breathed happily from the luxury of a British steam locomotive carriage, after the wooden slatted seats of the cattle trucks to which we had become accustomed, as clipperty-clack she sped me to my glorious four weeks' leave.

My reception likened to the return of the prodigal son, Ciss couldn't do enough for me, and was anxious to notify everybody of my wellbeing and availability, even Jack, that most undemonstrative of people, managed to enthuse on my reinstatement to the fold. But I wouldn't be totally happy until I had set eyes on that charismatic, swashbuckling Romeo of a brother of mine. It came with a ring of Ciss's doorbell on the early evening of Friday 12th September 1947, almost five years, give or take a couple of months, from the day he'd marched like a ramrod down our tree-lined avenue to start his overseas adventures.

He looked resplendent, standing there, upright and athletic as ever, in his now, officers uniform, that broad chest emblazoned not with just RAF wings but sporting two rows of campaign ribbons and the unmistakable close ranked diagonal pale blue stripes of the DFM. (Distinguished Flying Medal). Every inch, including his enigmatic moustache, was the exact image of another hero, Errol Flynn! But there was one distinct exception, this hero standing before me, was no canvas screen make believe cosseted actor. Len was real, and although like most of his contemporaries he would never discuss his part in the war, one day I would learn the full extent of his actions, and strive to record them and give honour to them.

But right now though, "Billy!" he chuckled, those steely blue eyes twinkling like two iridescent stars, as deeply they studied this towering comparative stranger before him. "You old bugger, how dare you be bigger than me!" Clasping my hand as though in a vice, before pumping it half a dozen times with excited enthusiasm.

THE WAY WE WERE

"Move over," he grinned, blithely stepping across the threshold "let's take a good look at you," all the while shaking his head in utter disbelief. Hovering just behind me, Ciss waited impatiently, ready to pounce and embrace him with all the fervour at her command.

Rank between family and friends meant nothing to him, with little in the way of civilian clothing, most servicemen were consistently in uniform. So here we were, the decorated RAF flight lieutenant meeting his private parachutist brother. Yet ignoring everything to do with his own service prowess he would gleefully enthuse to everyone how this kid leapt from aeroplanes, something, he said, he would find very hard to do, and ever thankful to Jacob (his name for God) at never having needed to master it.

That evening would be one of the most memorable of my life, as valiantly I tried not to let down the reputation of the airborne services, somehow I would need to hold my liquor against one of the RAF's most notorious imbibers.

He'd decided that only a glorious night on the tiles could cement our reunion, and to this end invoked the services of an army sergeant of recent acquaintance who just happened to have transport. I'm afraid his name escapes me, but I do remember he appeared slight of build and small in stature and, like brother Len, full of gaiety and giggles. We would squeeze into his little ten-horsepower runabout and whizz off to one of their newly acquired haunts set in Gidea Park. This was a delightful pub called the Drill Hotel lying just beyond the actual park itself and leading to my errand boy playground of Upminster. Big, posh, double fronted houses abounded everywhere, most, overlooking a lovely lake awash with wildlife, where mothers stopped to feed mallards and moorhens as they strolled with boisterous offspring. Youngsters crabbed oars whilst messing about in small boats, and courting couples canoodled within the depths of heavy foliage throughout this small piece of English countryside. Even today, it represents an isolated pastoral scene, despite the thunderous roar of twenty-first century traffic sweeping past its entrance gates.

A rotund slightly balding publican called Bob greeted us warmly on arrival; you could tell immediately he was a devout fan of Len's. That, coupled with a particularly buxom barmaid, who shot admiring glances from beyond the bar, was all that was needed to understand why this particular venue ranked among the favourites for both my travelling companions. Swiftly, as the banter flowed, Len couldn't wait to introduce his kid brother and insist wild horses wouldn't get him to jump from aeroplanes if he didn't have to. In turn I could only utter that my contribution to anything was as nought compared to his achievements. After which, the conversation hurriedly centred on girls, or the lack of them. Certainly for all his romancing Len still remained firmly unattached and to the best of my knowledge at that time had no one particular girl. He had finally caught up with Alex, that femme fatale of the written word, whose seductive missives had given him reason to stay alive as he fought high above the Fourteenth Army throughout Burma, only to have his love and sanity almost destroyed, by the receipt of her Goodbye Johnny letter, after bidding farewell to 152.

He declared in later correspondence from Peshawar, that it was entirely through the good auspices of caring companions, that he'd been rescued from a mad desire to desert, jump the first ship to Blighty, and put paid to her impending marriage to another. Now, having met at last, I think she was more the one to regret her hasty decision!

I'm afraid we left Bob's establishment rather the worse for wear, a condition that would be forcefully frowned upon today, especially as we piled into our chauffeur companion's box on wheels, with uncontrollable arms and legs hilariously spread-eagled, before scooting back towards Romford and the next watering hole.

That night became ever fuzzier, but I do recall holding my own alongside the others without passing out, a victory of sorts, earning giggling applause and much approval, a definite improvement from the gangling teetotal youth Len had left behind in 1942.

The following day being a Saturday, the family had arranged a gathering at 86 in honour of the safe return of their youngest clan member. Pop and his fairly new wife, Mary, had worked hard to produce a sizeable cake, complete with parachute wings, beautifully designed by Dad. They had encouraged and cajoled various family members to contribute as many of their precious food coupons that they could spare!

This must have been some of the harshest times ever suffered by our country, with respect to food stocks, and it spoke highly of everyone when I later learnt that Len had received this very same treatment on his homecoming the previous year. Sugar was the rarest of commodities, eggs almost unobtainable except in powdered form, dried fruit non-existent, and icing sugar unheard of. Yet still, with substitutes and imagination, they managed to produce a cake worthy of a king.

THE WAY WE WERE

All were there, brother John with wife Ivy, and growing daughter Peggy, sister Irene with husband Johnny and baby Maureen, wearing her uncle's hooded pink cape. Ciss fussed, Jack poured the drinks, and I circulated, while the prankster of the family kept everyone in stitches. Musical renditions would be performed by Ciss and our virtuoso John, and even Len tickled the ivories. This last enabled him to show off his big sister's teachings, by offering up selected renditions of "Clare-de-Lune" and "Moonlight Sonata", two popular classics of the time! It was a great gathering, and unused as I was to making speeches, I hope I didn't let the side down!

Among the many accomplishments achieved by Jack whilst I'd ventured abroad, had been, with the help of his grandfather, the removal of the dividing wall between dining room and lounge. Now instead of bricks and mortar, we had, with the support of a steel lintel, opening glass doors that hooked back to give 86 one long through-room. One has to remember most of these innovations were very new, so in all probability Ciss and Jack were not only the first to have a garage adjacent their property, but conjoined living rooms complete with television, and telephone as well. I also doubt if any other local resident was self-employed like Jack either! After tortuous negotiations with Romford's bureaucrats for the best part of a year, during which time he had struggled stubbornly on by using his trusty tipper as a hire and reward vehicle, he had finally managed to establish Norwood Motors on waste land adjacent the railway line off Crow Lane.

Unfortunately sister Elsie with husband Wally and at this time just five boys (Derek 14 years, Ron 12 years, then Brian and Robin right down the ages to little John) were unable to attend their uncle's homecoming, due to being evacuated, quite by accident, to Jack's family retreat of Stone.

This move came about during the days of Hitler's V-1 and V-2 attacks, and for some bizarre reason all had remained until now in a very nice wooden constructed single-storey chalet. This line of pre-war holiday dwellings lay just behind some of Stone's huge teeth-like tank traps set along the riverfront. Wally, meantime, remained firmly at Homestead Road in Dagenham, close to his place of work, the May & Baker pharmaceutical factory, except that this particular weekend he had journeyed to be with Elsie and the boys.

Ciss retold, with much laughter, the night of Len's homecoming, when he had brought with him a fighter pilot's dinghy, and when she innocently enquired how it worked, without further ado he'd mischievously activated the gas bottle and filled the hallway with rubber life raft!

William S. Smith

Events beyond our family circle still evoked the senses!

By 7th September 45,000 miners were on strike in Yorkshire, forcing the Sheffield steelworks to close, and French police stated they had foiled a plot by the Zionist Stern Gang to bomb London from the air. Perhaps it was me they were after! The Labour government was now spending our gold reserves to pay for imports, but they've given up on the idea, at least for the time being, of nationalising everything, because they hadn't got the money to do it with. Our money! Towards the end of this month a future Labour prime minister, Harold Wilson, joined the cabinet. He looked like a high flyer, declared Mr Attlee!

I had bumped into Bob Underwood, my next-door-but-one, ex-Morse-code neighbour, now demobilised from the Merchant Navy, and discussed with him our serious intentions of reaching New Zealand. Moves were afoot that would grant the Brits in particular passage to there or Australia, for a cost of only £10, but we were later to learn such opportunities would not be that straightforward.

I also managed a visit to Bill Russell. He had finally married his Sheila, and they both lived happily inside two rooms at her parents' home, from whence this lovely lass had nimbly stepped to the accompaniment of a pair of William Wolf whistles, as she swept proudly past Alcoe's Timber Mills.

Still enjoying the remains of his demobilisation leave, Bill was seriously contemplating joining the police force. His service career had been a bit fraught like mine, suffering illness and army nonsense, especially whilst stationed in Germany. I spent many an evening cosseted under their roof in deep thought about our future prospects and where they might lead us.

Before Len returned to Chalgrove, arrangements had been made for Jack to take Ciss and I on a visit to his station. This was to see for the very first time, the Battle of Britain Display. These displays would be held throughout famous RAF stations all across the country to commemorate the 15th September 1940, the very day Hitler had instructed Goering to finish off Britain's air defences. So many enemy aircraft had been deployed against us, that when Churchill accidentally popped into the main Fighter Command bunker, he was told in answer to a question on reserves, that none were available. Every fighter squadron throughout southern England was now airborne to meet the attack. It was a defining moment that turned the battle, and thereafter Hitler postponed any attempt to invade our islands!

Our brother had informed us he would lead off in one of his favourite

THE WAY WE WERE

Spits, a clipped wing Mark XVI, and I couldn't wait to see him fly.

Sure enough on the following Saturday he met us on the concrete apron in front of the control tower. He was dressed in a one-piece blue/grey overall, and for the first time I thought how serious and unlike the constantly playboyish Len he looked. He'd always admired Jack for not only his intuitive grasp of all things mechanical but also the way he persevered against adversity as he strove to better himself. Now he quickly led us to the static displays to invite both him and me to study close up, the mighty Merlin and Griffon engines that powered his beloved Spitfires. Also parked separately, and enclosed so that the viewing public remained at a safe distance, stood one of the latest jet aircraft, a twin-engine Meteor.

Enthusiastically Len explained how this machine had been fitted with one of the first prototype ejection seats, and that later in the display he was expecting a friend of his to demonstrate the first public viewing of an actual cockpit escape using the new explosive device. It would take place at a fairly low altitude and near the crosswind circuit to afford everyone a better backcloth and perspective.

Glancing at the sky, I remember thinking as Len bade his temporary farewell, that the weather appeared pretty good, and apart from the odd scurrying clump of cumulus, should be ideal for the day's displays.

It is hard to describe the feeling of quiet pride running through one's veins, when for the first time you hear a public address system announce the fine attributes of your very own brother. My heart missed a beat as the words fanned out across the tarmac from the strategically placed public address speakers, "Good afternoon, ladies and gentlemen," came the commanding voice of the RAF officer acting as MC for the day, "Flight Lieutenant Smith, DFM, whose service career has spanned not only this country but North Africa, Sicily, Italy and Burma, will now lead off our display in a Spitfire XVI."

All three of us had made sure of a ringside spot, watching closely as the Spit taxied effortlessly over the grass. Occasionally the Merlin would give a little blip causing its tail to wiggle, affording the pilot a better view, as first one way then the other, Len peered beyond the rim of his cockpit.

I watched intently, determined not to miss the slightest thing, even if it meant consciously trying not to blink. As he turned into wind I never doubted for a minute after the initial surge of power, that both wheels would be reaching for their under-wing housings before any of us realised there was actual daylight between them and the mown grass. I had always known he was a perfectionist and now I could witness the fact at first-hand.

Some two years from the turn of the millennium, Mary and I had the honour and good fortune to become invited guests of 152's ex-Sergeant Armourer on his eightieth birthday. Also at Ray Johnson's party were two ex-Black Panther pilots, with all three totally familiar and extremely fond of my brother. One of the pilots was Norman Jones, the very Jonesy who flew alongside Len as they dived on Focke-Wulf 190s during our landings in Italy. The other was another Norman, a colourful extrovert and charming man sporting a handlebar moustache and chequered waistcoat. Norman Dear, like Jones, had fought alongside Len throughout Malta, Sicily, Italy and Burma, and held a deep conversation with Mary that day. Afterwards Mary confided to me that among his many varied and interesting stories, was one concerning Smithy's flying abilities.

"We were seeing who could fly the lowest," he said, "and after watching a few of us, Smithy said, 'You call that low!' and without further ado proceeded to take off, circuit the field and streak in along our runway at nought feet where you could actually see his tail wheel just rubbing the ground! On return his eyes positively twinkled as he beamed towards all and sundry: 'That, gentlemen,' he chuckled, 'is low flying!'"

Another great friend of his, John Vickers, whom I have already mentioned, stated that. "Len was a compatriot who was very competitive with a great presence of mind".

Naturally I was oblivious to these sentiments in September 1947 as I watched my hero take to the air, but they did not surprise me when I heard them uttered years later.

In the far distance I saw his plane curve towards the earth until it disappeared below the horizon.

"Watch to your front," warned the MC, which we all obediently did, and none of us could see a thing. This phenomenon was entirely due to the curvature of the field, which allowed the approaching Spitfire to look as though it were rising from the ground, like the very phoenix itself, as it hove into view. But then, as imperceptibly its nose started to rise, so immediately did the plane begin to roll. At the halfway point through this manoeuvre with clipped wings now standing vertical to the body, everyone gasped, as its port tip appeared to almost brush the ground. At one and the same time a vortex of spiralling air streamed out from the extreme edge of each wing, creating a symmetrical pattern, something I have only witnessed since on high speed jets from a greater altitude!

After attaining an inverted attitude, Len reversed his controls and climbed away upside down so that you could clearly see him hanging by his harness.

If only I had been armed with a modern movie camera, what a shot that would have been, I even doubt the aerobatics facing the crowd would be allowed today, as all flying has to be kept strictly side-on for safety reasons. I am not sure it would have been allowed then, but I declare that's exactly what happened, because my neck was craned right back as Len flew no more than fifty feet above me. Reaching for the sky, the ground firmly below his head and the distant clouds scurrying beyond his feet.

It was a grand opening to a promising day and after a further eight to nine minutes of precise aerobatics the MC announced that Smithy would be flying off to another airfield to open their display.

Before long Len was back at our side looking as chirpy as ever and talking about the coming part of the show that involved the cockpit escape.

This was the first time any of us had seen a jet aircraft, and I remember thinking how much noise it produced compared to the magnificent purring throb of the Rolls Royce Merlin. Just as well perhaps that I remained ignorant of the portent this would have in the years to come as gradually our lives would become filled with ever more screaming jet engines.

At the moment its high pitched whine had reduced to a bearable hum, enabling Len's escaping friend to eject without too much slipstream pressure. The action was far enough removed so as not to allow us to hear the cartridge go off; all we witnessed was a sudden black blob shooting vertically from behind the pilot's position. This in turn developed into a parachute with the blob dangling on the end as fascinated we watched it drifting towards some distant trees.

Thinking quite naturally that this was the entire procedure, we were amazed when just prior to disappearing below the tree line we observed something fall from the blob and form into another parachute. This second chute hardly had time to deploy properly as swiftly it sank below the trees.

Len stiffened, becoming quite anxious. "Something has gone wrong," he grimaced. "He's left it far too late getting free of the seat." Now I understood how the entire operation worked. Obviously it was not possible to land strapped into the seat, no sooner were you free of the aircraft and safely supported by the seat canopy, you must release yourself and fall away to deploy your own chute. However this second escape had happened so low the chap must have hit the ground with tremendous force.

Having excused himself, hurriedly Len left and we were not to see him again that day, but we did learn over the public address that the man had survived apart from suffering severe injuries. When next we saw Len, the following weekend at 86, he was able to inform us that his friend had sustained two broken legs! Apparently he had misjudged just how far he'd floated towards the ground whilst still attached to the seat, and I can certainly vouch for that phenomenon, because without an altimeter it can be extremely difficult to gauge one's height. Nowadays of course everything is done automatically and as soon as the seat leaves the aircraft you are catapulted from it and your chute deployed in the blink of an eye. The most dramatic demonstration of this took place when two European jets during an aerial display touched wingtips. Even though colliding at fairly low altitude with one pilot observed to eject almost vertically downwards, he still only suffering minor back injuries due to the enormous speed and sophistication of today's equipment! If only such know-how had been available in 1948!

Back at Aldershot Barracks I was pleased to learn that we were going to be given vocational training to prepare us once more for civilian life. That is until I discovered it was just another word for cheap labour. They were going to send about half a dozen of us to a local farm to help gather in the autumn harvest. Immediately I made representation to see if I could get onto a mechanic's course, and when that failed, enquired after opportunities with His Majesty's Forestry Commission. Here I felt, because of my previous involvement with varying types of trees, there might be a chance, but to coin a phrase, that didn't bear fruit either! Whilst I was at it I even enquired about the possibility of going to Canada to become a Canadian parachuting fire-fighter, at least I was experienced at the jumping bit, but was told in no uncertain terms that only Canadian ex-parachutists could enrol!

So my month's vocation was spent gathering in the sheaves and stuffing them into a funnelled hopper, where hidden machinery separated wheat from chaff, throwing the corn into a side sack as it did so. The remainder, being tied into small bundles, were left propped up in military rows across the open fields, to be gathered later with huge twin-pronged pitchforks which we tossed high into the air to fill horse drawn wagons. In one corner of the field it all came together to form one giant haystack, sometimes two!

Actually, I thoroughly enjoyed my time down on the farm, especially helping the local experts build these last items. Ever since then I have deplored the passing of the haystack. Somehow they symbolised everything that was good, well built, and quintessentially English. Always they were great fun to frolic in, and later, as you grew older, a handy hidey-hole when courting your young lady!

At lunchtimes we would follow the yokels to their favourite pub and sup Black and Tan ale, listening intently to their village gossip as they played cribbage or shuffle board.

During my disembarkation leave, one of the items I'd purchased was a Norton motorbike. Having sent Ciss a weekly sum via the good offices of His Majesty's Paymaster, ostensibly to repay her and Jack in part for bringing me up as their own, I was not surprised when my dear sister promptly placed the money in a savings account for my return, insisting she wanted nothing to do with my hard-earned cash. I thanked her by buying the Norton, which she would now fret over each and every time I mounted the menacing machine, but it was handy having some personal transport which allowed me so much more freedom.

I could so easily belt down to Stone, instead of having to cycle most of the day, covering the seventy-two miles there and back. This way I was able to visit Sister Elsie and her boys, also Jack's mum and dad, Ma and Pa Rouse, who now lived a lot of the time in their wood and asbestos riverside bungalow. Incidentally in one of the fields opposite, the farmer always erected a haystack at the end of each harvest. It was during a playful fight on top of this in our youth, sparring with Jack's brother Frank that I lost my balance and slid headfirst backwards down the steep-sided roof, to land flat on my back from an eve height of about seven feet. The resulting impact drove every vestige of air from my body, causing me to gasp uncontrollably for many seconds as I fought hard to refill my lungs. I remember that at the tender age of no more than nine or ten the experience was quite frightening.

On another occasion, attempting to capture a nearby thatched cottage with pencil and paper as I sat propped against this soft aromatic haven, a gentle voice had spoken over my shoulder. "That's my bedroom you're drawing," I turned to spy a pretty little blonde girl eyeing my masterpiece. I guess by this time that I must have reached all of eleven or twelve, and certainly hesitatingly shy when it came to the opposite sex. I blushed and asked if she would like to keep my handiwork when finished. She replied in the affirmative, and I often wondered how long she cherished that amateurish

William S. Smith

sketch. It would be nice to think that perhaps after sixty years she has it framed somewhere as a reminder of her innocent youth!

Before Christmas 1947 my days as a burly paratrooper were definitely numbered, and before leaving camp had been informed to report back on the 5th January 1948 to receive release documentation, a civilian suit and overcoat, demobilisation money and final physical exam.

With barely a month gone since India's partition, 1200 Moslem refugees entrained from Delhi to their new country of Pakistan were slaughtered in an ambush by Sikh troops and armed Sikh civilians. About 600 others survived. Witnesses swore that the Hindu guards protecting them fired over the heads of their attackers, and that the only person who tried to save them was the British officer in command of the escort. He, they said, fired his machine-gun at the mob until his ammunition ran out, then he too was killed. The whole battle lasted three hours!

America was busy trying to find communist sympathisers or fellow travellers round every tree, and there was a big witch-hunt going on, particularly amongst the Hollywood actors. Ronald Reagan had been one of those brought before the Congressional Committee. The man who would one day become president himself during the reign of our own Maggie Thatcher warned sharply of delegating their own democracy in the pursuit of un-American activities.

Another piece of news emanating from across the Pond, as the Atlantic became fondly referred to, was the breaking of the sound barrier on October 14th by Chuck Yeager in his Bell X-1 rocket plane. Achieving well over 600 mph, the noise as he broke through the pressure wall equalled that of a large thunderclap.

On November 20th Princess Elizabeth married her Prince Charming, Phillip, newly pronounced the Duke of Edinburgh. Once again after the celebrations of VE day and VJ day, people lined the Mall fifty deep.

Just before Christmas day, on the 23rd to be exact, it was announced that the last of the Moslem refugees had crossed the Indian border into Pakistan. They were lucky, for it has been reliably estimated that something to the order of 400,000 people, Moslem and Hindu, have been slaughtered since partition. The migration was declared to be the largest in history with 8,500,000 soul's crossing over!

After five years of many absence's the Smith clan finally came together that Christmas. Len and I remained the only two in uniform, yet outside

THE WAY WE WERE

in the highways and byways the country still teemed with service men and women and a few Americans walked our streets. Of course thousands of military occupied defeated Germany, and much coming and going between the two countries took place.

I'd had the honour of welcoming my loveable brother when he arrived for the festivities. There he stood, resplendent as ever, crumpled cap set to a jaunty angle, eyes twinkling, cheeky grin a mile wide, sporting a soft leather holdall, with lying long-wise between its carrying handles a snuffling pug-nosed Pekinese.

"Hi Billy," he chuckled, "brought Foo Foo home with me, couldn't leave the poor old thing on his own over Xmas could I, tell me you old bugger, have you won yourself a popsie yet!"

Well I had and I hadn't, so to speak! (Oh by the way Foo Foo had been passed to him by one of his service pals, never did discover why, but the pooch would lie contentedly between the leather holders wherever he went, on buses and trains, and naturally always attracted the most glamorous of girls, truly amazing!) As far as popsies went, I had met sister Irene's Johnny's younger sister. Her name was Kathleen and she stood nearly six feet tall with a round bonny face and mousy coloured bobbed hair. Kath was the only girl amongst four boys, Jimmy, Charlie, Johnny, and a brother younger than her, Dennis. They hailed from Irish immigrant stock, and their father had worked right through the London Blitz as a stevedore in London's dockland.

In those days everything going on or off a ship had to be manhandled into and out of huge nets, which the dockside cranes would winch up and down and swing back and forth. It was back breaking work and every morning at about 6 am, hundreds of men would congregate at the dock gates hoping to be selected to work in one of the many gangs. Either they would be lowered into the ships' holds or left to scurry ant-like over the wharf, collecting and sorting off-loaded cargo into the waiting cavernous warehouses.

There was no such thing as giant slab-sided steel containers, piled like high-rise buildings on broad flat-decked seagoing transports, as there is today. Now, operating at ports beyond London, just a few men with giant machines can expedite a turn-around those from the past could only have dreamed about. And the docksides themselves bear no relation to their former noisy congested dirty image as they shine out majestically from their prestigious developments over sparkling clean Thames water.

However, the pay at that time, so I was given to understand, was exceedingly good, averaging perhaps two or three times a normal working mans salary for the period, which made the union card job, a virtually closed shop as far as outsiders were concerned. All the sons stood well over six feet tall, and while McCarthy senior toiled in the heart of our capital, the three eldest went to war. Each one as tough as they come and the salt of the earth. They had all been brought up in a four-story tenement block off Cable Street that ran through one of the poorest areas of London near the river, and the very Street marched down by Mosley and his Black Shirt sympathisers prior to the war!

Only some eighteen months ago in the year 2002 we lost Johnny aged eighty-five, the last of the three fighting brothers to go. Then within one month we heard that dear Kathleen had passed away too, leaving only Dennis whom Mary and I met after many a long year, at John's funeral.

I suppose you could say that Kathleen was my first love. Certainly we kissed and cuddled and were fond of each other's company, but that was as far as it went, besides which, being of strict Irish Catholic upbringing, any further temptations would be resisted for fear of a parents wrath. Whilst on the subject of wrath, I did incur my brother's because of my feelings for Kath. Early in the New Year he'd acquired a very snappy sports car, a Jaguar SS100, and during one of our few times together I asked if I might borrow his latest love to escort my love to the nearest bus stop. He'd momentarily hesitated, before acquiescing to my request, but unfortunately I got carried away with the excitement of the moment, and instead of journeying about 800 yards, drove Kath in swanky bravado all the ten miles to Cable Street and kissed her goodnight on her tenement doorstep.

On the way home, I was pulled over and investigated by the police, because they were decidedly suspicious of a private in the paratroops sitting behind the wheel of such an ostentatious car. Needless to say I had to talk fast to get out of that one, quickly explaining the good offices of my Spitfire flying brother in loaning me his transport to assist my damsel in distress.

It was the first and only time I ever witnessed Len in darkish mood, as he harangued and lashed me with a sharp tongue. For not only had I had the temerity to drive his precious Jaguar twenty miles to London and back, but give cause to Ciss and he to worry over what may or may not, have happened! My apology couldn't have been more profuse and thankfully he eventually calmed down. I often felt that secretly he came to appreciate that the action was probably not all that dissimilar to the type of behaviour he easily slipped into himself. Never the less it was the first and last time I was allowed to take command of the SS.

Kathleen did eventually marry a Bill, but not me. Her Bill became the master of his own tugboat, plying up and down the river Thames. A very interesting and rewarding job involved in many varied activities, from moving huge chains of Barges, to helping dock big boats. As far as I can tell they had a very loving and happy life together, with Kath giving birth to one baby boy also named William. But her husband was to die in only middle age, leaving dear Kath a youngish widow, never again to marry. I shall always remember her as a softly spoken, loving girl, very willing, and forever anxious to please.

By the turn of the year it was reported Russia had exploded its first atom bomb, the Labour government nationalised the railways on the 1st of January, and Mahatma Gandhi died from an assassin's bullet on the 30th. Gandhi, whom Ciss and Jack had driven me as a boy before the war to see waving from a balcony in London, had just completed one of his fasts! Fasting was something Gandhi became famous for, and on this occasion had inflicted such weakness on himself had almost died in his desire to bring Hindus and Moslems together. It seemed ironic therefore that the man who more than any other, had won India's independence from British rule, should be shot by one of his own kind!

My first venture back into civilian employment was not dissimilar to the time when I left school, lasting little more than two whole weeks. I found it soul destroying, having to sit alongside somebody else as we drove around the countryside stopping at isolated homes to change the occupiers' radio batteries.

Yes! Believe it or not, that is the way people had to live. Not only were they divorced from any form of electricity, but invariably not connected to a national sewage system, and very likely void of mains water as well, coupled with the high probability of no telephone. We would visit outlying districts on a strictly rota basis, calling usually once every two weeks to change large accumulators. These at least would keep them in touch with the outside world, but needed to be recharged back at the depot.

My job was to help hump these heavy lead monstrosities up quite often long front gardens, or round the back of rambling country cottages. Disconnect the discharged, approximately two feet long, batteries, and replace them with a bank of fully charged cells, struggling back to our poor overloaded tiny van with the old ones. I cannot remember how many we actually did in a day, and I wouldn't have minded if I could have at least driven between these sojourns, but certainly at the end of the first week I'd had enough, and began looking for pastures new! My driver said he'd been doing it since his demob about a year earlier, a fairly smallish quite pleasant chap, whose name escapes me. I know I thanked him and wished him the best of luck, as I hastily scanned the wanted ads.

The next venture meant a bit of swotting. I'd spotted a sign for taxi driver, and straightaway made a beeline for a Mrs Lomax. This somewhat flirtatious lady dwelt within what I believe to have been a disused stabling yard for an adjacent brewery. Ind Coop & Allsop had premises just at the beginning of London Road where it joined the Romford crossroads near the marketplace. Here you could journey north, up North Street, passing Eric Dubois's radio repair shop on your right. Or continue along London Road past the brewery until eventually reaching Alcoe's Timber Mills, and towards my sister Irene's home. Conversely you could travel in the opposite direction to Ind Coop's and end up in the marketplace. Finally if you wished to follow South Street it would take you to the railway station, where from the opposite side of this main thoroughfare, you could hail yourself a cab! I mention this last, because yours truly eventually wound up there! But Mrs Lomax had her own headquarters; she held sway in what must have once been a stable for a couple of shire horses.

Here she would lord it over four or five of us ex-service types who drove for her. All I had to do was pass the local authority examination by writing down the shortest distance between any given two streets or avenues that they chose to select. About half a dozen journeys altogether and you were rewarded with a licence. The area covered was quite extensive, going from about halfway to London to as far out as Upminster (my old stomping ground). Being a local lad with good knowledge I found the task less than daunting and passed with flying colours.

Our cars were a mixed bunch, from a 1934 Vauxhall 14 hp to a 1938 Austin 12 hp. And I think one Standard 12 hp. We had about a third of the old stabling yard to work from, where we swept in nose-first towards our ladyship's domain. I recall a slight downhill gradient leading to a tight left turn directly from a North Street access.

I immediately loved the job, the money was nothing special but you could keep all your tips, and for the first time I felt like a self-employed person.

THE WAY WE WERE

All we had to do was let the lady in charge do all the worrying while us lads dashed in and out as she took the phone calls. Of course in those days not many people had cars. I don't know from where Mrs Lomax may have got her money, and I didn't really care. She must have been about thirty, fairly tall, slim, plain looking, wearing little make-up, with light brown straggly hair, and to my juvenile mind, quite mature, but she had a pair of shapely pins, which she would cross provocatively whilst sitting on her desk, shades of my old English teacher!

With only bus transport as competition our journeys were many and varied. One shilling and threepence for the first mile and ninepence a mile thereafter. In new pence that is about six and half pence and four pence respectively, with very often a shilling (five pence) tip!

We used to take about four pounds a day on average and work 6 days, but the cars were seldom idle, with stand in drivers taking over on different shifts, right round until 2 am most nights. I never saw a Mr Lomax and never knew whether our lady boss had been widowed by the war or was divorced, but she always seemed quite happy and loved being surrounded by us young bloods. She must have put in a terrific number of hours, although one of the crew would stand in for her as necessary.

The retainer doled out came to a moderate sum of four pounds, for about a fifty-hour week, but tips could double this and in the beginning before our Chancellor got his greedy eyes on it, you didn't have to declare their value. When he did legislate he took a guess at our extra remuneration and demanded payment whether you'd been given that amount or not.

The funny thing was that having to give Ciss only about two pounds out of my eight, I began to feel quite rich. Working most evenings I had little time to spend anything, and if I went to the pictures it only cost me about two shillings, and don't forget there were twenty of these to the pound. A pint of beer was something to the order of eight old pence, round of golf one shilling and three pence, fish and chips about the same, and if you wanted to go to a local dance, no more than a nominal sixpence, if anything! A suit set you back about two and half pounds, in fact Burton's used to be called the fifty-shilling tailors! I remember buying a working camera at Woolworth for sixpence, this company being our sixpenny store. It was beautiful then, long side counters and short end ones, with an area set in the middle where lovely uniformly dressed girls waited on you. Each counter would be laden with untold goodies, sweets, bric-a-brac, toys, a bit like you see sometimes at car-boot sales, and nothing would be priced beyond sixpence!

I found it hard to believe that when Len came home for weekends or longer, he invariably tapped me for a few pounds, because practically all his pay seemed to be swallowed up in mess bills. Next time I visited Bill Russell and Sheila, he was studying to be a police constable at Hendon College. I thought Bill would be good at it. With his droll humour, and broad physique adding power to his height, he portrayed every inch the English copper!

Bob Underwood meantime had made further enquiries on the prospects of reaching New Zealand, but here the criteria required seemed to hinge around young families. Apparently, they felt young married couples with one or two children were more likely to settle and make the effort to stay because of their added responsibilities.

Another aspect of offering paid-for passages was trying to entice good tradesmen, such as carpenters, bricklayers, plumbers or anyone connected to the building trade or professions, like doctors and lawyers, to help their new country expand. So, as far as Bob and I were concerned, we looked very much, like non-starters!

I regretted it then, but not half so much as I regret it now. At the latest census, Britain's population has gone up by fifty percent to over sixty million, whereas New Zealand's current numbers stand at only 3.9 million, and they have a greater landmass than we do, with a very similar climate! Now perhaps my future great-grandchildren can see what I mean when I say our governments have short-changed us by opening our doors to all and sundry!

But I was happy in my newly found employment, although advanced prospects might be limited. I was young and single with very few cares in the world as I swept rapidly towards my twenty-first birthday, yet before I reached twenty-two my carefree existence would change dramatically!

Pop and our step-mum, Mary, set to and created another baked masterpiece for my coming of age, complete with a half-crown piece stuck firmly in the middle. Cheekily I quizzed them as to whether the coin was merely the top one of a piled high column of two shilling and sixpenny pieces Today this age milestone is eighteen, but back then every pertinent step reached in the cycle of growing up seemed to reflect much more significance and receive due recognition of achieving manhood, or womanhood. Nowadays they infer young people grow up quicker, I'm afraid I must demur from that sentiment. The age of responsibility to my way of thinking is now far later than twenty-one!

THE WAY WE WERE

By February 1948 we knew that although we had won the war against Hitler, Stalin and the communists in the East would now constitute another threat. Already they were flexing their muscles throughout the whole of Eastern Europe, setting up puppet regimes inside every country they had supposedly liberated, including half of Germany.

In Palestine British soldiers were still dying at the hands of the Jews, with twenty-eight killed and thirty-three injured when a Stern Gang land mine blew up a train on leap day. Just after my twenty-first birthday two explosions rocked the Arab quarter of Haifa, killing seventeen and injuring a further 150.

This is how things would continue until on the 14th May a Jewish state was finally born, eight hours before the British mandate was due to end. David Ben-Gurion would head a provisional government until elections in October, and President Truman had shocked the Arabs and British by acknowledging the state of Israel within seconds of the proclamation. All Arab states now bordering Israel were massing their armies in preparation for war.

On April 14th Len had celebrated his twenty-eighth birthday at Chalgrove before he flew next day with his squadron to Scotland. Here at Leuchars Air Station, just across the bay from the Royal Burgh of St Andrews he would remain as leader of B Flight.

They had been sent north ostensibly to assist the Royal Navy in gunnery practice over the North Sea, being charged with towing long strung out targets, well to the rear of (usually) Martinet aircraft. The other duties remained similar to Chalgrove, utilising the Mark XIX Spitfire equipped as it was for photographic work, and experimenting with its two oblique fuselage mounted cameras. This particular Spitfire had extra large wings and a five-bladed propeller driven by a Griffon engine. The increased wing area was to accommodate greater fuel capacity and the 2050 hp Rolls Royce Griffon provided the impetus to pull this latest Spit higher, further, and with a top speed of 450 mph, faster than any Spitfire previously designed.

Leaving his SS in Oxfordshire, Len was able to fly from Scotland and drive from Chalgrove, where, after a lightening visit to Romford, would invariably motor onwards to Southend, to challenge his Burma campaign Black Panther friend Vicky to strenuous games of squash. Vicky and his wife Bette were always pleased to set eyes on Smithy, but unfortunately as a consequence denied his much sought-after presence within his own family circle.

William S. Smith

Just about the time that Russia decided to play awkward and stop all the Western powers from entering their areas of responsibility in Berlin, so I came a cropper on my Norton. The mishap wasn't too serious, but it did leave me with my first scar, and considering all the things I had been up to throughout my growing years, where I probably deserved many reminders about my body, it was ironic that it should happen in this way. Unbeknown to me they had, only the day previously, laid down fresh tar and grit along one of our local roads, where innocently I had carried out my usual confident rakish banking turn. Instantly I found myself skidding violently to one side, as the bike lost all grip on the loose surface, thrusting my bare sleeved right elbow firmly into the goo, and causing it to gouge a furrow not only in the highway but into my arm as well!

Returning to present my dear sister with a bloodied and messy young William, she hastily bathed the whole sorry mess in hot stinging water, but try as she might the black goo clung tenaciously to the deep lacerations in my skin. "I'm sorry," she said; "no matter how hard I try I just can't get it all out."

"Never mind," I answered, gritting my teeth like mad, "just wrap it up like it is." Which means to this day, some fifty-six years later, I still have two black scarred areas of tissue where the tar has been healed in. I do believe the substance can act like an antiseptic, which is probably why I have never suffered any ill effects!

This year saw an increase in the number of babies born, the highest recorded number of births over the last twenty-six years, and twenty-one percent greater than that needed to maintain our existing population. Everyone, they reckoned, was trying to make up for the lost years of the war. And Princess Elizabeth was doing her bit by announcing the expectation of a baby in the autumn.

On June 1st the UN won an agreement from Israel and the seven Arab League states to conduct a one-month truce.

The day following, the Lords threw out a bill that was proposing the suspension of the death penalty for five years.

By the 8th Richard Strauss, the composer, was cleared by a court in Frankfurt of being a Nazi.

Two thirds of the way through the month, doctors had been sufficiently pacified by the Labour government to agree to join the coming National Health Service, but dentists were being advised by their association not to

THE WAY WE WERE

acquiesce.

As June came to an end so did any pretence by Russia of allowing the Western areas of Berlin to survive. Without further ceremony, all roads and rail links were firmly closed.

Surrounded, as Berlin was, by Russian occupation, with only ground link from West Germany to supply her every need, the situation appeared fraught with disaster. There was no way the Allies could allow western Berlin to collapse and by definition, fall into Russian hands. Only one answer remained, call their bluff and fly over the top. Bring in by air every mortal thing required to sustain life in this part of the city now so completely cut off. It wouldn't be long before over 800 flights were being made each twenty-four hours by Dakota, Globemaster and York aircraft, landing and taking off every four minutes from RAF Gatow inside the British sector.

Back home, there must have been much disaffection among the many stevedores at this time, because over nineteen thousand of them had decided to strike. Prime Minister Attlee, is furious, declaring that the dock workers were letting down the ordinary public, already the meat ration had been reduced to six pence worth of fresh, and sixpence worth of tinned meat.

Two hundred and thirty-two ships were held up and even their union had disowned the men!

Our well-known golfer, Henry Cotton, won the British Open for the third time, and on July 26th Freddie Mills, Britain's Light Heavyweight boxer, beat Gus Lesnevich, to become undisputed champion in front of 46,000 people at the White City stadium.

About this same time Len and I both fell in love, me with an American Indian motorbike, and he with a Scottish lass called Mary! I'm not quite sure how I came across the motorbike, but it was beautiful, with a big Indians head, complete with feathered headgear, painted on each side of the fuel tank. The machine was heavy and robust, with side platforms for your feet as opposed to the usual small pedals tucked to the rear. Other differences meant that you had a proper, hand gear lever, and foot clutch, instead of the Norton hand-operated type, and having to feel for the gear change with the heel of your boot. Handlebars were upright and wide and you sat on a big seat making it akin to riding from an armchair.

I managed to persuade Ciss that this latest acquisition would definitely be safer than the skittish Norton, and used to go roaring up and down Norwood Avenue just to show off its stability, even to the extent of holding my hands high in the air. I apologise belatedly to all our neighbours for my thoughtless exuberance, but at least it was only the one time, after which I calmed down and zoomed off to Stone. I feel sure the cc rating was about 750, which made the machine very flexible and powerful indeed.

Len's love was a softly spoken, golden haired, five foot, finely formed, resident beauty of St Andrews, who gradually danced her way into his affections during the local hop, held each Saturday night at the Town Hall. It wasn't long before he discovered she was a good swimmer and powerful diver from the high board too, which she accomplished with aplomb, down at the natural seawater Step Rock swimming pool.

Her hometown lying across the bay from Len's station, was a grey-stoned Royal Burgh, steeped in history. Way back at its birth, so the story goes, a Monk by the name of St Regulas carried from Rome, in a stout casket, bleached bones of the prophet St Andrew. The idea was to enable him to establish the Catholic religion and give guidance to those poor heathens way up in the north of the newly conquered Britannia islands. Unfortunately he became shipwrecked along the eastern coast north of a great river inlet, which eventually became known as the Firth of Forth.

After his rescue he vowed that he would stay and build a monument to his beloved Andrew, and this would be known as the St Regulas Tower, around which over many decades was eventually built a vast cathedral, where Scotsmen from far and wide came to worship the Catholic faith at the holy burgh of Saint Andrew. Placed on a blue background the symbol of the crossed bones of the revered disciple became the national flag of Scotland! This lovely cathedral now lies in ruins, not because of the passage of time, but because King Henry VIII, during his arguments with the Pope, had the cathedral bombarded from the sea. However, the one piece still left intact and in working order is none other than the old boy's 120-feet tall square tower, which I have climbed on more than one occasion to gaze upon the panorama that is St Andrews.

Another ruin atop the cliff adjacent this place of worship is the town's castle, also bombarded by Henry. Here lies buried deep alongside the cliff wall, the notorious Bottle Dungeon, so named because its slim round neck-like opening leading down to its bulbous curved bottom is very reminiscent of the old type of apothecaries' bottles. Nowhere is it possible to stand on a flat surface and the whole dungeon was kept in total darkness until its keeper lowered food on a rope to its pathetic incumbents. Here for two years

THE WAY WE WERE

until taken out and burnt at the stake was kept the Scottish martyr, George Wishart. Now they have a monument to him too! St Andrews had three main thoroughfares running from the eastern seaboard inland to the west. North Street and South Street, with Market Street lying between them: each ex-fish market thoroughfare is so wide you can park cars down the middle and nose-in at each kerbside. Except, that is, where Mary's family lived, and had done for nigh on a hundred years, just beyond the walls of the ruined cathedral and not far from the sea. At this point Market Street becomes so narrow that today local officials have been forced to make it a one-way traverse.

Built in part from rescued stone of the bombarded house of God, No. 8 Market Street lives on, 300 years from its inception. Three storeys high, it had a lovely curved ornate staircase leading to a spacious hall, and throughout our many visits, hosted a lovely old chiming grandfather clock, standing majestically along one of the inner walls. In fact most of St Andrews was one big chiming clock! No doubt emanating from times gone by when few people owned a personal timepiece. For the whole twenty-four hours and particularly at night you can hear the chimes.

Somehow the various instruments never seemed to synchronise where no sooner had the first chimed the quarter, half, or three-quarter hour, then immediately the next would start up, just in case you missed the first, then the third and fourth and so on. I think I have counted all of a dozen until my brain got used to the nightly renderings. Not forgetting the striking of the hour itself of course, telling you you were fast awake at two or five am, and especially midnight! There used to be a tradition where the town clock struck no fewer than 100 times at 8 pm sharp every evening, whether this remains so I cannot say!

Here, with their own family plot within the cathedral grounds, resided the clan of the Blacks: Tom Black with his wife Euphemia, together with their ten children. Tom, Peter, Jimmy, Aggie, Maggie, Phemie, Lizzie, Mary, Bella, Bob.

Of the ten children, Bella, born in 1893, after marrying her WWI sweetheart, William Inglis (pronounced Ingles), would give birth first to William Kenneth, 1922, then our petite Mary, 1924, and finally Jack, ten years later in 1934. So by the time my scintillating, soft-shoe-shuffling brother swept her around the dance floor, Mary had reached a very wise and informed age of twenty-four years! In fact it had not been that long since wee Mary had broken off her engagement to one John Orr, brother to her

William S. Smith

swimming pal and girl about town, Betty Orr.

Just around the corner from No. 8, almost equidistant from the sea, another Mary had once quartered in South Street: this was Mary Queen of Scots, who also greatly enjoyed the game of golf. It is a well known fact that St Andrews is the home of golf, founded as it was on the sands and dunes stretching inland from the West Sands beach area. This stretch of beach, curling round the complete bay towards Leuchars, is comprised of hard packed sand that when displayed by the receding tide becomes a quarter of a mile wide. In fact when the tide comes in, it can take that distance to reach a depth of water capable of covering your waist. A very safe beach indeed that had often been utilised amongst other pastimes for motorbike races.

Four courses stretch out in finger fashion from between each line of dunes, one of which is called The Old, famous as the venue of our British Open Golf Championship. Others include The New, Eden, and Jubilee. Local residents used to be able to play for free, and Bella (Isabella) spent most of her life striking the wee ball and became a past master at sinking it into the cup. She held the captaincy of the St Regulas Ladies Golf Club for many years, winning competitions and being presented with miniature cups to retain, now entrusted to our second son, Barry. When we lost dear Bella in the 1980s, Mary and I presented her club with a cup to be contested for, in her honour.

All golfing laws throughout the world emanate from the Royal and Ancient Clubhouse, standing proud and magnificent facing the first and last greens of The Old Course. Two historic facts proclaim St Andrews golf. Old Tom Morris, the local lad that became first Open Champion, and the picturesque little Swilken Bridge, known throughout the golfing world, that enables golfers to traverse the narrow Swilken Burn running across the first and last fairways of the Old Course.

Another trademark of St Andrews is its University, now even more well known, since our own Prince William has been in attendance these past few years. I guess he has paraded the aforementioned streets alongside other students in the bright red college gown. Whether it is still fashionable to stride to the pier head and back each Sabbath morning I don't know, but they used to make a striking picture as they wended their way in flowing flame coloured cloaks.

It is highly unlikely that Len gained a great deal of knowledge about his nearest watering hole, although he did make himself very welcome at No. 8.

THE WAY WE WERE

When he first met Mary she was one of her hairdressing father's assistants, working and living from the upper floors of Greensmith-Downes ladies outfitters. The large premises standing on the far west corner of Market Street where it met Bell Street, housed within the first level above ground, not only the select salon, but two residential bedrooms, with a further two bedrooms in the top floor as well as living, kitchen and bathrooms.

It would not be long however before Len would be roped in to assist in a sad upheaval, for Mr Inglis, suffering ever since WWI from a badly injured leg, found he was unable to hold the business together and the whole family would have to move.

Most of the members managed to lodge at No. 8, where during this period only sisters Phemie and Liz now resided. Mary would move in with her mother and brother Jack, whilst Ken worked away in Glasgow. Mr Inglis meantime managed to find fresh employment at the next largest town of Cuper.

Being extremely fond of animals it was not long before Mary could be seen striding round St Andrews being towed by quite often two or three large canine friends, as she took up a position with Mr Naismith the local veterinary surgeon.

Gradually Len came to know most of Mary's folks, and was surprised to learn that her brother Ken had actually been seconded to 152 Squadron in the photographic section during the time of Imphal. Ken was also an accomplished artist and pianist and became great friends with Len. He too was courting, dating a Glaswegian girl called Dorothy Cullen, whose family often commuted to St Andrews at holiday time.

During Len's forays home he would expand on his writings about Mary. "Gee Cissy," he enthused, "she's a great kid, you know that film actress, Theresa Wright! Well my Mary is the spitting image of her, and can she swim, we go together to Dundee now where they have a smashing pool, I think I'm really in love this time, no kidding."

Theresa Wright portrayed the kind of girl that was soft and inviting, filling you with a desire to protect her from every kind of evil. Her flowing tresses tumbled to her shoulders in shining waves that you just wanted to curl round your fingers. Her eyes glistened and lips pursed ever so slightly. Not at all like the brassy brazen tempestuous Hollywood actress, she was the typical gentle English rose, except Mary happened to be Scottish, but that was even better because it meant she spoke with the lovely lilting brogue that flowed from the county of Fife.

William S. Smith

Then straight away he'd start writing her even though it was only one day since he'd been by her side. I'm sure if it hadn't been for his devotion to Ciss and not wishing to upset her, he would have cancelled any thoughts of leave. Not that we saw him for long as he made plans to visit Vick and Bette, pouring out his longings and desires for this latest love onto their receptive shoulders.

Somehow it always appeared strange to me that despite the multitude of chaps I'd come to know throughout my service career, none seemed to reside nearby. That is until nearing demob at Aldershot where I became pally with a guy nicknamed Tye who just happened to live about six miles away at Ilford. Tye used to visit me at 86 and from there we'd jump on the old Indian and scoot off into the country, sometimes to Stone, other times to Southend, where we'd live off cockles and winkles bought from the stalls along the sea front. Then take a little train ride out to the end of the pier and back. There was very little security needed in those days, bicycles and motorbikes could be left anywhere, all I ever did was carry its ignition key with me. My newly found friend was a decent type, ages with me and similar in height, hair rather more fair with a fresh complexion. He would become a great stalwart over the following year, as did all of my friends.

Twelve years and two abandoned Olympic Games after Hitler's 1936 Nazi propaganda spectacular in Berlin, the London Olympics, held amid post-war austerity, have proved inexpensive, unpretentious and successful. Opened on August 14th 1948 they proceeded without the participation of the Soviet Union, Japan or Germany. Without any resources to build anything the organisers utilised all existing venues, such as Henley for rowing, Bisley for shooting and Cowes for yachting. However, Wembley, with its new cinder track, and nearby Empire Pool, provided most of the focus. Great Britain failed to win any of the field events, with America dominating procedures with thirty-eight golds; we did get a couple of rowing gold medals and one in yachting.

The athlete of the hour was a thirty-year-old Dutch housewife and mother, Fanny Blankers-Koen, who arrived in London holding the record for the high and long jump. Yet despite this achievement did not enter in either, but competed and won in four track events instead: the 100, 200, and 80 metre hurdles, and the 4 x 100 metres relay.

Back in St Andrews this same month, two events took place, the coming of the Lamas Fair that filled the three main thoroughfares with every kind of original fairground entertainment, from beautiful carousels to scantily clad dancing girls enticing you into the covered interior of their lairs. Whilst down at the Bruce Embankment, tucked between the Step Rock Swimming Pool and the start of the West sands, a bevy of beautiful women were about to launch themselves on the four mile annual round trip to the end of the Harbour Pier and back.

It was from a rowing boat that Len (suffering uncomfortable symptoms of a northern cold) snuffled and sniffled his way alongside Mary and Ken, to keep pace and cheer on their two favourites, Dorothy and Betty Orr! Both girls were handsomely built and well equipped for the cold waters of the North Sea. This was not Mary's forte, despite her preference for seawater, essentially, swallow diving remained her speciality. It would appear from recent conversation held with Dorothy that neither she nor Betty won that particular year!

As the month receded so Len began preparations for the forthcoming Battle of Britain day. Having finally bitten the bullet he had confided to our dear sister that he had proposed marriage and was over the moon that Mary had agreed. He would be a handful to take on, even he knew that, at the moment he was hoping for an American swap. This is where one of our pilots is transferred to an American flying unit in return for one of theirs, which meant Mary must be prepared to hang on to his coat tails as they were swept hither and thither. Fighter pilots could be in demand anywhere, the world was still a very dangerous place, as well we know in hindsight with the North Korean conflict not that far away.

Betty Orr had also befriended a flight lieutenant, a certain George Elliot who was second in line behind Len to take over B Flight just as soon as his superior stepped up to squadron leader. But George was already married and Len had reservations about this couplet. Not that you could really blame George, for Betty was a steamy raven-haired beauty with a saucy disposition who could trap a fellow as easily as looking at him. Already she had given birth to one child, Steven, whose father was Polish. St Andrews had seen many Polish servicemen during the war, at one time it had been heavily populated by them plus large contingents of RAF trainee personnel. Betty would one day marry a man connected to the diplomatic corps and travel the world including a posting to the Seychelles, a detail that she loved, swiftly becoming the beautiful bouncing gay hostess of many parties given for visiting dignitaries and their wives. When she passed away at the age of only seventy-five years her husband Danny wrote in the local Scottish paper that he had not only lost his beloved wife, but the best friend a man ever had.

On September 1st China's communist radio announced the setting-up of a North China Peoples Government, it showed the world that the Western favourite, Marshall Chiang Kai-shek, despite massive American aid, had all but lost. By the 3rd, Warsaw's leader, advocating independence from Russia, was summarily dismissed for his impudence, and on the 9th North Korea proclaimed itself a republic.

The evening was pleasant, not a cloud in the sky and quite calm, a typical autumnal British September, as arm in arm Mary and Len strolled almost the length of the bay. Despite having such a soft surface underfoot, still Len managed to convey springiness in his step, it was a trait always apparent in his bearing, like a finely balanced boxer about to pounce.

The air became so still you could hear the crack of club against ball as golfers teed off from way in the distance, it was the perfect setting for two lovers, yet Mary could sense a tenseness and irritation in her fiancé's demeanour. "Tell me," she queried, "have I upset you in any way?"

"No, of course not darling," Len quickly interjected.

"Well something surely has," Mary continued, "I can sense a tautness in your manner, please tell me what is bothering you."

In mid-stride Len came to a halt, turning to hold her close, annoyed with himself for not being more relaxed and causing his beloved unnecessary distress. "I didn't want you to know," he said. "It's just that today Pennie pranged my kite, you know, the one I use for the display!"

"Oh dear," she cried, feigning sympathy, when in reality Mary would be quite happy to see Len removed from the display, although her hopes could be short-lived. "Does that mean you cannot fly?"

"Not necessarily." He was studying her face now, trying to smooth away a troubled furrow creeping across her brow, "I'll have to speak to old Lover." (Squadron Leader Lover was Len's commanding officer.) "See if I can get him to agree to me using one of the photographic types. Anyway enough of that, lets talk about our wedding plans, because as soon as this Battle of Britain thing is out of the way I want the Banns posted at your church!"

Mary had met Flying Officer Pennie out at the Leuchars Mess, he seemed a nice chap, quite a bit taller than Len, now she began to feel sorry for him. She had visited the Officers Mess many times, and shared a few evenings there with Ken and Dot (Dorothy). Ken would entertain the pilots with his playing, and giggle along with them, when Smithy, (as Len was affectionately known,) joined in with the few classic bars Ciss had so painstakingly taught him.

Next time Mary joined him there, he wasted little time in whisking her over to see his sorry-looking Mark XVI Spitfire firmly supported on trestles, both undercarriage legs now dangling and looking decidedly the worse for wear.

"Damn fool," remarked her escort. "All that happened was a glycol leak." (This is loss of anti-freeze fluid.) "Needed to put his head outside the cockpit as he came in to land because the stuff sprays all over the windscreen, happened to me many a time. Once when I flew above the Kirthar Mountains to drop into India, my engine gave up the ghost; no excuse for a heavy landing." Suddenly he brightened up, his eyes showing that sparkle again. "But I have some good news, Lover has agreed to me using the XIX instead!"

I'd been tearing around all morning; Saturdays tended to be like that, and Mrs Lomax would rush to meet us before any vehicle barely had time to grind to a halt outside her office. Hastily she'd thrust a piece of paper in your hand and bark a few instructions and before you knew it a three-point turn had been executed and tally-ho, you were off again!

Ciss never could tell when I might pop in for lunch and on this particular Saturday I needed to run round the table a bit quick in order to collect my next fare. Before she'd had a chance to convey anything to me I was gulping down my last mouthful and heading for the front door again. A bit breathless she just had enough time to call out before I closed it behind me. "By the way, thought you would like to know, Len called in this morning on his way to Southend, he flew down from Scotland to talk about his wedding plans and now he hopes to get a game of squash with Vicky before dashing back to Mary tomorrow."

"Fine!" I said. "It's alright for some, flying backwards and forwards to be with their popsie, others have to work!"

I didn't really have time to contemplate my big brothers wedding plans, as deftly I let in the clutch on my 1938 Vauxhall 14, and roared off down Norwood Avenue.

It was September 11th, exactly one week before BB day 1948!

It emerged later that during that hectic game of squash with John Vickers, Len had spoken excitedly of competing the following Saturday against an

RAF jet. "Must show 'em what a Spitty can do," he chuckled. "I'm flying the XIX with the big Griffon engine!"

Always a great advocate of the Spitfire, Len never spoke kindly of the modern innovation of jet aircraft. Unfortunately, although it was correct to say the Griffon-engined Spit still managed to hold its own against some of the new types, in truth, engineering had more or less reached its limits where Len's love was concerned, whereas with the jet they had only just started to exploit its potential. The very cause of his delay in acquiring the American Green card would later be attributed to his not yet having flown British Jets.

Only this very weekend he had shown Ciss his latest creation in recognition of his love: three perfectly formed miniature planes carved, sanded and polished from perspex, emphasising its exquisite lines. These were to form the basis of an idea he'd been working on. "Look Cissy," he said, warming to his subject as expertly he drew his concept on paper. "These three little Spits will be fixed to curving finely polished supports, spreading upwards and outwards in a climbing open formation. The three spirals will in turn be fixed together centrally in a vertical standing circular base etched with clouds, this will give depth and perspective to the whole thing, which in turn will be anchored to a heavy base. What do you think, whoo hoo!! It's gonna make a smashing centrepiece for my Mary's sideboard!"

True to his word he collected Mary at No. 8, from where she took him to her church. St Andrews town church lay about halfway down South Street going towards the Penn's, an ancient grey-stone arch denoting the entrance to Mary's hometown. Every Sunday Aunt Phemie (Euphemia) journeyed with her niece to sit in the pew reserved only for members of the Black family. But with the loss of Tom Black senior followed by his wife Euphemia, and various sons and daughters leaving for pastures new, only the two of them took their places now.

Young Phemie some six years or so older than Mary's mum, was a slim, sprightly lady, who had a reputation for being the towns seamstress. Rumour had it that dear Phemie had been in love during the First World War. Right opposite No. 8 in the narrow section of Market Street they had built a barracks. Can you imagine all those 1914–18 soldiers billeted facing a doorway where every morning Tom and Euphemia's daughters stepped into daylight! But sadly the one that Aunt Phemie grew fond of was lost in one of the terrible battles and they say after her distress she just buried herself

THE WAY WE WERE

in work. Already she had started her favourite niece's trousseau by creating a lovely light blue dress for her wedding, together with two pink and white nighties trimmed with lace, and a beautiful midnight blue two-piece where the top nipped in before flaring over the skirt to accentuate Mary's tiny waist. This ceremony had all the hallmarks of an auspicious occasion, if I knew my brother half as well as I thought I did, he would have all his officer pals forming a guard of honour under the portal entrance to the church.

So regular was their attendance that the Reverend Armour knew Mary and her aunt by their first names, and was well pleased to be able to officiate, at such an endearing girl's special day. So all was finalised and he would make sure that the banns were read one week before the end of September to allow for a mid-October ceremony.

On Saturday September 18th my motor had hardly stopped running, with mums having completed their shopping and desperate to get home, while others wishing to catch the next train to London kept several of us tearing back and forth. All morning I had busied myself helping people in a rush, tying luggage on the rack behind, and heaving heavy shopping to front doors. This last not really a requirement, but apart from hating to see ladies struggle with such loads, my gentlemanly behaviour often brought forth a little extra gratitude in the form of perhaps the odd sixpence.

Considering the hectic nature of the early part of my day, I was pleasantly surprised to find myself taking lunch at the not unreasonable hour of 2 pm. At 2.45 pm the doorbell rang and Ciss hastened to answer it. There stood a telegram boy, holding forth a telegram. It was addressed to Pop, but as he and his wife Mary still resided within the Greater London Council children's homes, he always used 86 as his main address. "It's alright," called Ciss, placating Jack and me, thus allowing us to continue eating. "It'll be from Len notifying us of his wedding plans." Then all went quiet, before the torment of one terrible scream. A sound I never wish to hear repeated! Anxiously we both rushed into the hall to find Ciss trembling from head to toe and the telegram shaking uncontrollably in her right hand. Supporting his wife as best he could, Jack lifted the paper from her trembling fingers and proceeded to read it. "Oh my God!" he uttered. "Brother Len has been killed in a flying accident."

Suddenly my whole body went cold as though drained of all life, and for a moment I couldn't move, both legs were as made of lead, my stomach aching with contraction, my head spinning in disbelief. *Oh no it's not possible*, I kept repeating to myself, *it can't be, not Len not, dear Len.*

We all seemed to stay like that for ages as though desperately trying to turn the clock back, as though the mere thought of moving would become one fatalistic final acceptance of something that was impossible to accept.

I don't know what happened next, I only know I found myself once more behind the wheel, driving I know not where, until I found a quiet spot somewhere, where I could stop the car and sob my heart out.

In Scotland the trauma was much worse, only ten minutes before taking off Len had squeezed some money into Mary's hand. "One of my colleagues is giving public flights in our Tiger Moth," he told her. "I want you to take this and see what I mean when I talk about being up there," and he'd pointed towards the heavens.

She was standing beside some of his brother officers in their compound, as Len pulled from a 5000-foot power dive prior to entering a rocket loop from only 300 feet. Things happened so fast that it was difficult to distinguish one action from the next. But in essence black smoke was seen to envelop the front of the plane a split second before one wing swept back towards the tail, taking that with it, as the remainder of the machine dove at high speed into woods towards the far end of the aerodrome.

The speed would become the centre of argument. This Spitfire was designed and built to fly faster than any Spit before, but it was a well known fact that planes not built to withstand the extreme buffeting of sonic forces if they approached the speed of sound could very easily suffer the consequences. Is it possible that this could have happened, could Len have been trying to accomplish the impossible? Vicky seemed to think so when approached about Smithy sometime afterwards!

Yet it was rumoured that one blade of the five-bladed propeller had been located some greater distance from the remainder: could one propeller blade have come adrift and cut into the starboard wing, causing it to sheer? Wasn't Len too experienced to over-rev his engine? Eventually the Air Ministry investigation would exonerate the aircraft, leaving only its pilot to pick up the cause, but the matter for myself, and most of my family, could not so easily be laid to rest.

For poor sad Mary of course the cause would be academic, her life had disintegrated as fast as the aircraft, her whole immediate future torn to shreds. The man she loved, friends she had come to know, the existence of life in the RAF, happy times spent in the mess, possibilities of travel across the world, financial security, a picture book wedding, a wonderful honeymoon with officers' quarters provided when they returned. All gone in perhaps no more than four seconds, every dream cruelly wiped out.

After a hurried conference high-ranking officers decided the show must go on, a show that Len had helped organise, and their decision the one he would have expected them to take. Meanwhile Len's heartbroken lady must be taken home, to be cared for by Bella, Phemie and Liz.

But it wouldn't be long before reporters from the *Sunday Post* hunted her down, pressing her for the intimate details of her and Len's last moments together. How did he seem, what did he say, was he troubled in any particular way. With fortitude, Mary answered their questions, trying hard to retain her composure, behaving bravely like, she felt, an officer's betrothed should.

By Monday Sept. 20th a photograph of Mary from the waist up, showing her dressed in a bathing suit, down by the Step Rock pool, appeared on the front page of the *Daily Mirror*. To this very day she has no knowledge of how this was come by, but it showed an attractive girl, and the story beside it wrenched at the nation's heartstrings. Typically a small head and shoulders photograph of the lost pilot was squeezed between the printed words, that also gave brief mention of his flying career, not totally accurate as is usual in these cases.

Wheels of authority began to turn, Air Ministry annals declared the deceased serving officer must be given a full military funeral and be interred within a military cemetery in Scotland, next of kin to be duly informed. No one had apparently told them about Smithy's sisters! Ciss raised bedlam, joined in chorus by Rene and Elsie, Pop understood service matters but also showed concern at the possibility of not being able to travel such a great distance.

The RAF relented, Len's body could be transported to Romford, but from that point onwards affairs must rest firmly on the shoulders of his family.

Not good enough declared our three female champions, nothing short of a full RAF funeral to take place in Len's hometown could be accepted. Len had given his all for his service, now in return they would do him just honour or matters would escalate.

And believe it or not, that is precisely what took place. The cortege escorted by six of his brother officers would travel from Leuchars to Edinburgh and thence to London, before transferring yet again to the

Romford line, and to cap it all, Mary would not be forgotten. Travelling far south for the first time in her life, she remembers being chaperoned by a tall, gangly, gentle officer, who went by the name of Robbie! Almost a week had gone by since the tragic accident, a week that seemed to be filled with comings and goings at 86. So many letters of condolence had dropped through the letterbox that my dear distraught sister failed to inform me that she had received one from Mary's mother.

Along with her commiseration's, Bella had informed Ciss that Mary would be travelling with the cortege, and asked if it were acceptable to take in her daughter, and care for her during a short stay.

Ever since the loss of my brother I had eaten but little, so often food just seemed to stick in my throat. I tried very hard to put a brave face on things, whenever good humoured banter went round the taxi office I would join in, even if only half-heartedly. I still greeted the public with a smile, albeit forced, and each time I found myself with an empty cab, I could cheerfully have smashed it into the nearest wall and so ended the perpetual pain.

Learning of the imminent arrival of Len at Romford Station, I hurried to watch as they brought him through the terminal and onto the public highway. I distinctly remember how all movement of traffic was halted as solemnly the coffin, draped with the Union Jack was carried from the station to a waiting RAF tender. Standing erect in the centre of the road a flight lieutenant snapped to attention coming smartly to the salute as reverently the coffin was slid into place. Other officers were quickly shunted into waiting vehicles with the whole assembly moving slowly away towards Hornchurch Aerodrome and its chapel of rest, where Len would be placed.

At no time did I observe Mary or Robbie, and Mary says she does not recall seeing the coffin taken from the train. I should imagine passengers would be unable to alight until these proceedings had taken place.

However the timings came about, the end result somehow brought me to the door at the sound of Ciss's bell, where I came face to face with a lovely young lady dressed in blue. Unaware of Mary's arrangements, and with a uniformed officer standing discreetly behind her, all I could think of was, this must be Vicky and his wife Bette! Why I should think of Vicky, when John Vickers had already left the service and would clearly have been attired in civvies, I do not know. Much to my embarrassment Mary was forced to enlighten me of my error. What a stupid way I thought, to greet my brother's fiancée for the very first time!

THE WAY WE WERE

My immediate impression was of her Scottish lilt, of how delightful it was and how melodic and delicate, Len must have loved that, and how soft and shiny her golden tresses looked. Then to experience the power of her perfume as she brushed past, to discover later that the captivating fragrance went by the name of mischief, something I have never forgotten in fifty-five years. Then quickly to become lost to me, as without ado, she became caught up in my sister's embrace, and commandeered into telling all about her relationship with dear Len, whilst Jack and I were left to exchange pleasantries with Robby.

By Monday September 27th Dad and Ciss had been notified that Len's final ceremony would take place on Thursday the 30th. There was to be a large contingent from Hornchurch, including a Firing Party and the Central Band of the RAF would be journeying from Uxbridge, with the whole cortege forming up in Norwood Avenue, escorted by his brother officers from Leuchars. Ciss had one last request to make, could she have her dear brother's body removed from the Chapel to lie in state in her front room the night before, to give those who wished to say farewell a chance to do so. Although most of the family did just that, I was loath to see Len lying at rest, I needed to remember him as alive, flamboyant, that forever devilish twinkle in his eye, the beaming smile, the gay abandonment that he had always displayed. That is my memory!

Of course Ciss could cater for Mary, there had never been any doubt, Len's younger brother would vacate his room, "Bill," she said, "will manage just fine on the dining room floor!"

It would be a gesture sorely felt by Mary, yet it was one I was only to happy to provide, both during this period and later when Mary would return to us.

I shall not dwell here on the lying to rest of brother Len, suffice to say that I doubt if Romford, either before or since, has ever witnessed a funeral of such magnitude. It was a proud day and a sad day. When many years later I asked my eldest sister how she would describe Len, she simply said. "I feel sorry for all those who never knew him." I think that is as good an epitaph as any!

But Len's hold on family life was not to end there, for Mary secretly let it be known that she was pregnant. At first such news became withheld from their young brother whilst earnest discussions between all three sisters took place in out of the way places. When Jack, who tended towards a

Victorian outlook; became aware, he showed strong displeasure. But in fairness he wasn't the only one, for in the beginning only Elsie who herself was expecting her sixth child, showed any real sympathy. Even Mary's own mother did not condone her daughter's actions. Without a doubt Mary seemed surrounded by disapproving adults, and it must have been a terrible time for her! Nowadays nobody would bat an eye; in fact the out of wedlock situation is more normal than the other way round.

Ciss began to think fast, what could possibly be the best thing to do, it wasn't too late, Mary was only two months into pregnancy, and I believe hot baths were advocated. But by the time Mary was due to leave once more for Scotland, baby Smithy still clung desperately to life!

I had been able to escort Mary here and there, once to London to Madam Tussauds, and even managed to burn her shoe on the exhaust of the Indian when giving her a lift. When I learnt of her predicament, my immediate reaction was one of heartfelt sympathy. I in no way considered her to blame, I felt sure my brother would have been in full command of his actions, although all three sisters implied otherwise, and his pending marriage was one of duty rather than love. I have steadfastly refused to accept that view, but then my sisters being women felt their reasoning held greater sway!

But Mary was such a beautiful girl I felt sure someone would snap her up. On her return home many letters were awaiting her, some from across the world, all from men who, having eyed her picture in the press, were now pleading to save this damsel from her distress.

Somehow I never put myself in that category, my outlook, although today Mary would be shocked to know it, was that I couldn't possibly aspire to fill Len's shoes. Let's face it, he was the epitome of everything I wasn't. Good looking (as I have already mentioned, not unlike Errol Flynn). A natural-born dancer, clever artist, in both drawing and carving. A perfect swimmer and skilful diver. A leader of men, having conquered each of our enemies in single combat, German, Italian and Japanese! And the one thing I always aspired to emulate, without success, puff out his cheeks and talk hilariously like Walt Disney's Donald Duck, leaving everybody doubled up in stitches whilst imitating the cartoon bird!

Not that I deride myself, for I have always been confident about the things I can do, but back then I did not sense that what I could offer a beautiful woman in anyway matched up to the man Mary had so recently lost!

There was bound to be a thousand types she would prefer before settling for little me, so I quite literally admired this lovely girl from a distance, and continued walking out with two or three fairly plain Janes of my own discovery.

Firstly there was tall, handsome Catherine, very nice but no real passion had developed between us, which in fairness was probably my fault. Then Ivy, sporting a slight hare lip (an amorous girl I'd met at Mrs Lomax office) and lastly diminutive June (a publican's daughter who had the personality of a damp squid and a handshake to match).

Mary wrote to me from St Andrews, a letter that much to her surprise I still possess. It tells of Ciss's concern that I am still off my food, and refers to my love of flying. This is something I decided to do after speaking to Vicky at the funeral; he suggested I visit him and Bette at their Southend bungalow so that he could introduce me to the flying club. This flying field sat literally at the bottom of their garden, and all day you could watch the little high wing Auster aircraft take-off and land. I must try to find the small blue logbook Bette bought me at the time. I used to nip down there on the Indian with Tye clinging to the pillion, I remember on one occasion the dynamo must have packed up and being winter it was virtually dark as we set off home.

I turned to Tye and said that we could either poodle down the Southend to London dual carriageway and let everybody pass us hoping they didn't hit us up the backside. Or I could swing to the outside lane and overtake all those we encountered, using headlights from their vehicles to help us scoot past them before they realised we were there!

He agreed we do the latter, which we did in record time. But one must remember that throughout the twenty-six-mile journey I don't suppose we had to pass above twenty vehicles. What a difference today where you can pass that many in 200 yards, or metres!

Dear Mary also mentioned seeing the planes flying low over the town after taking off from Leuchars, she found it upsetting and was rather hoping she had overcome that feeling. She finished by referring to beginning to feel a little tired as young Smithy continued to sap her strength, and suggested that as she now had to eat for two I could at least try to eat something despite my sorrows, then signed off hoping to see me soon!

Yes! My anxious sister had invited Mary back to 86 for Christmas and beyond, Len's Scottish lass had written to many admirers and actually dated a few, but to date still nothing positive had loomed for her or the baby's future.

Around this period, in fact it may have been just prior to Mary's trip home, I'd tentatively approached Jack on the subject of acquiring my own taxi. I could see the potential, and quite honestly so could Jack when I explained matters to him. For all that had been said and felt about Jack, because he could be very strict, and sometimes downright brutal, I still give him his due. Providing you were prepared to put your back into things and pull your weight or more if possible, then he would always be more than willing to help. So I was reasonably confident that if I put my case over in sound form it may bear fruit. It did mean asking an awful lot because the 1936 12 hp Austin taxi that had come onto the market was commanding a £500 tab. The trouble being that £350 of it related to the licence.

Licences were actually issued free except no more were available, so the only way to acquire one was to obtain a possible transfer from a previous holder. Owners were naturally aware of the difficulty and would sign them over only at a premium.

One must remember that back in 1935 Jack had only paid £600 for 86, now here was I asking for almost an equivalent sum for what today would be classed as a box on wheels, albeit now a veteran.

My winning argument would have to stem from a grasp of mathematics. We averaged 500 miles per week, and by my calculation easily achieved one shilling per mile for half the distance, this being outward journeys of mostly two miles. Quite often you picked up a fare for the return trip, maybe as many as twenty-five percent, so to the total of 250 shillings you could add another sixty making 310 or £15.10/-. Add to this sum our average amount earned in tips of £4 and you could expect something to the order of £19 or £20 per week. Next came the cost of fuel, currently two shillings a gallon, with a consumption rate expected on the Austin of twenty-five miles, totalling forty shillings, equal to two pounds per week! Jack agreed with my suggestion that £3 should more than cover other running costs including both road tax at £12 and insurance at £20 per annum. This meant a conservative profit of £14 per week, which compared favourably with my current £8 including tips.

The whole exercise could only be achieved by Jack taking out a further mortgage on 86, something to my great relief he seemed prepared to do. The house had risen in value to at least £1500 and it is possible with Jack's past earnings he owed very little if anything on his existing borrowings. "Seems fair enough to me Libby," he acquiesced. "You will have to pay any interest of course, currently at five percent; I reckon four years at £150 a year should do it."

The outcome presented me with my first car that coincidentally held the first three letters of the winning race team, British Racing Motors, BRM! Although BRM may have looked a bit boxy, she had been well maintained, mechanically she couldn't be faulted, and her body and paintwork remained in excellent order. No speed king with a maximum bone-shaking fifty mph, and like all her contemporaries void of any form of internal heating, she was nevertheless ideal for the task asked of her, and initially I gloried in her attributes.

I remember the cost of my flying lessons was £3 per hour dual and £2.10/- solo. Having found the long lost logbook I can also confirm that I started on October 24th 1948 with 46 minutes of straight and level flight, then climbing, gliding and stalling turns. I can also state that my baptism towards solo flight came after a tentative eight hours and thirty-two minutes on the 9th January 1949. Thirty-seven years later at the defining age of fifty-nine, I was to use this same logbook to describe the microlight experience!

On November 3rd as Mary tried hard to placate her mother and aunts in Scotland, so Harry Truman became elected President for his second term. Against all the odds including Dr Gallop's dire assurances that Governor Dewey would win hands down, Truman romped home forcing the good doctor to tie himself in knots on American radio. Profuse with apology he fought in vain to explain how he could get things so horribly wrong.

As they stared into the future our government announced they intend to build 1000 miles of motorways, the age of the motorcar was truly coming!

By the 12th Tojo and twenty-four of his cohorts were convicted of war crimes, before Xmas he alongside six others would be hanged in America.

Princess Elizabeth gave birth to Prince Charles on the 14th and King George, her father, was forced to cancel a tour of Australia because of a rumoured blood clot!

By the month's end, London was suffering one of its worst fogs ever, already three trains had crashed and four people been killed. Both police cars and buses were removed from the roads.

This was the time when driving a taxi came into its own. People at our rank would sort themselves into groups going in similar directions and ask us if it was acceptable to travel together if each paid for his total journey. I know it seems hard to believe today, but I have actually driven cautiously behind one of my own fare-paying passengers as he or she peered through the murk to guide me for perhaps a couple of hundred yards, and then happily paid me for the privilege. Sometimes it would be the guy next to you sitting there with his door partly open to keep a check on your distance from the pavement. This way with four passengers you could get two shillings from the first plus tip, then three shillings from the second plus tip, and so on. The only difficulty was finding your way back to base, but with little other traffic to worry about we had become dab hands at this, being able to steer a straight course whilst leaning far over to the left and following the just visible kerbside.

One of the most memorable inventions of 1948 occurred when the Bells Laboratory of the USA proclaimed the birth of the transistor. This remarkable little device duplicated all the work currently performed by the thermionic valve used in most electrical equipment. Being no larger than the average thumbnail, immediately we had entered the age of miniaturisation, nothing to equate with the silicon chip of course, but for its time a significant step forward.

As Christmas approached so did Mary, journeying once more from Leuchars railway station, changing at Edinburgh and then London, to be met by BRM and me as she alighted at Romford. Sitting beside me, wrapped this time in Scottish tweed and heavy outer garments, she was well protected against the ravages of a 600-mile winter journey, yet still managed to pervade the air with the unforgettable fragrance of mischief.

Feeling more at ease I began to appreciate how we conveyed two kindred spirits entwined by the one common denominator, our love of Len. I'd had time to reflect on the terrible heartrending sequence of events that had brought us together, although still totally convinced that before long Mary would find a beau capable of filling her emptiness.

That Christmas was one filled with work, thankfully for me at least, the period, owing to being self employed for the first time, meant heavy commitment every day, in most instances until well into the early hours of the next. The net result left little or no time for Mary and me to renew our acquaintance and apart from enjoying one or two excursions to meet possible suitors, Mary became more involved with my sisters and their predilection for psychic powers and seances.

I don't know for sure how this came about, but I do remember seeing an elderly lady holding court the other side of the dividing glass doors leading to the sitting room, an area where Len had lain in state. So devastated had Rene, Ciss, and Elsie become by our brother's demise, all three were desperate to cling onto the slightest possibility of life after death. I'm afraid I only observed these tantalising and tormenting efforts into the occult from afar. Even though from a very early age I had been subjected to religious teachings, attending Sunday school and receiving yellow stars for perseverance, having to kneel by the side of my bed to say the Lord's Prayer every night up to the age of probably twelve years. Yet still I could not bring myself to believe that what my sisters, and now Mary, were chasing, conveyed nothing but pipe dreams. But I did know in my heart, that it helped them across a very difficult threshold.

With the advent of the New Year I began flying again in earnest, and on one trip much to his chagrin, left my friend Tye behind in order to let Mary hang onto my waist as we swept down the dual carriageway. She hadn't seen Bette and Vicky since the funeral and they noticed a slight thickening in Mary's waistline. Upon being told the news both became very supportive but extremely concerned for her future. That evening after Ciss and Jack had retired Mary stayed downstairs helping me to prepare my usual bed on the floor for the night, something she constantly apologised for, and I would airily dismiss. After all, with the ungodly hours I kept, it was just as well I lodged on the lower floor; at least it saved disturbing others. Suddenly I took the opportunity to ask how she was making out with these types who wrote to her, some of which I knew had called, even at 86, to take her out, although I hadn't actually been introduced to any of them. She remained fairly non-committal, saying that to be perfectly honest she didn't think any had wanted a lasting relationship, and for her part had not found any of them particularly appealing. The omens I felt did not look good, now nearly four months since the tragedy, and almost six months into her pregnancy, yet still no decent future loomed on the horizon.

Before the end of the month Ciss began badgering Jack, trying to seek out his feelings towards adopting Mary's child when born. His answer did not beat about the bush. No, he firmly stated, he had no wish whatsoever to become a father to someone else's child, even if it was her brother Len's. The problem for dear Ciss stemmed from Jack's inability to father a child and because of it he had been quite prepared to support me. But I had grown up and to start all over again with an infant younger even than I had been was like an anathema to Jack.

After my enlightenment into Mary's thoughts I began to look upon her as a girl I might indeed have a chance of loving. Although they say you should never marry a girl older than yourself, the truth was she had been four years younger than Len, which left her only just under three years older than me! Yet in spite of my new found feelings I was so shy and retiring, as introvert, as my brother was extrovert, that any advances would surely have to derive through Mary.

Arriving home as usual very late one night I was surprised to see her curled up on one of the armchairs deeply engrossed in a novel. She appeared completely wide-awake yet the hour must have been about 2 am. "Hi," I said, "you're very late tonight missy, must be a good book!" Mary stirred herself, tucking both legs even tighter to her bum so that she showed just a glimpse of a provocative thigh as a tight skirt rode higher.

"I stayed down to make your bed," she whispered, ever so softly. "I still feel damn awful about turfing you out of your room, I hate to think of all the trouble I've put you to!"

Once more I tried to shrug the whole thing off, "I'm just going to have a quick wash and get myself a cup of tea, can I get you one?"

"That's okay," she murmured, "you get yourself cleaned up, I'll make the tea."

Well! I had to strip to the waist quite close to her, as she worked in the kitchen, but there was nowhere else I could go because I would have hated to disturb Ciss and Jack by using the upstairs bathroom. Feeling refreshed after a long stint behind the wheel, I squatted on the floor to sup my tea, as Mary once more buried herself into the bowels of the chair. Reaching forward with one hand, she beckoned, tapping a vacant portion of cushion. "Come and sit next to me." That Scottish lilt was as captivating as ever, whilst mischief kept sweeping over me, from both the perfume and those smouldering eyes.

Two in one seat seemed a bit cramped, so I just dragged my buttocks across the floor to be closer, and more readily able to gaze into those deep-set blue-grey eyes. Then we kissed, her moist lips sending tantalising tingles down my spine and I pressed harder, before pulling back and smiling like a cat who's just swallowed the cream. "That was nice," I said. "I've been wanting to do that for a long time."

"Me too," said Mary, and imperceptibly loosened her blouse, taking hold of my left hand to rest it enticingly against her breast. There was no trace of a bra and the sensation was of warmth, smoothness, and deliciously round firmness.

We stayed like that, embracing and caressing one another for a long time; sometimes I would run my fingers through her soft silk-like hair, until gently,

THE WAY WE WERE

Mary disengaged herself from my clasp, prudently arguing that perhaps she should retire, just in case Ciss or Jack awoke and wondered what on earth was happening with all the lights still ablaze. I agreed and bade her a hasty goodnight. The ice had been broken and I slept a happy man, but I had reckoned without the family!

For a week after that I couldn't concentrate on my job, all the time I was anxious to get back to my beautiful Mary, but I had commitments and a certain amount of money had to be earned. Unfortunately taxi work is something you can't hurry; customers only came to those who were patient enough to wait. And wait I did, from 10 am to sometimes right round the clock until 2 am the following morning. I didn't know how Mary felt but, being kept apart began to weigh heavily on my nerves, like a very slow Chinese water torture, if this was love then I had a huge dose of it. As I parked the cab quietly into Jack's drive each ungodly early-morning hour, I forever prayed that my secret love would be waiting, wrapped in breathless desire to greet me.

But the secret could not last, and after one midnight rendezvous, had Mary warning me that Ciss suspected something. She had implied that Mary was deliberately staying up late to entrap me and was very displeased because I was still young and vulnerable, and she would not condone such behaviour.

I tried hard to override these stupid objections and told Mary in no uncertain terms that I was master of my own destiny and fully capable of making my own decisions. But poor Mary felt unable to go against Ciss's wishes, because my protective sister had given so much support to her, and out of respect, from now on she would be retiring earlier. Naturally I was furious, but understood her dilemma, so we would have to see less of one another, which on reflection may not have been a bad thing because I could concentrate more on work, which was something I'd been loath to do of late!

Before long however, I found myself bombarded on all sides by sisterly love, as each in turn spoke of the dire consequences that awaited me should I continue with my amorous pursuit. "Billy," implored Rene, "can't you see, you will be lumbering yourself with not only a wife but a child, and all before you've had a chance to settle into life." Elsie would offer similar sentiments. "Yes, it's not nice for Mary," she argued, "but she will soon find an older man, one more suited to her requirements, perhaps with more stability to offer!" And so it went on, with all the time Ciss of course desperate to save her little Billy from a fate worse than death!

I went to gain solace from my friends, Bill Russell and Sheila, and lo and behold dear Sheila was also expecting her first child. Each in turn would be sympathetic and try to be wise, advising me to think extremely carefully before going any further. I thanked them, but knew that they or anyone else could not deflect me from my chosen path.

I'd even warned Ivy, the one with a slight hare lip, which she couldn't help, bless her that I would not be able to go out with her anymore because of Mary, and much to my surprise young Ivy went almost into hysterics, why, I cannot say, because our friendship was going nowhere.

With less than five weeks to go before the birth of young Smithy, I confronted Mary one afternoon in Jack's conservatory. Here, at one end, we'd erected a dartboard, and casually I picked up a spare dart, glancing towards her as I did so. "I tell you what my gorgeous," I grinned. "If I should score a bullseye we shall definitely be wed!" I took careful aim and launched the dart, the point of which could not have struck more centrally had it been guided by wire. To this day, fifty-five years later, Mary does not know what would have happened if I'd missed, and being the devil I am, I have never enlightened her!

Immediately the die was cast so my endearing sisters rallied to Mary's side. Ciss strongly advocating that we should remain with her at 86 and to that end use the upstairs back bedroom where Mary currently slept, as a sitting room come bedroom combined, and the little front box room utilised as an office by Jack would become our kitchen. All the family instantly joined forces to help set up our future residence. In austere Britain we only needed the basics anyway, what else could two people so deeply in love possibly wish for!

But we must hurry if we were to beat young Smithy to it, with three weeks required to obtain a licence. We needn't have bothered, well inside those weeks Terrence Leonard John forced his way prematurely into the world, one of the bonniest babies I'd ever seen. At the registration of his birth I broke the law by solemnly declaring I was his father, a deception Mary was happy to go along with! All day I had been rushing around 86, constantly at the beck and call of my eldest sister and the midwife, even journeying to the local chemist for a bedpan. It had to be April 1st. So Len could have the last laugh!

Exactly two weeks prior, to the very day, on Friday 18th March, I had reached my twenty-second birthday and five weeks later, on Monday 25th April, Mary and I stood side by side at Romford Registry Office. Here, we tentatively took our vows, before an assembly of Ciss, Rene and Pop, plus sleeping peacefully towards the rear, our son, cradled in the arms of my sister Elsie.

Dear Elsie was now well versed in such matters, having herself given birth to her sixth son only the previous November. A child who would be christened Leonard after his famous flamboyant uncle. Yet, although barely a year since that uncle's death, so once again our family would be struck by tragedy when Elsie's husband Wally, at the tender age of thirty-five, succumbed to tuberculosis in the following August! From that moment my fiery sister, known as such for her strong personality, brought up her six boys single handed, with a rod of iron. But the firm kind upbringing produced men of which she and Britain could be justly proud!

Our marriage could not have been simpler, still able to squeeze into Phemie's masterpiece after Teri's emergence, probably due to his being a mere six and half pounds, Mary positively glowed. I had driven both of us to the registrar in BRM without a semblance of a ribbon, where only Mary displayed any kind of flower, pinned prominently to her pretty blue dress. There would be no photographers, no wedding cake and no reception. Even the ring itself, had been handed down by her mother! Afterwards I would take my new bride and baby, snug in his carrycot, straight to our honeymoon destination of Stone.

Many years later, probably about the time of our silver anniversary, Mary confided to me that feeling apprehensive of the forthcoming nuptials, she had spoken with Rene regarding lovemaking so soon after giving birth. Smiling happily, Rene had assured her that not only was it perfectly fine, but she must also add, that in her humble opinion, of the two brothers that had so recently come into her life, Mary was definitely getting the most gentle and faithful one! That, I felt, was a lovely comment for my sister to make at such a moment.

But despite the low-key nature of our marriage, Mary and I were still nervous and excited as we each pledged our troth to the other with due solemnity. It was a time of life far removed from today's world that often treats rituals of this nature with light regard, we in comparison, were making an extremely serious life-long commitment!

My last flight took place on Sunday March 27th. Mr Whellam, the chief flying instructor, had suggested some crosswind take-offs and landings, before setting me free on my own to practise a few forced landings away from the field. I used to love this part of flying, gliding in low across designated ground, then advancing the throttle to zoom skywards again. This then was to be my final farewell to a spendthrift freedom I had come to enjoy. I would reach fifty-nine years of age before flying solo again, in a machine far removed from the conventional, and whose concept had yet to be thought of!

With scant time to prepare for our life together, the second sacrifice had to be my Indian motorbike, today I believe they can command a fortune, but I settled for £35. With this huge sum burning a hole in my pocket, our first purchase was the all-important bed/settee. It came in a mottled brown and pulled out nicely into a six-by-four-foot sprung divan. Next on the list was our one attempt at luxury, a second-hand radio-record player, housed as one, inside a handsome wooden cabinet standing three feet tall. Having acquired two very tasteful inlaid walnut door panels, I proceeded to make Mary and me a useful wardrobe, an essential addition to any couples trousseau. With this standing to the right of the little bedroom fireplace, the music centre taking up the opposite recess and our adaptable divan reclining handsomely on a brand new carpet supplied by Ciss and Jack, we both felt extremely grateful and lucky, to be experiencing such a wonderful start.

Stone, on the river Blackwater, that last week of April could not have welcomed us better. With clear blue skies and gentle warm breezes, it was almost as though nature itself rejoiced in our happiness. I remember stopping to have a kiss and cuddle against the sun-warmed sides of a last autumn haystack, depositing a sleepy Teri in his carrycot, safely atop the car roof as we did so!

I say it was before we actually arrived at our honeymoon destination, but Mary insists that it took place during our homeward journey, four days later. It doesn't really matter either way, for we revelled in glorious sunshine, and strangely enough have found the temperate weather conditions repeated time and again, over the many anniversaries since.

Its funny how so often it's the little things that gel in the mind. I can recall as though only yesterday, stopping at the small dairy farm atop the narrow lane leading to the riverside resort, to collect two freshly pasteurised pints of milk. You could actually follow the process from milked cow through to the pasteurising and bottling. From the thatched cottage near where Jack's twelve-foot caravan was parked we would purchase newly laid eggs, sometimes with straw and dirt still sticking to them. And our first evening meal consisted of that day's caught fish, fried and accompanied by home made chips, prepared and wrapped at the all purpose store down by the waterfront. That meal would

THE WAY WE WERE

be washed down by Tizer, a red coloured fizzy drink similar to lemonade. Alcohol was definitely not on our menu, in fact the only time this came to the table was usually at Christmas, and only then in the form of Advocat to make snowballs for Mary, whilst I settled for a glass of ginger ale.

Fortunately when it came to T. L. J.'s christening, someone had the foresight to take a few pictures, and here we can see not only Mary and me but godfather John Vickers (the reason for Teri's third name) posing alongside Mary as she cradles her two-week old son.

Within three months Mary had confounded all her critics, for apart from becoming the most adorable, delightful girl any guy could have wished for, she continuously exhibited all the attributes of a true forties wife. Totally uncomplaining and never demanding, her one aim in life centred entirely upon myself, our baby and the home.

One of my great joys that summer of 1949 occurred when with a swishing gingham skirt, off the shoulder blouse and high-heeled white shoes, she would occasionally push Teri in his pram all the way to the station to visit me at our cab-rank opposite. There she would drape herself lovingly by my side as patiently I waited my turn to move forward. Having reached prime position, she would uncurl those shapely legs, toss that shining hair, and with a cheery smile, swing wide the rear door to bid my beaming fare bon voyage. I know she never even gave it the slightest thought and today would cast doubt upon my memory, but I write the truth when I say my contemporaries simply drooled at the sight of her, and envied me like hell!

Never was a husband so proud as I at times like these. With just a delicate touch of the merest makeup to enhance her elegance, it was my constant boast to all and sundry, that when emerging early in the morning from between the sheets, my Mary looked as though she'd just stepped from the shower!

Her coiffure of course remained her crowning glory, not for nothing had she been her father's hairdresser. Although she would constantly complain at not having naturally wavy hair and spend precious time curling and brushing it, never less than a 100 strokes daily. Small wonder that it so constantly glistened. How tired and lifeless some of today's styles look in comparison, notwithstanding the unglamorous clothes that are worn. Why! I reckon my Mary would have beaten them all, hands down!

Cooking, shopping, and washing clothes compared to today, was very hard work, yet Mary threw herself into these tasks with gusto, while still retaining her outward beauty and poise.

William S. Smith

Persil could easily have used her washing line to advertise white nappies, yet the only automatic washing machine you could get in those days was an open topped aluminium tub that heated the water. After that you had to agitate everything by turning a handle on top to rotate a single blade back and forth. Rinsing had to be done in the sink and until we managed to acquire a hand wringer all removal of water was derived from the twist of a strong wrist!

Shopping needed to be carried out each and every day, with stewed rabbit high on the menu, a dish that was not only cheap but also extremely tasty. I have always insisted that the public lost out when government suggested that the killer virus myxomatosis had to be introduced from Australia to save our British farmers!

If I had any criticism at all of my adorable wife, and I suppose to be completely honest I must name one, it stemmed from my beloved's knack of feeding you quite often the same food, just because you happened to say you liked it. In fact it didn't always pay to be too enthusiastic about a particular dish as you could end up with it forever more. I'm sure the boys can vouch for our many bowls of chicken noodle soup, and rice creamola pudding! But to be fair it was only because of her constant desire to please, and we loved her for it! In May that year Russia finally relented and allowed the Allies once more to service West Berlin from the ground. At last the world was able to breathe a little easier. But by the third week in September she exploded her first experimental atom bomb, and everyone started to feel apprehensive again!

This was also the age of the Comet, the first jet airliner, which despite Britain's austerity had enabled us to steal a march on the world. Yet while we could achieve universal acclaim for our inventiveness, our sugar ration had been reduced to eight ounces a week, and milk to two pints! And as Russia showed off her prowess, so Britain's pound had to be devalued dropping from four dollars to two dollars eighty cents, a colossal 30.5 percent reduction.

Factors about the changing habits of British people compared to before the war made fascinating reading: we now drank more but were less likely to get drunk. We spent less on food but ate out more. Marriage also seemed somewhat precarious with ten times the number of divorces compared to 1937, and one of the phenomena suggested it was the men instigating proceedings in greater numbers rather than women! Finally, crime was rising, but convictions for drunkenness were only half pre-war levels! With Jack's help, I had organised Mary's tiny kitchen for her, even handcrafting a crockery rack, which meant with that and the wardrobe, a quick gaining of knowledge in carpentry had needed to be acquired!

Tucked up cosily to my beloved, both in deep slumber one early morn, we were suddenly awakened by an almighty bang, a noise that had us leaping up in startled fashion. Rushing towards the source, we were astounded to see Jack with feet firmly set apart, staring at our kitchen floorboards, with a nine-inch flame pointing towards his crotch. "I was trying to find that smell of gas Mary told me about," he wailed, sheepishly. "Thought I'd light a match to try locate it!" We didn't know whether to laugh or cry, but it was no laughing matter for dear Ciss, because unknown to any of us, most of the blast had gone downwards and Ciss's beautiful piano now supported half the sitting room ceiling.

It is true to say that Jack had experienced many escapes throughout his life, so many that when it came to the final tragedy, each previous traumatic event took precedence for the reason of his hospital incarceration. On each occasion we would inform dear Jack the particular adventure recalled had occurred sometime in the past, until he suddenly visualised the truth!

He was to survive for six weeks after being crushed by his own JCB vehicle, a manner of life and death occurring many years hence I shall relate to later! Already more than a year had elapsed since my brother's terrible crash and apart from a short visit soon after her first arrival south, Mary had never been able to set foot again in Scotland. I felt heart sorry for her, yet not once did she complain. What with my work and constant cash crisis there was faint hope of sending her on the 1200-mile round trip.

I believe it was her Aunt Phemie who paid us a quick visit once when she needed to journey to London. Apart from this Mary had remained completely isolated, yet despite having become a wife and mother in a strange land; it would still be some considerable time before she finally let her true feelings be known about severe homesickness. Bottling up her fervent desire to be reunited with family and friends not to mention her beloved St Andrews, Mary had fought hard to avoid passing her distress over to me, knowing how difficult my life had become. Whatever happened it was more than obvious that I could not stop working, for the only time I did it invariably involved attending to BRM. But apart from these obvious desires and difficulties we both remained deliriously happy, love they say conquers all, and in our case it certainly had!

And then I went and let my darling down! So much so that it must have only been by the grace of God she was not prematurely widowed.

Servicing of one's motor car was usually carried out by the owner in those days: until, that is, entrepreneurs like Jack sprung up. It was only natural therefore that I should accept any assistance offered by him and his Norwood Motors workshop, and it was to this end in early October I innocently pulled off Crow Lane to pay him a visit. The usage of his facilities was something I had enjoyed on many occasions and one of the tasks requiring constant attention on vehicles of this era was keeping a watchful eye on gearbox and back-axle oil levels. The trouble with these gear housings stemmed from the small sized filler holes provided, usually sealed by threaded square-headed plug-type bolts. The idea was to remove the bolt and if the thick oil didn't immediately ooze out, then you needed to check there was sufficient lubricant by inserting a piece of wire, or some such, to get an indication of just how low it might be. The next difficulty arose should a top-up be essential, was on how to pour the damned goo into a sideways-on hole. Up to now I had managed this athletic part of the operation with dexterity and much swearing. Either having to make a right-angled tubular funnel, which invariably required you to unbolt the floorboards to get at, or attempting to trickle in a spoonful at a time from beneath the car!

Making my presence known, I had borrowed a ratchet jack and raised the front end of BRM prior to investigating the levels, when Jack appeared alongside, carrying a five-gallon drum. "If you need oil," he advised, "use this," and pointed to the upright canister. "Made this up special," he said. "Soldered a tyre valve into the top, and welded in an outlet with a tap at the bottom." Jack was one of those guys who could always circumvent a problem. He'd also connected a long tube to the bottom tap. "Now all you have to do is put twenty pounds of pressure into the drum and when you turn on the tap, hey presto, it will push the oil through the tube. Piece of cake," he grinned, handing me a tyre gauge and the airline from the compressor at the same time. "Save you all that messing about!" I thanked him profusely, as I grabbed the airline and pushed it onto the valve standing a good two inches tall atop the drum. For a few moments I let the pump do its work, then bent down to apply the gauge. In that split second my and Mary's world changed, with one almighty bang I found myself reeling across the workshop floor, sensing only vivid colours of black and red. The black was oil, and the red my blood!

I do not recall losing consciousness, yet have very little recollection of Jack dragging me into the back of his little works runabout van and driving hell for leather the 800 yards to the beginning of Crow Lane and the entrance to Oldchurch Hospital! I do remember being laid on a ward trolley and beginning to shiver alarmingly when after what seemed an age no-one had come to attend me. Then someone kindly wrapped me in a blanket and said I could not be touched until a surgeon had carried out an inspection. I had this vague feeling of a squashed nose, and managed to put a hand to my face feeling nothing where it should have been, only to discover it lying against one of my cheeks. I must have looked an awful mess, covered in thick black oil and caked with blood. Eventually a guy came and gave me the once over, peering into my right eye with an instrument—an eye that I couldn't really see out of—then gently he started to push my nose back towards the centre of my face, until, satisfied he couldn't really improve matters further, he leant over and whispered, "Can't do anything with the nose old chap, right eye is hanging by a thread behind the ball, you're going to have to lie flat and not move for a few weeks to see if it will mend!"

Oblivious to this trauma, Mary innocently went about her preparations for dinner, feeding and changing Teri and getting him nicely settled, enabling her to be free for Daddy as soon as he arrived home. Except it was only Jack who stepped through the front door, and in a matter-of-fact tone suggested she need not bother with my lunch because he had taken me to the hospital about three hours ago!

Poor kid, what a shock she must have received, but Jack could be like that, very little sympathy. In fact he was probably cursing his luck because not only was his precious invention blown apart, but he'd had to spend half the morning clearing up, and he'd lost all his oil into the bargain!

"Damn fool," he muttered, "put too much pressure in the drum, blew the bottom clean out!"

He forgot to mention that if the two inch valve sticking out of the top had struck my head, I'd probably have been killed, and how could I tell what pressure I'd put in until checking it with the gauge, which I was about to do! But in those days you took responsibility for your own actions, and I was obviously an idiot to have held the airline in place for so long. Today I would probably receive thousands. Then I had to worry about earning a living and providing for a family whilst flat on my back in hospital!

Mary came to see me that evening along with Ciss, while Elsie looked after Teri. At least they had cleaned me up and my head was now swathed in bandages to protect my right eye. In fact I was in an eye ward which must remain hushed at all times as the eye surgeons insisted on virtually no noise whatsoever in case it affected their delicate work.

During my time with Mrs Lomax I had come to know and befriend a young woman by the name of Maisie, she was a sweet little thing who I'd felt heart sorry for, because I believe she had been married to what I can only describe as a rotten type! Maisie herself stood about five feet nothing, like Mary, but there the comparison ended, because in the attractive stakes poor Maisie had dipped out. But she had a heart of gold and I think a soft spot for me, at least I hoped she still might have after she saw what air pressure can do to someone.

Ignoring my state of health but thinking rationally of our predicament, I suggested to Mary she try to contact Maisie to see if the lass could do any driving for us, something that fortunately Mary was able to do. Sure enough before that week expired Maisie paid my prostrate figure a sympathetic visit, falling over backwards to do all she could to help Mary and I.

It was ideal, from her point of view, she said, warming to her subject, because Mrs Lomax had put her on a day shift, which meant she'd be delighted to drive BRM for Mary every night. Also she suggested, "I will take money from earnings to pay for fuel and am happy to work for tips only!" This was a very generous gesture indeed, and I insisted she should only do so provided it was worth her while. True to her word Maisie worked each evening, very often until quite late, keeping the car so as not to bother Mary too much, and would call at Mary's convenience to pass over her takings, less fuel tickets which she always religiously kept.

As far as Mary and I were concerned it was our saving grace. I don't know whether I still had to keep my payments up to Jack during this period, it is possible he may have agreed to defer the money until I was back on my feet, but it certainly helped to keep our head above water!

Every few days, the bandages about my head and pads over my right eye would be removed. This was to allow for a personal inspection by my attractive nurse. Upon each occasion I would glance towards her and say, "I can see two of you nurse, one up there and one down here," and I'd point in the general direction. And each time she would answer, "Lucky old you!" This fun exercise went on for weeks with me beginning to despair of ever seeing straight again. Then, on the 25th October, just to add insult to injury, somebody came round the ward telling us they'd just heard over the radio the Chancellor declare he was increasing the fuel tax by two and half pence in his

THE WAY WE WERE

next budget. This would push the price of petrol up to two shillings and threepence a gallon. No one, it seemed, groaned louder than I did!

By the middle of November I became really anxious, Christmas and New Year was fast approaching, one of the busiest and thereby most lucrative times of the year and still I lay in hospital. Then one fine day towards the end of the month I nearly leapt out of bed and kissed my nurse. "Nurse!" I cried, "Nurse! I can only see one of you!" My eye had finally repaired itself and that meant I could soon go home. I remember having to take things pretty carefully and still let Maisie do the night driving until the eye strengthened further, but I was back behind the wheel and at home with my Mary again.

Without my nasty accident I'm sure Mary would have been pining to be celebrating in Scotland, but we were so pleased to be reunited it didn't matter where we were. By the time the festive season did arrive I was back in full control, driving far into the night, getting back on our feet once more.

I had started to experience some breathing problems and when I saw the doc he suggested another stint in hospital, this time for a nasal resection, a removal of a small piece of bone which was damaged and causing me to snuffle and snore, which was not very nice. I asked him point blank if they could make my nose right again while they were at it and his reply was. "It looks fine to me, I don't know why you are so concerned, besides which, if they try to reset the bone, then forever after, the slightest knock will cause your nose to break again!" It was a prediction I had no knowledge to argue against, although I believed it to be untrue, but for now I could only hope my beautiful wife wouldn't feel cheated having to live with a less than perfect husband. It was another doubt I need not have fretted upon; Mary felt and acted exactly the same towards me. Never could I have wished for a more devoted girl!

We had reached the end of the forties, decidedly a dramatic decade. What then would the fifties hold! The hope as we raised our glasses towards our sleeping nine-month old child was of love, happiness and with any luck, prosperity. Straight nose or otherwise!

William S. Smith

Left: 1940. Len is finally allowed into the RAF and gets his picture taken by hitting the bull's eye at Blackpool at the RAF Induction Centre.

Below: 1941. Billy Boy gets into his ATC uniform with long trousers at last aged 14 years. Photographed with Jack's family and Ciss at the Rouse family home in Plaistow.

THE WAY WE WERE

1941. Brother John enters the RAF.

1941. Brother John's family. Ivy, Peggy, Raymond and Rodney.

William S. Smith

Hundreds of Homeless In London Blitz Trek

See bottom
Sister Irene   'DAILY SKETCH' REPORTER

HOMELESS families, victims of the fiercest attack on London since the City fire last December, their salvaged possessions loaded on barrows and handcarts, early yesterday started the trek down devastated streets in one area to new temporary quarters.

These front line soldiers—grey-haired women, mothers with babies in their arms—held their heads high.

No hysterics; they had faced the ordeal of thousands of incendiary bombs and high explosives of the night before with philosophical calm.

Many went to join their relations, comforted on their way by firemen—exhausted, grimy and sooty—driving back to their stations on A.F.S. trailers.

Berlin radio claimed that 10,000 incendiaries fell, that the attack was "unprecedented and far exceeded Coventry."

Hospital in Ruins

But as I walked through some of the areas that got the worst of the attack the tired faces did not conceal the Londoner's indomitable spirit. There were still smiles and wisecracks.

Five hospitals, a convent school, a tabernacle, a police station, three churches and hundreds of houses were hit.

One Nazi raider was shot down, two others were so badly damaged that they probably did not reach their bases.

Black eyes set amid wry smiles greeted me in the devastated corridor in one of London's best-known hospitals.

Hundreds Rescued

They were on the faces of tired doctors and nurses who had battled through piles of twisted steel to rescue hundreds of buried patients.

As I stood among heaps of nurses' capes, blankets, torn sheets, surgical instruments and a cage of guinea pigs catapulted from the "path. lab.," the medical superintendent said:

"Here was my hospital... 467 patients were here yesterday."

A.F.S. Girls' Bravery

Many homes were saved through the bravery of two 20-year-old A.F.S. girls—Ethel Argent and Irene Smith.

Incendiaries and an H.E. crashed on their station. But they did not quit. Calmly they continued to receive messages and direct firemen to the fires.

1941. Irene joins the Auxiliary Fire Service and gets a mention for bravery.

Above: 1941. Len draws his Harvard training plane whilst in Canada.

Left: 1941. Len creates model to commemorate his flagpole incident.

Below: 1942. Len poses beside his Spitfire when flying from Rednal near Shrewsbury.

William S. Smith

1944. Ciss and Jack at ease in 86 showing television, now obsolete.

1944. Len shows off his captured Italian sword when stationed in Burma.

THE WAY WE WERE

1944. Burma, 152 squadron Harvard.

1944. Bill becomes a paratrooper.

William S. Smith

1944. Panthers are born

1944. Spitfire Panthers are born with pilots posing beside the cat!

1944. Panthers at Ramoo, Burma.

THE WAY WE WERE

1945. Bill and friends gather in front of a Dakota before jumping from it. (Bill centre rear).

1945. Len and John Willoughby Vickers snapped while executing a grog (Gin) run from Burma to Calcutta.

COPY.

HEADQUARTERS 221 GROUP ROYAL AIR FORCE.

DO/SFV/1/377

22nd January, 1945.

Dear Smith,

    Many congratulations on the award of the D.F.M. which has come through this morning.

    It is very good news, and you can join the comparatively few who have the honour to wear the D.F.M., as so many either reach Warrant rank or get commissioned and, therefore, get the D.F.C., and in my opinion the D.F.M. is worth more than the D.F.C. as there are definitely, partly for the above reason, far fewer per hundred N.C.O. pilots with the D.F.M. than there are Officer pilots with the D.F.C. and, therefore, one has to get the D.F.M. quicker. (Rather a tangled sentence, I find, on reading through!)

    Wishing you the best of luck.

                      Yours sincerely,

                            S.F. Vincent.

F/O L. Smith, D.F.M.,
No. 152 Squadron.

1945. Len receives DFM recognition from AOC Vincent.

THE WAY WE WERE

Above: 1946. Bill arrives at Quassasin in Egypt with pals.

Left: 1946. Bill 19 years in Palestine complete with revolver. (Now PIAT gunner).

Below: 1946. The road to Nazareth.

William S. Smith

1946. Nazareth.

1946. Palestinian Fort.

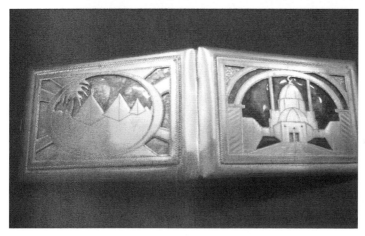

1946. Cigarette case acquired by author from German p.o.w. made from service mess tin.

THE WAY WE WERE

Left: 1947. Bill and Tye home again at 86.

Below: 1947. Portrait of a PIAT gun weighing 27lbs.

Bottom: 1947. Len beside his SS100.

1947. Len and Bill together again after 5 years.

1947. Dad with new wife Mary.

THE WAY WE WERE

1948. Sister Elsie with husband Wally 'and in order' Derek, Ron, Brian, Robin and John with probably baby Leonard in pram.

1948. Len with Mary Inglis in St Andrews.

William S. Smith

1948. St Andrews. Mary, Len, Betty Orr.

1948. Len checks out the MK X1X before Battle of Britain Display.

THE WAY WE WERE

News columns from St Andrews Citizen & Romford Times papers.
Also featuring
Daily Mirror front page Headlines of Monday 20th Sept.
following the Saturday 18th Sept. Battle of Britain Display.

Scots Girl Sees Fiance's Plane Fall

BANNS WERE TO HAVE BEEN CALLED TO-DAY

A 24-year-old St Andrews girl, Miss Mary Inglis, saw her fiance's plane crash ten minutes after the Battle of Britain air display began at Leuchars aerodrome yesterday afternoon.

Her fiance, 28-year-old Flight-Lieutenant Leonard Alfred Smith, Norwood Avenue, Romford, Essex, was killed instantly when his Spitfire, the first to take the air for an aerobatics show, came to pieces 500 feet above the crowd.

The banns of their marriage, which was to have taken place on the first Saturday of next month, were to have been called at St Andrews to-day.

Their Last Chat

Seen at her home, 8 Market Street, St Andrews, Miss Inglis told a "Sunday Post" man she had been speaking to her fiance in his quarters before he left for the take-off.

"He liked the idea of opening the display," she said, "and was his usual cheerful self.

"Something which had troubled him was the fact that the Spitfire he should have flown crashed in a rehearsal during the week while being landed by another pilot.

"The Spitfire he flew to-day was a number 19, a heavier type."

Miss Inglis was taken home by car immediately after the accident.

Wing Falls Off

The Spitfire flown by Smith had done several aerobatic stunts before it failed to pull out of a power dive. It was first seen to be in difficulties right in front of the control tower.

Smoke began pouring from its engine, and the starboard wing fell off. Fragments of it showered down among a lone line of aircraft, and hundreds of people who were inspecting them.

A sea of upturned faces saw the aircraft continue east at 400 m.p.h., 200 feet up with smoke continuing to pour from it.

There was a minor explosion when it hit the ground about a quarter of a mile away, out of sight of spectators.

At the scene of the crash on the perimeter track wreckage was strewn around for several hundred yards. Only the engine could be recognised.

Fire Engine Mishap

On the way to the crashed plane the trailer of one fire engine became detached and crashed at a turn, but no one was injured.

After a hurried conference among high-ranking officers, the programme continued as planned. Minutes later, with the wreckage of the Spitfire scarcely burned out, the pilots of two Moths took off to do synchronised aerobatics. Thirteen other flying displays followed.

Flt.-Lieut. Smith had taken part in several air campaigns, including the Battle of Britain. He was a holder of the D.F.M.

D.F.M. Killed In Exploding Spitfire

Receiving a telegram from Scotland on Saturday, Mrs. J. Rouse, of 86 Norwood-ave., Romford, expected it to contain a message about the wedding plans of her brother, Flt.-Lt. Leonard Alfred Smith. Instead it gave the news of his tragic death whilst flying his favourite 'plane, the Spitfire, in a Battle of Britain display—in full view of the girl he was to marry in only three weeks.

The incident was at Leuchars, Fife, and Flt.-Lt. Smith's 'plane was the first off the ground.

EXPLODED IN MID AIR

It was only 300 feet up, when, pulling from a power dive, it exploded in mid-air. Flt.-Lt. Smith, who was 28, had been in the R.A.F. since the beginning of the war, and made his home with Mrs. Rouse, his eldest sister and her husband, while on leave. "His whole life was in flying," Mrs. Rouse told the Romford Times, "and he could never look forward to the time when he would have to leave the R.A.F." He had made many models of the "Spitfire" for her, the plane in which he won the D.F.M. in Burma shortly before he was commissioned. He had 12 planes to his credit then.

His fiancee, Miss Mary Inglis, of 24 Market-street, St. Andrews, Fife, was watching the display. They were to have been married in three weeks and Mrs. Rouse, who had never seen her, was planning a reception for them.

Mary Inglis

Wished her pilot fiance "good luck," then saw him die in air explosion

Five minutes after wishing her fiance, Flight-Lieutenant Alfred Smith, 28, good luck in the acrobatic display he was about to give at Leuchars (Fife) RAF station on Saturday, Mary Inglis, 24, saw his Spitfire explode in mid-air, killing him.

Miss Inglis, who lives at Market-street, St. Andrews, said yesterday that the wedding had been postponed from the beginning of this month because of rehearsals for the display.

Flt.-Lieut. Smith

Death roll in the Manston RAF crash on Saturday, in which a Mosquito aircraft hit a line of cars, increased to twelve yesterday. Marie Allen, 21, of Merrick-square, The Borough, London, died in Margate Hospital. Her fiance, John Higgins, 25, gravely...

1948. Headlines describing Len's tragic accident and Mary's plight.

William S. Smith

```
HW          Sloane 3467
     TELEPHONE:
                 Extn............
     Any communications on the
     subject of this letter should
     be addressed to:—
     THE UNDER SECRETARY
     OF STATE, AIR MINISTRY,
     and the following number
     quoted:—  P.437433/S.14.Cas.B.2.
     Your Ref...............
```

AIR MINISTRY,
2, Seville Street,
LONDON, S.W.1.

14th December, 1948.

Sir,

    I am directed to refer to the loss of your son, Flight Lieutenant L.A. Smith, and to say that a full report of the circumstances in which he lost his life has now been received, and it is thought you would wish to have the available information.

    Your son, who was briefed to carry out an aerobatic display in connection with the annual Battle of Britain commemoration, took off from Leuchars airfield at 1.45 p.m. on 18th September, 1948. After climbing to approximately 8,000 feet, he dived to 500 feet, following the dive with an upward roll of two full turns. He dived back over the airfield, climbed to 5,000 feet and again dived, this time with the intention of doing a rocket loop. He levelled out at 400 feet and appeared to be flying normally, when the starboard wing was seen to fold backward and upward. Various pieces then broke off the aircraft, which dived into the ground and disintegrated. Your son must have been killed instantly.

    The primary cause of the accident, it is believed, was the failure of the starboard main plane. The aircraft was completely serviceable prior to the flight, and examination

/of

J.G. Smith, Esq.,
   52, Hillingdon Street,
      Walworth,
         S.E.17.

Contd. overleaf.

of the wreckage by technical experts has disclosed no reason for the failure, which can only be attributed to the strain imposed by pulling out from a high speed dive. In forwarding this information I am to express the departments deep sympathy with you in the loss of your son.

    I am, Sir,
      Your obedient Servant.
        A W Rivington

1948. The Air Ministry's reference to the accident.

THE WAY WE WERE

The R.A.F. tender bearing the body of Flt. Lt. Leonard Alfred Smith, D.F.M., killed when his Spitfire exploded at a Battle of Britain display at Leuchars, Fife, twelve days ago, is seen in this Romford Times picture moving slowly up to the gates of Romford cemetery. Having moved off from the home of his sister, Mrs. J. Rouse of 86 Norwood-avenue, Romford, on Saturday, the cortege, which included a firing party and a large escort from Hornchurch aerodrome, and six of his brother officers from Leuchars, and which was led by the Central R.A.F. Band from Uxbridge, turned into Dagenham at the slow march.

As they approached the gates the band broke into two files, allowing the procession to pass through and into the cemetery, where a short service was conducted in the chapel by Rev. F. A. Stroud, rector of St. Andrew's, Romford. Many sympathetic neighbours gathered at the graveside to hear the salute fired and the Last Post and Reveille sounded. Among the mourners were his fiancee, Miss Mary Inglis, who travelled with the body when it came under escort from Scotland. Also there were his father, Mrs. Rouse and her husband, and brother, Mr. John Smith. Many wreaths included one from Commanding Officer and officers at Leuchars, one from warrant officers, N.C.O.s and men there, from the C.O., officers, W.O.s, N.C.O.s and men of 277 (P.R.) O.C.U.; and one from the Drill Hotel, Gidea Park.

Arrangements were by S. F. Egginton, of North-street, Romford.

Above (and left): *1948. The cortege at Romford.*

Below: *1948. Bill and Mary together in London.*

William S. Smith

1948/49. Mary's profile in collage form.

Mary as I first saw her.

Mary and Betty Orr, St Andrews.

Mary with John Orr.

Mary executes a swallow dive at the Step Rock Pool.

Mary and friend. St Andrews.

An angel and cherub.

Cherry picker.

Proud parents.

245

THE WAY WE WERE

Top Left: *1949. Mary holds her new baby.*
Top Right: *1949. Angel and Cherub.*
Above Left: *1949. Proud parents.*
Above right: *1949. Cherry pickers.*

William S. Smith

1949. Teri's christening day with Godmother Irene and Godfather Vicky. Cis holds young Teri while Mary and Bill are either end.

1949. Mary sits on Grandpa Rouse's switchback wall while sister Ciss holds Teri at 86 Norwood Avenue.

1949. Mary in doorway of number 86.

247

THE WAY WE WERE

1949. Ciss and Jack with Jack's family.

1949. Mary in glam pose taken by her brother Ken, a professional photographer.

William S. Smith

1949. Sister Irene poses beside my Auster aircraft at Southend Airport.

1950. Teri has his first driving lesson in Bill's Austin 12hp Taxi.

THE WAY WE WERE

Left: *1950. Peggy, Ciss and Teri.*

Below: *1950. Teri, Teddy and Mary.*

Follow your Heart and Hope
Reaching for the Mid-Fifties

Mary and I didn't listen to the news a great deal and thankfully in those days it wasn't thrust down your throat every five minutes! Mostly we played our 78-rpm record player, enjoying lots of Glen Miller, Bing Crosby and newcomer Frank Sinatra. I also remember a recently acquired disc that played "Horo-Staccato" on one side and "Bumble Boogie" on the other, sending the two of us jigging above my sister's dining room. What news there was seemed full of dictators, prime ministers and presidents telling the world what they proposed and what they didn't, very similar to today really!

Attlee said we would now recognise Mao's China, and Truman declared he could not offer anymore military aid to Chiang's nationalists. India's prime minister stated his country was now a republic, with Stalin chiming in much to France's disgust, with his recognition of Ho Chi Minh's North Vietnam. Then Attlee spoke of submitting himself to a general election in February, with the hope of hanging onto power!

On the whole, life for us was full of love and contentment, and we invariably managed a visit to the cinema at least once a week. It was in January 1950 that we saw *The Third Man*, I can't believe it was that long ago. In any event neither Mary nor I were overly impressed with the zither music, which seemed monotonously repetitive to us, although since then we've seen nothing but rave reviews about it, in spite of which we both stick firmly to our first impressions.

By February 24th Labour were back in power, but only just, the result had produced the closest for 100 years, with Labour on 315 seats, Tories 298, Liberals nine and Others three, giving Labour a majority of five. Churchill spoke strongly of Parliament being unstable and that a return to the electorate must be a foregone conclusion.

Soon after Teri's first birthday but well before our anniversary, I received advice on my forthcoming nose job. This would turn out to be a horrible experience where, after the operation, I came out of the anaesthetic with yards of narrow gauge gauze stuffed up each nostril, and just to cheer me up, the surgeon had decided the shape of my nose didn't warrant any improvement. Mary brought her young brother Jack to see me as I lay there looking for, all the world like a badly mauled boxer, with two heavily bruised eyes, a somewhat flattened nose, and grotesquely extended nostrils.

During her following visit she passed me a loving note to digest after she'd said her farewells. Within it, she'd written to say how badly she was missing me yet how deliriously happy her life had become and did I remember the way we'd never stopped laughing the previous April on our honeymoon at Stone. Finally to express her guilt at not being able to pass this joyous mood over to young Jack who seemed forever wrapped in a kind of depression?

The visit had been arranged to give her company for the two weeks of my incarceration, which I was very pleased about. Yet despite her euphoria, the reunion had touched a nostalgic chord that left my beloved hankering more than ever, after her distant homeland and absent folks! I was not surprised therefore, that after we'd waved farewell to her sixteen-year-old brother at Victoria coach station, that Mary should turn her misty eyes towards me and beg for the chance to follow him later that year.

Certainly coach travel proved much more economic, as is so often the case today, the fare then being, about £5 return to Edinburgh from Victoria. Unfortunately not only could I not afford even this reasonable sum for myself, but with so many lost revenue days in hospital, there was no way I could take any more time off!

Once again government intervention did not help, when in the spring budget our Labour Chancellor suddenly announced petrol duty would increase by ninepence, making the overall cost of a gallon now three shillings. Sometimes I swear the country achieved success not because of government but in spite of it. In most instances, the populace felt money wrought from the public was squandered on pet theories that encouraged other people to strive less!

Personally I had been investigating various opportunities of increasing my income, and this latest imposition merely pushed me harder. One idea stemmed from carrying out wedding hire, which had the distinct advantage of covering fewer miles to achieve a slightly higher income. Every Saturday cars would be sought to perform this service and joining forces with one or two others I'd managed to do quite a few. At fifteen shillings a wedding it meant you could earn a cracking forty-five shillings for a possible total of only twenty-five miles, as opposed to the normal taxi mileage of seventy-five to achieve similar returns!

We'd got the format down to a fine art. Between three of us we could get the bridesmaids and bride to the church, and whilst the vicar conducted the ceremony, nip off to fetch wedding parties for the second service. Timing meant everything, arriving with the second bride just as the first began leaving the vestry to take up position for the usual photographs. This gave two of us sufficient minutes to retrieve our third party, and as we dropped these at the church, so the second group would be ambling out to have their pictures taken. Then hurriedly we would whisk number one bride and her entourage away, rushing back for the collection of the second just as they finished taking final snapshots.

Sometimes it wasn't always the same church, but as most churches were only a mile or two from where the bride lived, then any church within three or four miles of your first wedding would allow ample time to fit everything in.

The beauty of those days was that everybody wanted to get married, well nearly everybody, and cars were not easy to come by. But swiftly times were changing as those entrepreneurs amongst us saw the potential and began looking for bigger and better streamlined cars to make sure we didn't lose the market we'd so painstakingly built up!

On the odd occasion, Bill Russell and I would meet at the Hainault links for a round of golf. This was a beautiful country course just outside Romford, full of mature trees and rolling hills, where usually the only other occupants were rabbits. Could you imagine such a phenomenon today! Sometimes on a still day it was so quiet you felt completely alone with nature. We carried what meagre equipment we had in small tube-like canvas bags, which Mary smiled benignly upon, after witnessing, even in those days, the many faceted club-heads used on the St Andrews links!

It was during these sojourns that Bill expressed his dissatisfaction with the British constabulary. Apparently the salary left a lot to be desired and some of his duties were not to his liking. So I would speak glowingly of being my own boss and always having a motor car, a benefit not to be sneezed at! Gradually he began to ponder the idea and he, Sheila and I would spend hours mulling over the pros and cons of my suggestions. Their first son Raymond had been born in the previous May just over a month after Teri so circumstances were very similar to Mary's and mine. Not having a father of his own to turn to,

THE WAY WE WERE

the reason for which I have no knowledge of, Bill suggested he and Sheila approach her parents with a view to discovering what chances, if any, of them doing exactly as Jack had done for me!

Whilst we young families struggled with these latest decisions, so petrol rationing came to an end on 26th May, it had lasted ten years! A couple of other bits of news filtering through in the spring of this year, was the declaration by the USA of voting Alaska to become their forty-ninth state, while over here a survey declared only forty-six percent of British households had a bathroom. Yet everyone always looked crisp and clean, elegance and smartness seemed more apparent then than it is today in 2005.

Things began coming together just as Mary and I found the wherewithal to send her and young Teri scurrying up the A1 to Edinburgh. It had been a sad farewell, more so from my point of view, being suddenly wrenched from the two people nearest to my heart. Mary's separation was at least tinged with excitement, knowing she was returning home after eighteen months, a legitimately married young lady with a bouncing boy. Someone who could now hold her head high, and proudly show off her fast growing son, and what a striking lad he was, dashing around with inquisitive fingers in every pie, except when Mary tied him firmly into his hired pram. A bundle of energy just, waiting to be spoilt by delighted aunts, not forgetting doted upon by Grandma Bella!

My next news was a message from Bill saying his father-in-law had agreed to loan him sufficient cash to get him started with his own cab, and that he had already sat the exam to qualify as a taxi driver. It wasn't long before he'd persuaded a multiple owner to part with one of their licences, but the car was a bit rough and Bill said he'd like one as good as mine before fully committing himself.

It was another crossroad rearing its head for me, a golden opportunity to obtain a later saloon and help Bill at one and the same time. Once again I approached Jack for ideas!

And it didn't take Cissy's husband long to check out potential limousines. He knew that Eric Dubois's brother Arthur was a second-hand car dealer, and one day whilst Mary still enjoyed her holiday up north, he took me to see a handsome looking 1939 six-cylinder, right-hand-drive, American 16.9 hp Hudson at Arthur's depot. I must say compared to the average British car, it was great, sleek and curvaceous, in black livery, as ninety-nine percent of cars were!

William S. Smith

The bonnet sloped forward in one piece and hinged upward from just in front of the windscreen so that the entire engine could be easily seen and worked on. Gear change was via a lever protruding at right angles from just beneath the left side of the steering wheel, making it one of the first cars to have steering column change. Styling of the dashboard was much more futuristic and the brown leather interior compared to little BRM oozed sumptuousness. The front seating stretched as one, as opposed to the individual style currently experienced, and the whole concept cried out for a bride brimming with white silk and intricate brocade, to spread herself seductively inside the cavernous rear compartment.

I couldn't wait to try it out!

One drawback arose with a few blemishes in the paint, something Jack said could be rectified at Norwood Motors, where he now employed a sprayer-fitter. So the stage was set, Bill could purchase BRM and for a few extra pounds I could acquire my American beauty and surprise my other beauty when she finally returned to my side.

All was well with the world, but alas life is never that straightforward!

Having spent most of the day polishing the resprayed Hudson it was decided that evening I should take Ciss and Jack in my new car to one of the local cinemas. Entering the parking lot I couldn't help but notice an open truck stationed nose in almost opposite and casually remarked to Jack that it might be prudent to leave the cinema promptly as I could just see this guy backing into my lovely taxi. To which Jack replied. "Don't be so bloody silly!" Sure enough as we retraced our steps after the film, the truck was still firmly in place. Then just as I was about to reverse round so Jack yelled. "Stop!" but not for my benefit, because he had leapt from the car as he did so, just in time to see the tail-end corner of the truck's flatbed carrier slam into the curved offside rear corner of my Hudson, gouging a horribly elongated shaped hole. Immediately Ciss and I were trying to restrain Jack from attacking the burly driver with my starting handle. Heated words were exchanged before we finally managed to calm things down. I think after that Jack always felt I was psychic!

Hardly had Mary set foot in England to coo over my latest acquisition, when North Korea invaded the South! This time it was America's turn to enter the conflict first when Truman ordered the US fleet to aid South Korea. With the Soviet Union absent from the United Nations, a call went out for everyone else to help the distressed country. By the end of June, Britain's Far Eastern fleet was put under the command of American General Douglas MacArthur. Within a month as Churchill warned of a third world war, British troops were on their way!

In this atmosphere Mary and I renewed our life together; thankfully I was not going to be subject to recall into the paratroops and could consolidate my little one-man business. I remember during this period, Bill and I decided that Monday being our quietest day we would enjoy ourselves together with a round of golf in the morning, followed by a relaxing vapour bath at the Ilford Spa. Here, after squatting naked in the steam room for a good thirty minutes soaking up vast quantities of the aromatic essence and sweating like pigs, we would emerge to grit our teeth as we plunged headfirst into the customary ice-cold pool. Afterwards we would take turns to subject ourselves to water torture by jet. Standing valiantly at each end of the pool, whilst one of us pointed a fierce stream at the other via a hose projecting from the wall! The bit I enjoyed most was the tea and biscuits afterwards as we each reclined, swathed in heavy luxuriously warm white towelling. Evenings were given over to our respective spouse's for trips to the cinema, where my sister's Ciss, Elsie and Rene would generously take turns to babysit for us.

Although I had realised the Hudson was going to be thirstier than BRM, the figures were somewhat disappointing. Wedding calculations came out fine, but constant queuing at the rank, having to move in small increments to keep station, soon soaked up the juice! After about six weeks I had to confide to Mary that my average consumption had worsened from twenty-five to about eighteen miles per gallon, this coupled with the Chancellor's increase in petrol tax did not augur well! I'd even taken to pushing the heavy limousine along the rank to eke out expenses! Now if only I could have afforded one of Ford's newly announced Consul or Zephyr range at 1.5 litre-four-cylinder or 2.3 litre six-cylinder respectively, at the unobtainable price of just under £650!

One piece of gossip Mary brought from Scotland was the impending marriage of her brother Ken to his fiancée Dorothy, due to take place the following 2nd March. Was there, they'd enquired hopefully, any chance of Bill bringing her and baby Teri to St Andrews for the ceremony? It was a tall order, which my darling seemed hesitant to encumber me with. I felt the date could have been a bit more propitious. It was bad enough to travel a thousand miles there and back on what was then only A and B roads with few dual carriageways, including one driver compared to two carried by coaches.

But to do so at the end of February when conditions were liable to be pretty hazardous would need some careful planning!

By the turn of the year I'd definitely decided to take the car, even though my longest journey to date had been Devon and back during the war, about half the distance I was now contemplating. I should average twenty miles per gallon on the long journey, totalling about seven pounds ten shillings for the round trip. So not only would petrol costs be less than the coach fare to Edinburgh and back but we could enjoy the use of our own transport whilst in St Andrews. Providing we got there in one piece!

Working long and hard to help save for the trip, Christmas came and went almost before we knew it.

Meanwhile events in Korea progressed steadily from bad to worse, as far as we in the west were concerned. By the end of September China had openly stated that any attempt of the allies to invade North Korea (something MacArthur had been advocating) would bring swift intervention on their part!

The General's idea was quickly scotched by Truman, but sometimes I wonder if we would ever learn, for once again as with Hitler, all we did was put off the fatal day. MacArthur was livid!

By 16th December Truman was declaring a state of emergency when UN forces suffered more setbacks, and watched Tibet's Dalai Lama flee his country on Christmas Day, as China prepared to invade it! On New Year's Day they invaded Korea as well, crossing the thirty-eighth parallel just north of Seoul!

Britain's contribution to world events was to pull out of their much-publicised groundnut scheme in Africa, losing thirty-six and half million pounds of our hard-earned cash in the process, only to announce a couple of weeks later that our meat ration was to be cut again owing to failed talks with Argentina, and we must now all survive on four ounces per week.

Towards the end of January, alongside America's second atom bomb test in the Nevada desert, Attlee declared he would now spend £4700 million over the following three years so he could recall 255,000 reservists!

To these monumental utterings I gave scant thought, what was the use of bothering my head over such matters when I had a winter safari to prepare for!

Sister Elsie's eldest boy Derek, now seventeen, when hearing about the venture, quickly volunteered to join our marathon. I had to admit I was not averse to him tagging along. Another pair of strong hands might come in

THE WAY WE WERE

handy. In my limited experience this was akin to a moon shot, everything north of Norwich being mostly foreign to me!

The journey would need to start at 4 am and averaging 100 miles every three hours take a good fifteen hours to get there, but I needed to rest at sometime and I reckoned three twenty minute breaks should do it, adding another hour overall!

We went well as far as the Midlands, with me constantly getting updates from my copious notes stuck to the sun visor immediately above my head. I must complete 400 miles by 4 pm or thereabouts.

Mary had warned me that if I took the straightest route via Edinburgh I had the Firth of Forth ferry to contend with, so I headed west towards roads leading round Glasgow and northwards to Stirling Bridge. The detour led me hopelessly into mining areas and remote villages, which left my head spinning. One thing my darling always admitted, when it came to map reading she would prefer to cook! Fortunately a young Derek was on hand, but bless him he was no Tonto Indian guide.

By a spot of good fortune and past navigational skills we eventually left B roads and isolated villages as we headed over the Cumbria hills to reach Shap and the A6 going north.

Snow had lain pretty thick on the high ground and sheep tended to clutter the winding narrow-track highways, lying quite often in the centre of the road to keep their underbellies dry, but at least there were sheep, because otherwise we motored alone.

Pre-war cars tended to suffer from a deficit of heating, so we huddled, shrouded in wool blankets. I drove comfortably showing only the points of my shoes beneath covers that wrapped tightly round my legs to keep out the biting weather. Giving the instruments an occasional glance, I suddenly noticed—horror upon horror—that the charging needle on my ammeter, instead of the usual input, showed a slight discharge!

For a fleeting moment I pondered on our plight, we couldn't have been more isolated and the temperature outside was well below freezing with a light fall of snow. Pulling onto the roadside I raised the bonnet to check on the fan belt, it seemed intact and the temperature gauge showed normal so I knew the fan still worked. I carried spare water, petrol and oil, but none of these was going to help; also, a few important tools that could do most jobs: screwdriver, pliers, adjustable spanners! It had to be the dynamo—hell! What now, if I took it apart we could be stuck here for ages, too risky! I decided to continue and take a gamble on life in the battery, after all it had been charging since leaving home.

But one thing I could do, every time we came to a reasonable down gradient, I'd switch off, select neutral, and let her freewheel for as long as possible, quickly switching back on, shoving her into third and letting in the clutch before she slowed too much, then with a small kick as she fired into life, off we'd roar again.

As Stirling Bridge hove into view the evening sky was already pitch black, and with both head and sidelights blazing the ammeter needle hovered many amps on the discharge side. With crossed fingers and silent prayers, the motor kept humming along and we were now entering the county of Fife, even the snowflakes had stopped falling. Halfway between the Forth River and St Andrews the engine gave an abrupt cough and began to splutter ominously. Hastily I switched off the headlights to increase electric current and allow her to pick up again. Now I really was anxious, my neck ached something awful, and Mary and Derek were also feeling the strain. But our nearly two-year-old son, bless his cotton socks, slept on, oblivious to all drama.

The time had reached well past 6.30 pm and we'd been travelling for more than fourteen hours with only a couple of short breaks. The dynamo had been out of operation since approximately 4 pm, I had no exact idea of where we were and doubted if the nearest garage lay within ten miles, and even then rarely did any stay open beyond early evening! In desperation to keep sufficient current running to the spark plugs, I had to take the risk of switching off all lights, yet miraculously we never saw another vehicle.

Reaching a junction the sign became impossible to read and dexterously Derek leapt from the car to shin up the post, shining his torch with one hand as precariously he clung on with the other. "That way," he pointed, before quickly diving into the back of the car again. All the while I had been toying with my right foot, using all my wits to keep the engine revs going, which began to receive power from only five of the six cylinders. We continued on, feeling our way carefully down winding roads guided only by shadowy banks that loomed ghost-like on either side of us, until I suddenly discerned a glow in the distance. Immediately the engine began to hunt and went alarmingly out of balance, I was down to four cylinders only! Excitedly I turned to Mary huddled by my side. "Does St Andrews have blue street lighting?" I practically screeched the words into her ear. Poor Mary, the question seemed lost upon her, but nevertheless I swung without hesitation towards the eerie

THE WAY WE WERE

iridescence hanging in the night sky. Suddenly it was her turn to cry out in excited fashion. "This is it! Turn here, it's the Penns! We've come in via the Kinkell Braes Road!" An observation that meant absolutely nothing to me!

Hastily I swung hard left as we swept under the arch and into a wide well lit street. "Turn here and here." She was beside herself with relief and directions were literally tumbling from her. "This is it, this is our house, pull up here." I ground to a halt opposite a tall grey stone building, pulling tight against a flat wall because at this point the road seemed so very narrow. But as I reached for the ignition my wonderful oh so helpful Hudson engine gave a final choking grunt and cut stone dead. It was nearly 8 pm, sixteen hours from Romford! In the light of a small bluish street-lamp Mary and I looked towards each other in a half smiling sigh of relief. Then as if by way of welcome, snow began collecting once more on the windscreen!

Already aware, as a raw army recruit stationed at Alexandria near the banks of Loch Lomond, that Scottish hospitality was extremely generous, it came as no surprise when Derek and I were feted like long lost souls.

I found Mary's mum Bella to be a loveable, charming woman, full of fun and good humour, we became great pals almost immediately, and from then on I am sure Bella looked upon me as her daughter's knight in shining armour. Often down the years my darling would shrug unbelievable shoulders at her mother's acceptance of my words. "My mother," she would say, her eyes ablaze with fire, "thinks the sun shines from your backside!" I could only laugh and kid her even more. "Hell! Mary, can I help it if I am always right!" Bella encouraged my golf, striding out over the links whatever the weather, everybody in town knew her, this robust slightly plump lady with the rosy cheeks and sparkling eyes. If and when she went shopping for her messages, as she called them, you could bet your bottom dollar that by the time she stopped to pass the time of day with all her acquaintances, what should have taken her ten minutes would finish up nearer two hours!

Aunt Phemie (Euphemia) was not so well built as her sister, she was more the tiny gentle character, she oozed sweetness and neatness. Never at a loss to please, always asking how she could help. She also of course knew everyone and they her, especially for her sewing skills. But to be honest St Andrews could be a bit like that, perhaps more than other royal burghs, being such an enclosed city with citizens having lived within its walls most of their lives.

Liz, (Elizabeth) was definitely the tallest, a slim, very upright lady of strong character. I never had an awful lot to say to Liz, but certainly whenever our paths crossed she was always very kind and courteous and never seemed to stop busying herself. In fact many is the time we have left a job undone returning later to finish it, only to find the table cleared, or washing done, or fire lit. Mary often remarked, "The fairies have been here again."

They were all charming and I loved them dearly!

Following our traumatic arrival I had slept like a log, whilst Mary complained of a night full of dreams driving down dark tunnels with no end in sight, to which I apologised profusely.

Removing the offending dynamo I dumped it in the nearest garage, a mere five minutes' walk away, where I later called to collect it. A cheery little Scot in grey overalls glanced up from his littered workbench as I approached. "Dirty armature!" he grinned. "Cleaned out the grooves, and although they weren't bad fitted a new set of brushes while I had the genny apart."

"How much?" I ventured.

"Altogether," he mused, "that'll be two shillings and sixpence." (In today's money that is precisely twelve and half-pence.)

Reconnecting the generator I turned the ignition key. Had the battery, I wondered, after a night of idleness enough current left in her to spark the plugs? Installing the starting handle I gave it a yank, and lo and behold she immediately fired on all six, and what's more the ammeter shot up to a charge of thirty amps!

The day was Thursday the 1st March, tomorrow Ken and Dot were getting married and I must take the aunts as well as Mary, Teri and Derek through to Glasgow for the big day. To cap it all they want me to say a few words in place of Ken's dad who was unable to attend!

The car and the wedding went smoothly and I found Mary's brother and his new wife very friendly and truly a lovely couple. Her younger brother Jack had acted as best man and carried himself well.

Touring St Andrews before heading home, I told my beloved I had fallen in love with her ancient city. From its broad expansive beaches to its rocky cliffs, it's historic grey-stone buildings, to the everlasting rolling dunes and links. The colourful students and the performance of Scottish country dancing in the Younger Hall, all a fascinating insight into the life and times across the Firth of Forth. To arrive back in Romford after such an eventful journey and picturesque surroundings, seemed a poor substitute indeed!

It must have been sometime in August that Mary let it be known she was expecting another child, a prospect we were both thrilled about and had deliberately set out to achieve. If this was so, I reasoned, it looked very much like another April celebration.

But soon after, Jack dropped a bombshell. Unbeknown to us he had been discussing at some length with Ciss the possibility of moving. Intransigence on behalf of the local authority had a lot to do with it. Although many had rented land to set up business near the railway track, as had Jack, it would now appear local planners had other ideas. Rather than sit back and see a hotch-potch of buildings utilise the area, in their wisdom they felt it should be reclaimed and a nice clean uniform development put in their place.

To say Jack was incensed would be an understatement. He realised that any buildings erected by officials would not only be unsuitable for his purpose, but damned expensive into the bargain. Immediately he started to scour the country; come hell or high water, there was no way he would stay and be dictated to by what he considered were a load of half-baked upstarts who wouldn't know how to earn a living if it was thrust under their noses!

Keeping him company we would travel the length and breadth of England and Wales searching for a suitable habitat that he could throw his energies into. Scrap yards and caravan sites were his main enthusiasms, much to my sister's alarm, for she hated the thought of a scrap yard!

At one time we thought he would end up with a small holiday camp including a riverside pitch incorporating punt hire. That was up in Norfolk somewhere; then another time it was a small petrol station down in Dorset. But eventually with my sister's blessing he settled on a deeply in debt business, operating alongside a big Victorian house, standing in just over one acre of ground, on the outskirts of Christchurch in Hampshire.

The venue suited him admirably for it was a vehicle body repairers and sprayers.

The owners, Roberts and Sons, had mishandled the enterprise badly and installed too many staff. To alleviate their difficulties they were prepared to accept £7000 for the freehold property that ran alongside part of the eastern boundary of Christchurch Airfield, to a depth of 600 feet, with the front elevation consisting of a double width total of 105 feet, facing the main road leading to town.

We came home with Jack bursting with ideas, ready to exploit this new venture. If necessary, he argued, Ciss could rent out some of the rooms in the big house, and as the grounds seemed to be one vast apple orchard, income could easily be exploited by selling these fruits at the kerbside! Then he turned to me. "How about you Libby?" he questioned. "Need to sort out what to do with you, Mary, and the little 'un!" I hadn't actually had much time to digest it, but matters were obviously going to move pretty quick from now on.

"Tell you what," he said, sucking through the gap in his front teeth like he sometimes did: "I'm prepared to knock up a chassis for the biggest caravan allowed if you can build the body!" The idea appeared daunting, but I was usually game for anything and Mary had no objections, providing I felt confident enough.

"Where could I park it?" I asked, without being unduly obstructive.

"Think that should be okay," he responded, thinking hard for a moment. "Know a chap in Crow Lane with a bit of land to spare could probably do with a few extra bob."

So the die had been cast and our future lay firmly in my hands, especially when it came to saws, screwdrivers and chisels!

Houses for rent were pretty scarce so most married couples ended up living within their parents' households.

One could argue that surely for me to purchase 86 would be the logical thing to do. But alas 100-percent mortgages were as yet disallowed, and even if they had been available, to reimburse Jack for the taxi as well as buying his house, now valued at four times the original purchase price would be an impossible burden.

The funny thing was that it would be his brother Frank who gained that opportunity when, Pa Rouse, paid a substantial deposit on behalf of his youngest son. After demobilisation Frank had taken vocational training as a toolmaker and with no children as yet, it meant Yvonne could continue with her nursing career, and thereby their subsequent joint income proved enough to sustain a mortgage.

Of the two remaining brothers, Jim having been lost at sea as previously described, Ted would marry a very attractive lady called Kay. Both would soon move to Wakefield where Ted found employment inside Wakefield Prison as a photographic technician. Kay, very much a gay bubbly character, would sadly die many years before Ted from breast cancer.

Bob married a matronly lady known as Mimm and once again with assistance from his father, now well established in the wholesale grocery trade, set up a corner store in Plaistow, where both his third son and Mimm lived and worked.

Within a few days Jack had acquired the chassis from a three-ton Bedford, and proceeded to cut and carve the U-shaped channels, extending them to the maximum allowed dimensions of twenty-two feet overall length and seven feet-six inches width. Centrally to this configuration he welded a sprung loaded tubular axle, supporting lorry wheels with cable braking system running to the front tow-bar and hitch mechanism. No corner jacks would be fitted, because, as he profoundly pointed out. "You won't be going anywhere, so you can make do with a concrete block under each corner!" Such a suggestion suited me fine, owing to the added expense saved, now all I had to do was build the thing, and I couldn't hang about either as my brother-in-law laid immediate plans for his acquisition on the south coast.

Fortuitously one of the businesses near Norwood Motors happened to be a local entrepreneur building small caravans, someone who quite often looked to Jack for assistance with mechanical or welding work. It was an ideal venue for all the timber, aluminium, ready-made windows and glass wool that I would need for the construction.

Money and time were obviously going to be at a premium and one of the things that had been weighing heavily on me was the running expense of the Hudson. A big drawback stemmed from it being American; every time a part was required, I needed to journey to the far side of London for the nearest stockist and there was little, if any, delivery service, owing to insufficient demand. That and the way she drank petrol kept me constantly living from hand to mouth.

Taking the plunge I parted with my lovely streamlined beauty, replacing her with a later version of BRM, a long-nosed 1938 Austin 12hp. It turned out to be a disastrous move! Not initially of course, with petrol consumption now a reasonable twenty-five miles per gallon, and spares stockists round local corners, life became a lot easier, and I still managed the odd wedding. Actually I'd made a bit of profit on the deal and this came in handy for material purchases for our new home, now uppermost in my mind.

Bolting the main timbers directly onto Jack's framework, I quickly had the joists and floor planking in place, allowing recesses for the wheels. To this base layout I was able to fix the four corner sections and roof timbers, and soon had the outline taking shape. After two weeks between long bouts of queuing on the eternal taxi rank I was ready to line the inner walls. These facings were positioned first, so that glass wool insulation could be set between the framing from outside, especially so in the roof where it could be easily placed on top of the interior hardboard ceiling. I'd had to create a slight curve to both the front and rear of the roofline to allow water run-offs. Finally in sheets of eight by four feet the exterior aluminium was secured with copper pins, beading, gutter rails, and alloy screws, hundreds of them without unheard-of automatic screwdrivers, only hard wrist work! With windows inserted and home-made doors fitted I stood back to look at my handiwork and felt justly proud, now all I had to do was make the empty shell into our first fully fledged independent home!

With twenty-two feet to work with I decided to split it into three, with the largest section in the middle. After all the dimensions still constituted almost twice that Ciss, Jack and I had survived in during our stint in Norfolk! At the front end would be our tiny kitchen, five feet in depth with an exterior door leading from it.

Under the kitchen window above the towing hitch I built a sink unit and small worktop with cupboards both above and below. To the left of this slotted in our reasonable sized butane gas cooker, with its fuel bottle cradled outside atop the tow-bar. Waste from the sink would run to a small soakaway to be built some distance from our home!

To reach the kitchen you opened an internal panelled door on the extreme left, to the right of which, stood a tiny cream ceramic coke burning fire, facing inwards towards our lounge, come dining room, come bedroom, come bathroom! This fire had two little heat resistant glass fronted doors, and an asbestos chimney running through a small airing cupboard that opened in the rear wall of the kitchen. Below and protruding from this same wall Mary had a hot water tap screwed into a tank built onto the back of and heated by the fire.

Next we had an area that could only be described as a cupboard, housing a chemical toilet towards the far right of the kitchen and alongside the outer door. Behind this toilet wall and facing the twelve by seven feet room adjacent the fire, I'd built a shelf unit that one day might hold a small radio or even a television but we couldn't afford either as yet. Both the central wheel arches, now boxed over, Mary and I had padded to form seating.

Standing six feet tall inside a panelled frame attached to the rear wall division I had painstakingly produced a purpose built double bed that pivoted neatly on home made steel pins set eighteen inches off the floor. Still made up ready to jump into, it slotted nicely into the accommodating recess. As this masterpiece swung into the horizontal it rested solidly onto the offside, or right hand padded seating over the wheel arch!

THE WAY WE WERE

To turn our bedroom into a dining room, a tabletop complete with collapsible leg clipped neatly to the underside of the stored bed, so that it finished up, standing squarely between both wheel-arch seats.

For a bathroom, a five-foot tin bath kept conveniently beneath the caravan was to be placed in the middle of the multipurpose room floor, which we would then have to laboriously fill. Thank goodness we were young, fit, and totally in love! After this ritual, Mary would need to help me empty the sudsy water out of what fortunately ended up as our back door. (This happened because when siting the van I'd decided to reverse into position ready for any future circumstance, which turned out to be excellent thinking on my part!) The other factor taken into account was the blocking up of the axle so that neither tyre would have to support any weight during our long period of stay. What I failed to do however, was to protect them from the rays of the sun!

The last five feet of space beyond our recessed boudoir acted as Teri's nursery and shared wardrobe facility. Clothing in those austere days, with rationing still very much in evidence, was of a limited nature. Today we could not house our very necessary wardrobe inside the entire structure, let alone five by seven feet of it!

Tom Lister, local chimney sweep, looking not unlike Fagin from the film *Oliver Twist*, would be our parking lot benefactor. He and his long suffering wife Winn, lived on one of those pre-war smallholdings in Crow Lane just before the turn off to Norwood Motors and almost opposite the end of the cemetery fence. I suppose in the past Thomas and Winifred must have been young and handsome people, but to Mary and me, apart from being a very generous and honest couple, they appeared middle-aged and weather-beaten. I always remember how Winn, a tall gangling lady with straggly hair, tried hard against the perpetual soot-encrusted world she had to endure, to keep her humble home liveable. To be honest what Mary and I had seemed like a palace in comparison.

Their little nineteen-twenty something dwelling called Crowley lay set back and sideways on to the lane. Apart from an area utilised for Tom's bags of soot, a vicious-looking chained-up black bull terrier, and an enclosure for chickens, the rest of the ground seemed more or less overgrown and empty.

Towards the rear, near the right-hand side border with our neighbour, stood a lovely oak tree, to the left of which could be established a reasonable site for our new home. Tom and Winn would allow us to share the one external toilet they possessed, whilst a cable running from their home, would supply

William S. Smith

our electrical requirements of three lights and two sockets. Mainly for Mary's new iron! Water was to be supplied from an external tap attached to the outer wall of Crowley's washhouse. To assist Mary I eventually set up an old milk churn with a tap welded near its base. This I kept topped up with water for her daily requirements and stood on a wooden stand, just outside our kitchen now-come front door.

To say it was modest by to-days standards would be a gross understatement, but to us, just a few years after WWII, it symbolised freedom and control over our own lives. Yet we had no running water, no in-house flushing loo, no mains gas supply, no bathroom as such, and as yet no radio let alone television! Ground rent to Tom amounted to seven shillings and sixpence per week (thirty-seven and a half pence in today's money), and we moved into our newly painted blue and grey home and oak tree surround, sometime before the turn of the year.

During all this upheaval and hard work the world had not stood still. Long ago Truman had decided to sack MacArthur for his constant insistence to overrun the North Koreans at the 38th parallel. There was no way the American President was going to be accused of starting the third world war. Hold the line became the order and not a step further!

By May, Britain's first V-bomber flew, the Vickers Valiant! At one and the same time British and Australian troops repelled a Chinese lunge at Chunchan into South Korea. Then before the month was out two British Foreign Office workers disappeared, confirmed at a later date to be that of Guy Burgess and Donald Maclean, both of whom had been spying for the Russians! In June, Russia spoke of brokering a cease-fire, which came as a large chunk of cheek considering they had encouraged the North Korean adventure in the first place.

July saw Randolph Turpin shake the boxing world with his middleweight win over Sugar Ray Robinson, to become our first champion in that weight since the legendary Fitzsimmons in the previous century!

It had been reliably stated that the average housewife worked fifteen hours a day preparing meals and housekeeping, and that Friday seemed to be her normal shopping day, when she spent between ten shillings and two pounds on food!

On August the 27th 1951 both sides in the Korean conflict were optimistic about a cease-fire.

Maureen Connelly (Little Mo) at the tender age of sixteen became the youngest winner of the USA Tennis Championships on September 5th.

267

THE WAY WE WERE

Winnie was back! Yes! On October 26th Winston Churchill, at the age of seventy-seven, became Prime Minister of Great Britain once more. And the number of homes with TV sets was expected to double from the current 344,000 in the next two years!

On November 28th an eerie calm had settled over the battle zone in Korea during an informal truce. But two days before Christmas everyone was trying to discover the fate of 50,000 allied prisoners taken by stony-faced Chinese and the equally uncooperative North Koreans!

In the following early spring, while Mary still felt able to travel, we visited Ciss and Jack in their new home. Much to Jack's disgust, we found Ciss feeling horribly homesick and longing for the three of us to be beside her. Although Christchurch lay a mere three-hour drive away, it may as well have been on the far side of the Moon for my dear sister.

We found Jack having had to be ruthless in his business dealings, gathering staff about him to inform them they were all, bar one, to be made redundant. Only Norman would be retained as the paint sprayer, because as Jack pointedly explained to the perplexed remainder, he alone was quite capable of handling the rest of the workload!

On February 6th 1952 King George V1 died in his sleep and we heralded our new Queen Elizabeth II. The Princess had been staying at the Treetops Hotel in Kenya where her husband the Duke of Edinburgh, soon to be Prince Phillip, broke the sad tidings to her!

The time for Mary to enter labour was fast approaching. Teri had enjoyed his third birthday and we were beginning to wonder if my love might receive a gift for hers in the shape of a newborn babe. She only just missed this experience when I rushed her to Oldchurch Hospital after midnight, on what had become the 30th April. Elsie had been celebrating the day with her and strongly suggested she take young Terrence home in case Mary needed to enter hospital. Despite it being my darling's birthday I had still kept working the rank, so when I returned from a late night stint on the 29th, rather lower than I would have liked on fuel, I became a trifle hesitant when Mary suggested I run my sister and Teri to Dagenham.

My dilemma arose because cars did not adjust easily to carrying spare fuel alongside public luggage, and garages were never open in late evening, which meant I must take a calculated risk. It was sods law therefore, when in the early hours, things began to happen, leaving me feverishly pulling on my pants and bundling everything into the car, including Mary, before roaring off as far as Tom Lister's front entrance, where effectively God and my stupidity combined to cut the motor stone dead!

In desperation, I could do nothing other than disturb poor old Tom from his slumber, what chance of fuel, I wondered! Winn was beside herself, "God bless her', badgering her, beleaguered husband to get a move on and help the young ones as fast as he could! I honestly cannot remember whether we had to siphon petrol from his van or if Tom actually had some spare, but we got a drop from somewhere. I didn't need much; a cupful would have got me the 1000 yards I needed to go. At a pinch I would have carried my beloved, but in the end I drove us through the gates. In those days, Matron wouldn't tolerate a husband anywhere nearby a wife in labour, and in matriarchal manner dourly dispatched me. "Go home Mr Smith,"she ordered, as she ushered me ungainly towards the exit. "You can't do anything here, you'll just get in the way, now be off with you!"

I wouldn't know a thing until the following morning when they finally allowed me to see my darling, now sitting bolt upright, looking all pristine and glamorous, her face literally glowing as she nursed another bonny boy. Apparently, so I learnt, Mary had given birth to six and half pound Barry, within thirty minutes of my enforced departure, and here was I, fretting for the rest of the night, thinking only of my love in torment! (Oh, for a mobile phone, but we were at least forty years too soon!)

So we had a son on the first day of the month, and now we had another on the last day too, and with Mary's birthday on the 29th plus our anniversary on the 25th, April was surely going to be an expensive and busy month from now on!

1952 was also the year that Oxford won the boat race in the middle of a blizzard.

That Mary and I left our two boys with Elsie, in order to see Gene Kelly at the local cinema, perform in *Singing in the Rain*. (Was it really that long ago?)

That Britain exploded its first atom bomb and the cheese ration was reduced to one ounce per week. When America signed for the official cessation of the Pacific War, and agreed Japan could finally govern itself again. Britain's meat ration climbed to the dizzy height of one shilling and seven pence worth per week! The Allies launched their biggest air strike yet in the month of May, to force North Korea to the negotiating table.

The release of Anne Frank's diary exposed the trauma of a living hell under German occupation, where alongside eight members of her family she had hidden and survived in one tiny attic room for two years, to eventually be discovered and perish with so many others in those terrible camps. With only her father and her diary surviving the holocaust!

In July, Argentineans learned of the death of their adored Eva Peron (Evita) champion of the underdog, who'd fought hard and long to better their lives. Clothed in a beautiful white dress, the way she always met her public, and in which after her lying in state, she would be interred.

A census report published this year declared that one household in three still lacked a bath, while one in twenty had no piped water! We were not alone!

Having become the latest victim of an army coup, overweight King Farouk fled Egypt in his luxury yacht from the port of Alexandria.

With most of north Devon hit by a massive storm, it had been reported that a large part of the beautiful harbour village of Lynmouth had been devastated and swept away.

Speed ace John Cobb died in his jet-engine speedboat, *Crusader*, when it disintegrated after having built up pressure waves doing 240 mph on Loch Ness.

During the Farnborough Air Show, John Derry, test pilot for De Havilland, with his observer, Anthony Richards, were killed when their DH110 blew apart as it entered the sound barrier. One of its jet engines, screaming at supersonic speed, tore into part of the watching 150,000 crowd, killing twenty-six and injuring a further sixty-five.

That summer, ever anxious to see her daughter, especially after having so recently given birth to another son, Bella paid us a visit. I remember gazing from the caravan window with her at my side, whilst the granddaddy of all electrical storms beat about our ears. I can honestly say I have never witnessed such a phenomenon, before or since. How Mary's mother felt cooped up in our small alloy home during such a frightening experience, I never knew. For she became as I, utterly transfixed at the gyrations and angry striking flashes interspersed by tumultuous thunder claps that were being continuously emitted from the heavens for at least thirty terrifying minutes. As far as I recall, Mary had shut herself in Teri's bedroom endeavouring to cover the ears of both boys at one and the same time!

During her stay I had taken the opportunity to drive the four of us to Christchurch, where, with my sister's help and guidance, we visited Corfe Castle, Swanage, Durdle Dor, and the Blue Pool. Soaking in the vistas and pleasures of this part of England struck a particularly strong chord with Mary, estranged as she was from her distant seaside home. But in fairness she was not the only one, as Bon and Eric, Mimm and Bob, and Jack's youngest brother Frank and his wife Yvonne, all began to fall in love with Ciss and Jack's newly found territory. Indeed this was the year that Bon and Eric decided to forsake their heavily mortgaged bungalow and swap it for a humble caravan similar to my home made effort, after Ciss had persuaded them both to park on her and Jack's land. This move was all the more surprising as only recently Bon and Eric had enhanced their life by adopting a baby girl called Lynda!

Each time I managed to cover the journey, I would settle more payment with Jack, but because of being forced to build and finance our mobile home it had become harder to meet this debt and I had fallen badly in arrears. I tried explaining the simple truth to both Mary and Ciss who still hoped that one day we might settle beside her, that I could not in all honesty consider any move south until I had at least honoured Jack's assistance. Even then there was the question of giving up my self-employment and finding alternative work.

Not that running my own taxi service was all downhill; there were many facets to the job that could help the day along, like the time a lady hired me to follow her husband! She'd stepped in from the rank and requested I drive to her home but wait out of sight while she spied on her spouse as he drove off in their car. Immediately this happened she ran to the cab uttering the immortal words not many of us get to hear, as swiftly she launched herself onto the back seat. "Follow that car!" she commanded, her manner and demeanour now quite menacing! So I did just that, all the way to Southend, by which time night had fallen. During the chase she'd kept up a stream of invective against the guy we were trying to hold within our sights, until arriving at the seaside resort he swung into some dark back areas where immediately she cried "Douse your lights, I don't want him to know we've been following."

This was great; I hadn't had so much fun since doing figure-of-eights over Southend pier in the little Auster, except this time I would get paid!

After winding our way around various avenues and side roads, keeping a discreet blacked-out distance, her husband eventually stopped beside a row of terraced bungalows, where having vacated his vehicle he quickly approached one of the illuminated doorways. In less than a minute the outline of a female form appeared silhouetted against the hall lighting.

My fare couldn't stop thumping the back of my seat in excitement. "Got 'im!" she kept repeating. "Got the son of a bitch! Okay driver you can take me home now." Suddenly she'd assumed a calm and more down-to-earth demeanour.

"Do you know who it is?" I asked, feeling like part of the conspiracy.

"Not exactly," she said, "but I have a fair idea. This has been going on for some time, but I could never get the so and so to admit to anything improper, now the bugger will have some explaining to do!" I felt almost sorry for our caught-red-handed miscreant, I could just imagine all hell being let loose on his return, probably been explaining his absences were something to do with work! On second thoughts I suppose you could make a connection, just happened to be nice work if you could get it!

Other fares that sometimes turned out to be lucrative were the ones we picked up from the greyhound track. This track was near Alcoe Timber Mills, the venue of my youth.

Opposite its main road entrance a stall vendor used to set up a coffee and sandwich bar, mainly for us drivers. Taxi drivers were always fair-minded and if you arrived at the pick-up point first, latecomers would queue behind you. So Bill Russell and I used to park our vehicles about half an hour before the track closed and indulge in a bite and a natter by the roadside until the punters came pouring out. Most gamblers would be down on their luck, but occasionally a joyful character climbed in beside you and couldn't wait to spill the beans of his good fortune. Sometimes spread a little of it around too, on the nearest person or thing, which very often meant a thumping good tip!

I'd arrive home anytime between two and three o'clock in the morning, it must have been a terrible time for Mary, having put the boys to bed some seven or eight hours earlier, and to begin with life in the caravan was still devoid of even a radio.

Before bidding farewell to Bella at Victoria coach station, it had been tentatively agreed that somehow we would send Mary and the boys to Scotland for New Year. The thought of being isolated from our growing family at such a time did not sit comfortably on my shoulders, but I realised how desperate my precious was to have her folks around her, during what was then essentially a purely Scottish holiday.

To make life a little harder my latest motorised acquisition, Austin 12 hp, letters FLH 283, had begun to falter, so to carry out the necessary repairs that kept cropping up I had installed a concrete ramp in front of our home that I could drive up. This adaptation at least afforded me sufficient space to work beneath. By laying flat on my back with a cushion supporting my head it enabled me to remove with hands held uncomfortably high, the likes of clutch and thrust race, including sometimes the gearbox after having first dismantled both from the drive shaft.

I forget the number of times I needed to accomplish this task, as first the thrust race on the clutch would grind and grate, then the clutch itself begin to slip and even at one time suffer from a gear slipping out of third. Each time of course meant money spent and working hours lost, so invariably I would carry out these repairs during the night with the aid of a light bulb cabled from the kitchen window, at least that way precious time and thereby money was saved. I recall episodes during mid-winter when snow lay heavily on the ground, that I needed to struggle with a grease-laden grimy engine. I would be helped in these endeavours by a pressure-fed paraffin heater placed comfortably only inches from my nose, and lying flat on pieces of old cardboard to stop the damp cold from encroaching into my body. They were not the best of the good old days! Yet despite these difficulties Mary and I remained deliriously devoted and extremely happy. In fact when Mary wrote to me from St Andrews on New Year's Day, describing her tiring journey and ensuing festivities; she made me fully aware of her undying love and prayed I did not experience problems with the car whilst she remained so far away and unable to comfort me. However, after several days without receiving word, instinctively she guessed I had suffered further mechanical trouble. At the time Ciss and Jack had been paying a Christmas visit to the family, during which I had managed to keep FLH running. But as the New Year approached I suspected a serious engine fault and decided to follow both my sister and brother-in-law to Christchurch before it gave up the ghost altogether. Once again Jack had the ideal facilities to overcome whatever problem persisted, and it transpired I had made a wise decision when we diagnosed a faulty engine block!

It seems laughable now but when I wrote to Mary about the unfortunate circumstances and the price to put things right, she expressed horror at the tremendous cost of £21. "Never mind," she penned, "maybe it will mean things will finally come right for us in 1953!"

The aunts and Bella couldn't do enough for Mary and the boys, Teri was quite the lad now, running around in his one-piece blue siren-suit with matching hood, and Barry became the apple of everybody's eye! I had to admit both lads were very photogenic and Mary kept them immaculate. I've always felt that despite little money in people's pockets and still under the constraints of clothes rationing, the fifties nevertheless managed to mark out the decade as one of the most smart and elegant. Maybe it was because prior to this almost everyone had been in some sort of uniform and the girls couldn't wait to dress up in lovely coloured frocks and swirling skirts. Whatever the reason, I say the age represented a romance and glamour that has fast receded ever since!

1953 marked another year of momentous events, when Tito became elected President of Yugoslavia, and Marilyn Monroe graced the front cover of a glossy magazine entirely nude, very saucy for the early fifties! The resultant exposure of the provocative lady led to her nomination as America's number one pin-up. She certainly won my vote, although to be perfectly honest, I already had, entirely to myself, Scotland's answer to the vivacious American!

It was also the year that saw a hurricane tear along the east coast and devastate most of the holiday sites in that area. A disaster that, in not many years hence, would see me involved in part of its rejuvenation.

On March 5th Stalin died of a cerebral haemorrhage at the age of seventy-three, and it looked very much as though Nikita Khrushchev, who currently headed the Politburo, would take his place.

Before the month ended we lost good Queen Mary, wife to George V and grandmother to our present Elizabeth II. They say that for fifty years Queen Mary never changed the style of her attire!

As April loomed to pronounce the fourth anniversary of our honeymoon, and birthday celebrations of Mary and the boys, so news from around the world invariably reached us through the auspices of the cinema. In Africa Jomo Kenyatta, scourge of British rule in Kenya and terrorist leader of the Mau Mau, had been captured and given a seven-year sentence of hard labour. I cannot remember whether such punishment was ever completed, I only recall Jomo becoming the first black President of Kenya.

On April 16th Queen Elizabeth launched the new Royal Yacht *Britannia*, and on the 24th Churchill was invested as a Knight Companion (I bet the old boy loved that).

But at the beginning of May disaster struck when our wonderful streamlined world-beating jet passenger plane, the Comet, crashed during a thunderstorm twenty-five miles from Calcutta. A fourteen-year-old witness said he saw a plane without wings flying just above the trees before exploding in a ball of fire. All forty-three passengers and crew were lost and the unpredictable accident did not bode well for our supremacy in new-age jet travel.

William S. Smith

Gradually Britain was beginning to suffer from all those impatient souls now wanting to flex their muscles and govern themselves, Egypt being next in line to control the Suez Canal! To be fair, this enterprise, although thought out and designed by both British and French engineers, did come about because of vast numbers of Egyptian workers. The income now generated for the Anglo-French consortium looked too tempting for some nationalists to resist.

All the time our rulers appeared to agree and show willingness towards the self-expression of these various groups, but it wasn't always easy. Britain felt and affirmed that it couldn't just hand over and walk away, leaving all our previous efforts of government in uncontrolled hands, such a step would be looked upon as a dereliction of duty.

Once again, I personally, in my limited knowledge and experience, do not think we were all bad in our dealings and controls of our various nations in the Commonwealth. Fifty years later one has only to look at most of Africa, where in a majority of instances they were worse off! One of my brother Len's Black Panther associates actually trained on Harvard aircraft in what was then Rhodesia. Ken Plumridge met and made many friends in that country, staying with a white farmer and his family in particular. Although his black staffs were obviously subservient to him, they were extremely well treated and cared for, and wanted for very little. Gradually these early beginnings could be improved upon, but today under President Mugabe in what is now known as Zimbabwe, life leaves a lot to be desired.

So before the end of May British families were advised to vacate Egypt!

Cricket made the record books in May this year, when wicket keeper Arthur Wilson, playing for Gloucestershire, caught all ten of the opposing Hampshire batsmen out, in one innings!

June entered with a bang when we all heard that Edmund Hillary had reached the summit of Mount Everest with his faithful Sherpa Tenszing by his side. It came just in time because the following day the whole country rejoiced in the coronation of our Queen Elizabeth the Second!

We never really had what you would describe today as a holiday, but with Ciss and Jack firmly established at Christchurch, whenever the opportunity presented itself we would make tracks in that direction. Travelling along the London North Circular Road, we would head for Slough, turning off the old A4 onto the A30 and run down past Virginia Water, Camberley and Hartley Witney.

No sooner had we joined the A30 we felt we were in the country.

THE WAY WE WERE

Sometimes the North Circular could be a little busy, there might be as many as four or five cars in front of you, but driving towards Virginia Water meant we were unlikely to see another vehicle for at least a mile! Eventually we would get onto the old A31 past Alton and New Alresford with the road entirely to ourselves, before circumnavigating round Winchester and Southampton to reach the New Forest at the A35. It was a journey we loved, and became familiar with, every inch of the way. In spring, summer and autumn, even sometimes in the dead of winter. In mists and rain, snow and high gales, but mostly the weather would be pleasant. Once when we'd left the boys with Ciss for a week and began travelling back to collect them, my motor started to overheat halfway through the forest, I could see nothing but clouds of steam coming from the radiator. "Oh hell!" I said to Mary. "What's gone wrong now?"

Immediately I lifted the bonnet and checked the hoses I could see they were okay but then I noticed the fan belt was missing. I always carried emergency water, but that wouldn't last five minutes without an operating fan or water pump. Then I remembered something Jack had told me a long time ago, "If you ever get in a situation like this," he'd said, "and Mary is with you, ask her nicely if you could borrow her stockings, tie them round the pulleys and at a pinch they could get you home. But I have to say," he chuckled, "they won't be much good to her afterwards!"

Plucking up courage I poked my head through the driver's window, entreating Mary to slide off both her precious nylons. In those days it could be quite a sexy act because ladies held them up with a suspender belt, a slim piece of soft material circumventing the waist, supporting four small hanging straps that clipped to both front and rear of the stocking. To see a skirt raised high enough to expose a shapely leg and watch her dislodge this piece of equipment was enough to send a type heading for the nearest cold shower. Mind you I had to quickly explain why I needed her to perform this act whilst parked on the public highway!

Entwining both garments together I passed them round the crankshaft, water pump and dynamo pulleys, stretching them tight and finishing in a reef knot. They worked too, holding together just long enough to complete the seven or eight miles we still had to go. And to give some idea of traffic conditions then on the road from Lyndhurst to Christchurch, all the time Mary was stripping off and I worked under the bonnet we never saw another vehicle.

Bon and Eric and adopted daughter Lynda were now well ensconced in my sister's grounds. I believe at this time Eric had rented a small shop in Boscombe to continue his television and radio repairs, but beyond this there was talk of him and Jack joining forces to create the first motor auctions in Christchurch. I think the idea originated from a travelling auctioneer who said he could put Christchurch on his circuit, and all that was required was plenty of parking space and a clear workshop in which to erect a rostrum, plus local permission of course!

The venue could also work well because it was possible to drive vehicles through the front of the existing building and after pausing in front of the auctioneer for bidding to take place, leave by the side doors towards the rear. By the middle of '54 this latest venture had taken root and it was quite interesting to see how the whole thing worked. First of all the workshop had to be cleared of all vehicles currently under repair, by 5 pm every Friday evening to make way for the auction. Then the sectional dais for the auctioneer would be erected centrally towards the back of the workshop, and a small kiosk just inside the front entrance made available for Eric's bookings and my sister's scrumptious home-made sausage rolls, for which she became famous and sold dozens! Jack's task in all this was to make sure every vehicle had sufficient fuel and battery power to actually cover the few yards required.

Such a requisite may sound silly, but I was amazed how, after collecting their numbered ticket from Eric, some people would walk away from their vehicle leaving a teaspoon of petrol in the tank and a suspect battery. Customers were able to bring their vehicle anytime, which meant some could have been parked there all week!

When we finally managed to move south I became one of the hapless drivers taking cars through this procedure every Friday evening, and I shall never forget the lessons Jack taught me on how to size up quickly a vehicle's unwillingness to start! If you spun the engine over more than twice he would be shoving his head through the driver's window asking if you'd checked the fuel situation. If the answer were in the affirmative, he would ask you to try the start button once more after he'd raised the bonnet and wrapped his fingers round one of the spark plugs. If he didn't leap into the air, he'd say, "I think the distributor is damp." He'd remove the distributor cap, lift out the rotor arm and rub the brass end hard on one of the tyres, blow inside the cap, put the whole lot back together, clench the spark plug again and say, "Try it now!" When the engine fired he'd do a little jig, shaking his fingers and grinning like a Cheshire cat, before calmly waving you into the auction room. "Off you go

THE WAY WE WERE

Libby," he'd say, "and don't stall it in front of the public!"

Ted Sealey was one of the other drivers, fresh out from the wartime Navy where he'd served on a minesweeper. A strong, fair-haired, dapper little chap, who would turn his hand to anything. Ted had become a ministry fire fighter at the nearby Hurn Airport and did odd jobs for Jack almost from the day Jack had acquired Roberts and Sons. Incidentally he had now renamed the site Viking Motors, using the helmeted head as his insignia, in recognition of the Nordic influence over the local area.

I would one day join Ted as a fireman who continued working in his spare time for Viking Motors, and later after the loss of dear Jack, served Ciss well into her old age. After a quadruple bypass in the eighties, we eventually lost Ted some ten years later. His wife, whom we knew as Dot, and one of the gang, along with other firemen and their wives, told us how he had choked on a sandwich and died before her very eyes! Back at the Listers', Tom had very kindly allowed me to erect a small open-ended outhouse out of odd scraps of wood and materials I'd managed to salvage. This gave us somewhere to store our gradually increasing amount of paraphernalia. There were a few toys of Teri's, a foldaway playpen where he or Barry could play happily without too much worry for Mary. Teri's pram now extensively used for Barry and various bibs and bobs for the car, accumulated over the course of time. It also came in handy for the odd repair because I could at least get the front end of the car under cover.

Another helpful piece of labour was the lying down of a concrete circular path near the oak tree. This enabled Teri and later Barry to have some hard standing on which to pedal their Mobo toy, a black and white horse standing on its hind legs supported by one wheel that turned as you applied pressure to the reins. The boys sat in a buggy seat pulled by the horse, and in turn had great fun with this, as opposed to the usual pedal car.

On a rare occasion Bill and Sheila with their now two boys, Ray and Geoff, would join the four of us on a trip to Stone. The Blackwater site was still very much the way it had always been except Jack's mum and dad, now retired, lived permanently in their prefabricated home, and his brother Bob, having purchased a plot alongside, had built himself a chalet.

But despite these sojourns Mary and I still hankered after the south coast, having seen and enjoyed it so many times. Each of us was quick to admit that our rather run-down patch of ground left a lot to be desired, even if Romford itself was still a lovely country market town.

William S. Smith

Today though, I would fight hard to get away from the area, Romford having become overgrown and part of metropolitan London! But if ever the opportunity did present itself the one person and pastime I would sorely miss was going to be Bill Russell and our weekly rituals of golf and vapour baths.

Apart from the first two days of euphoria, June had not been a particularly good month, at the age of seventy-nine Winston had suffered a rather bad stroke, leaving his left side partially paralysed, plus some loss of speech with his doctors advocating a month's rest for the old war-horse!

By the middle of the month, trying to outwit the Allies before the signing of the expected armistice, China had launched a 30,000-strong offensive against our positions in South Korea.

But at least the signing did take place on the 27th after three years and the loss of two million lives. Today North Korea is reported as developing more nuclear capability and the West is threatened yet again fifty years on!

With military leaders deposing ex-King Farouk's young son King Fuad in Egypt, it looked very much as though the army would take over. In the end it would be Colonel Gamal Abdel Nasser who was to win out and cause our new Prime minister, Anthony Eden, so much grief!

But the Soviets did not have things smooth either, when 100,000 German workers rebelled against their oppressors in East Berlin!

One of our wartime escapee heroes, Airey Neave, had won a by-election seat for the Conservatives. Such a bright and brave man and yet in the course of time his car would be sadistically blown up by the murderous IRA as Airey prepared to drive from the Houses of Parliament car park.

On September 12th John F. Kennedy, America's future President, married Jacqueline Lee Bouvier at Newport in Rhode Island. John was the eldest son of Joseph Kennedy, wartime US ambassador to Britain. The family were to suffer such terrible tragedies, including the murder of both President John F. Kennedy and his brother Robert, as well as disasters to other members, that people referred to the Curse of the Kennedys.

Car prices made the headlines in October when Austin announced that their new A30, at £475, would be £6 cheaper than Standard's 8 hp car, and that Ford had abandoned austerity with the new Anglia selling at £511. However Ford then surprised everybody with the spectacular unveiling of their new Popular car selling at only £390 including purchase tax!

Guy Fawkes Day started with a pledge from the government that all rationing would end next year. We had survived well on the meagre amounts

THE WAY WE WERE

granted us, and in all probability looked and felt fitter for it. Little did we realise then, that as the scientists and big business conspired to control nature's food supply, that gradually we would be indoctrinated into consuming vast quantities of synthesised and chemically grown food and fifty years later worry about the obesity of our grandchildren. So much for the advance of modern thinking!

This Christmas and New Year I enjoyed the company of Mary and the boys, and with Teri fast approaching the age of five and Barry two, we began to revel more in the festive season with them. I cannot recall what Santa brought the boys that year, but I do know the following Christmas I took great pleasure in building them a model railway on a six-by-two-feet board complete with, farm, buildings, trees and roads, as well as track, signals and station. The whole thing was a masterpiece of miniaturisation, and I distinctly remember simulating a ploughed field by using wood filling paste furrowed by drawing a fork through it, before applying brown water colouring. Another toy Mary and I had lots of fun with was a pair of bows that had arrows tipped with rubber suckers! During one madcap spree, Mary took refuge in the kitchen whilst I commandeered the boys' bedroom. From these opposing positions we loosed our missiles towards each other, ducking hilariously behind our respective doors so that the arrows stuck harmlessly onto the wooden panels. I can visualise it now, both laughing our heads off as first one then the other opened their door and fired, retrieving as we did so each other's arrows!

Having finally installed a radio, I would try to coincide my evening break to listen avidly along with Mary about the everyday story of country folk titled *The Archers*. The plot portrayed a farming community whose continuing antics are still broadcast today, except in this politically correct world, I doubt if we would be happy with the storylines!

By now it had been a year and a half since Mary had seen her folks, so we decided that a change of season would grant better weather. September would give the boys and her a chance to stroll along the wonderful beaches and cavort amongst the dunes down by the West Sands. Also if possible with aunts and uncles in tow, scramble the odd visit to some of the local beauty spots, Craigtown Park with its boating lake being a particular favourite. I still ran my latest Austin, FLH! But it had become the devil's own job to keep her free from trouble, culminating, each time she broke down, in loss of valuable revenue.

Unfortunately what tended to aggravate even more was watching my faithful BRM in Bill R's capable hands, consistently purring along as it covered the average 25,000 miles per year with hardly a hiccup!

By the 10th September Mary's first letter arrived from St Andrews. Apparently Barry had bitten the cheek of her cousin Betty's baby Brian, a custom he was inclined to resort to through excessive love! Although chastising him for over-zealous behaviour Mary was quick to emphasise how everybody had fallen in love with our angelic looking child! Teri however would consistently outdo his brother by being the essence of a perfect little gent, ever commenting on the wonders and merits of St Andrews. All he wanted, he kept telling his mum, was for Daddy to come north so everyone could live happily ever after! Daddy would have loved to, but where would we live and what work could I do? No! I think if I was going to make a cosmic change it would have to be south alongside my sister.

In Mary's next communication she showed anxiety for my news, it was now a week since I last wrote and she wondered if I'd found myself another girl! Little did she realise it was me that harboured thoughts of a lecherous ex-boyfriend taking advantage of my beautiful wife, whilst living it up 600 miles from her protector. It is heaven to have an attractive partner, but imagination can play havoc during a separation!

This time she extolled the delights of warm sunny days and frolics by the sea, with Barry coming a cropper at the water's edge and bawling his eyes out as he lay there, rompers and top soaking wet. But in no time, being the competent mother, she had him dried and dressed in fresh clothing propitiously packed for just such a mishap. For her part, working as she did in a toyshop, Bella had the boys constantly plied with goodies, little boats, dinky cars, and every kind of beach amusement she was able to lay her hands on. Mary said the boys thought she was Mother Christmas. No wonder our eldest son didn't want to leave!

In a further communication Mary told of being unable to bring herself to take young Teri on a visit to Leuchars, and wished I were there to hold his hand. "We journeyed past the Officers Mess," she says, "and everything looks just the same, it hardly seems possible that six years have passed since that terrible day!"

Our parting would last for three heart-wrenching weeks to cover her mum's holiday and give my precious a chance to enjoy St Andrews with her. But before the extra week was up my beloved was pining for me and neither of us could wait to embrace the other. It was a tortuous decision and one we must both endure because of the distance that separated us. I said to myself this would definitely be the last north-south divide we would experience; from now on, whatever it took I would remain by her side!

Plans were being laid for Teri's first venture at school and as soon as everyone was safely back home Mary would take him to see the headmistress. He was now well turned five and Barry two and it wouldn't be long before I had to contemplate how we were all going to fit into our tiny residence!

Whilst they were away Rolls Royce announced the first tentative steps towards vertical take-off when their Flying Bedstead paved the way for Britain's famous Harrier jump jet!

With our beautiful Comet grounded after two more crashes and many fatalities it had been proven that metal fatigue was to blame and Great Britain's lead in jet transport took a severe knock!

Before winter set in we journeyed once more to pay Ciss and Jack a visit and this time my brother-in-law had what he reckoned was some good news.

"Got just the car for you Libby," he said. "1935 25 hp Chevy, don't let the size or the fact it's American put you off, it comes from the General Motors stable and is equivalent to the British Vauxhall. Parts are cheap and interchangeable and it shouldn't be too bad on gas!"

It had been brought into his works for auction and he reckoned it might get under the hammer for a fairly low price, whatever that meant! I must say she looked nice in her deep blue livery; it was right-hand drive with brown leather interior even including the roof lining, and sported six cylinders with floor change. It was going to be a difficult decision, always Mary would go along with whatever I decided, but I had experienced so much rotten luck with my car changes that I was naturally cautious.

Practical as ever, Jack said, "Look, I think if you ever do decide to come down here you'll need a car capable of towing the van. Well this is the tool that can do it; I'll even fit a heavy steel plate behind the rear bumper and attach a tow-ball just in case!"

I remained hesitant, then he suggested he'd give it the once over just to be sure and if it passed muster would bid for it in the coming auction. I was to ring him to discover the outcome.

The following week I had become the proud owner of a Chevrolet, I had driven to Christchurch on my own and after removing my taxi meter and licence plate from FLH, drove back the same day in the Chev. It had a Scottish number plate, JS5023, so I was hoping that might be a good omen. She passed into my hands at the knockdown price of £40!

We always had to deliver our change of cars to the Meter Depot on the far side of London, just off the Great West Road, where the instrument would be fitted and calibrated. This was now my third pricey changeover procedure.

Under Jack's capable management FLH actually fetched more than JS, the surplus of which I promptly suggested he put towards my indebtedness and payment of recent help. With all the various mishaps and extra expenses since 1949, my original hoped-for clearance within four years had flown out the window and I realised there was faint chance of honouring the loan this side of 1955.

That Christmas and New Year I had a smooth and trouble free run. I relished my newly found transport and quite a few of the guys were also impressed, she performed well, was roomy, quiet and powerful!

On January 14th they announced another hike in the duty on petrol by five pence per gallon, bringing the precious liquid to four shillings and sixpence, or two pounds-fourteen shillings to fill a twelve-gallon tank! I began to seriously consider a change to our future. My first tentative moves towards relinquishing my self-employed status did not augur well. Taxi licences were not commanding as much money as just after the war. I had now reached a figure of £140 to clear my debt, and it was sod's law that I couldn't find a taker above £175, half the price I had paid in 1948! Once again I discussed the consequences with my beloved, who without hesitation said she would stand by me come what may. If necessary, she said, she could always get part-time hairdressing work to help us out.

I made one more trip to Christchurch, visiting De Havilland, the aircraft manufacturers on the edge of Christchurch Airfield, but to no avail. Only aircraft fitters or similar who had learnt their trade whilst serving in the RAF could apply. Ciss and Jack were sympathetic, readily agreeing to let me park our home within their apple orchards at a moderate rent, just as Bon and Eric had done. Then without my asking, Jack made a suggestion. If all else failed, he said, he could offer me employment at the garage. I would have to turn my hand to anything and everything, helping with engine overhauls and various other mechanical jobs, also preparing work for Norman his sprayer, plus of course assisting in the weekly auction.

But he could only afford to pay me £6 per week!

Whatever I decided would change our lives forever, the prospect did not look rosy. I must swap a steady self-employment, albeit of late hours and much heartache, for a grease-covered and dusty existence bringing in barely sufficient funds to look after my family.

Before the end of March I had taken the plunge, Bill Russell and Sheila could not believe it, all they kept saying was, "You know what a tough taskmaster Jack is," and that I would regret losing my independence. But my mind was made up, at least our family would be beside the sea, and I was never one to be afraid of work. Why! I thought, who knows, I might even be able to help Jack build up Viking Motors!

At least my purchaser did not insist on buying JS with the licence, so I made preparation for our move south. The first thing I must do was stand the caravan on its wheels to make sure the tyres could take the weight, then I loaded everything we possessed inside and spread items throughout the floor. I needed to balance her just right so that she became slightly nose-heavy. She was certainly that all right, despite my physique it was all I could do to raise the front high enough to drop the hitch over the ball, immediately the car groaned and sank on her knees, but everything held!

There was little opportunity for a test drive, once I pulled out of Tom and Winifred's entrance that was it; there was no going back. So we said our farewells that evening and I warned Mary we needed to place the boys in the back of the car wrapped in blankets for a 4 am departure. Whatever happened we must miss the London traffic because I would be taking the shortest route, straight over Tower Bridge!

I had no idea how heavy our home might have been, but the Chevy took a bit of enticing to roll forward, then we were on hard tarmac and making steady progress at a galloping twenty-five mph.

Within thirty minutes on empty roads we approached the church standing in the middle of the highway at the Stratford traffic lights and well on our way to the bridge. Suddenly without warning I saw with dismay through my driver's mirror the whole offside of the caravan slowly sink to the floor as JS shuddered alarmingly to a halt, right at the lights.

Hell! What a dilemma!

Trying to placate Mary's concerns, hastily I leapt from my seat to check on the cause. There, right below the trolleybus wires, we had suffered a completely flat tyre, but the worst part was the van now lay so close to the carriageway I doubted very much that the car jack would get underneath, and even if it were possible I had no spare!

Gingerly I stuck my head through Mary's side window to impart the sorry tale. "I'm going to raise the front end of the van and leave it propped on the jack," I explained, "then I can use the car to find a garage, but I doubt if any are open this early of a morning." It was now nearly 5 am!

We searched for half an hour to no avail before finally returning to our lopsided home. Of course none of us had breakfasted up to then, so the stress on Mary and me was beginning to tell. If I recall correctly both boys slept soundly, oblivious to the dawn drama.

At 6 am the trolleybuses started running and with their overhead pylons able to swivel, just managed to cling to their electric current as they squeezed past on our right. Fortunately other traffic could overtake on the left.

Then a miracle happened, someone had alerted the bus breakdown service to our plight and before we could say "Bless you!" they had the whole thing in the air and were dismantling the wheel. I'd spotted a garage in my earlier search about half a mile further on, so slinging the offending wheel on the floor beside the boys,

I made a dash to see if they were open. It was 7 am!

As luck would have it a young mountain of a guy was just opening the gates and, taking one look at my harassed expression and big wheel, took command in firm manner.

The tyres on these wheels were held to the rim by an open-ended circular band of steel. This band was levered off as you gradually worked round the circumference. After dislodging this you could easily release the tyre and remove the large inner tube.

"Perished," Tarzan said, eyeing me quizzically. "Got this size, shall I fit a new one?"

"Certainly," I said, "and what's more as soon as I can get going I shall stop here so you can do the other one." There was no way I was going to chance Tower Bridge with a suspect tube!

As he hammered the steel rim back in place and pumped in air to expand the tyre it gave an almighty bang, then he was raising the whole thing above his head and throwing it across the yard as a final test. "That's okay," he grinned, "she'll hold."

By 8 am, thanks to Hercules and the caring bus staff, we continued our journey towards Christchurch, yet even as we did so I felt the clutch start to judder!

With Tower Bridge looming, I realised I'd made another mistake as morning commuters began crowding round. I didn't mind this so much but progress was painstakingly slow and now each time JS tried to pull away so her clutch bearing began shaking alarmingly. Whenever I needed to edge forward, I prayed she wouldn't fail me, not now, not after everything that had happened so far. I could see poor Mary's knuckles going white every time our queue moved nearer the bridge, leading to a convulsive staccato leap from the Chevy!

But I am pleased to report everything held and we all breathed a sigh of relief when I could let her roll down the far side of London's landmark!

Gradually the roads became less congested, and provided we could keep moving by leaving a reasonable distance between us and the vehicle in front, the bearing might just survive, but as soon as possible we needed to stop for sustenance. Mary reminds me now that at the time I looked quite ill. I had reached my carefree brother's age of twenty-eight years, but unlike him I had a wife and two small sons to care for, with an uncertain future before us. However, we were comparatively young and very much in love, a combination that with any luck would hold us in good stead.

Viking Motors hove into view at 4 pm, exactly twelve hours since leaving Romford, on what was then normally a three-hour journey. Jack was there to greet us and waved us to a spot allocated behind a few apple trees. "That'll do for now Libby," he grinned; "we can sort out a more permanent position another time. Oh and by the way, you've missed Ciss and Bonnie, they've gone by train to London, visiting the Ideal Home exhibition!"

When my grandson Daniel first asked me to record a few memories, he basically wanted to know how it came about that the family ended up in Christchurch. He expected a couple of pages describing the reasons in cryptic form so I apologise for taking nearly 290 to achieve his wishes.

I could have said that it was because his great-great-grandfather decided to walk from Newcastle, or that his great-grandmother died at a young age whilst her youngest child was still a nine-month-old-baby. Or that his Great Aunt Ciss married a mechanical entrepreneur. That Hitler started the Second World War and his great uncle, having survived that war, met his grandmother in St Andrews.

It's because of all these things that we ended up where we did, but I might be able to put in more condensed form why, after a further fifty years, we were still in almost the identical spot to that in which we arrived!

William S. Smith

1951. Bill Russell and me holding our first-born sons Raymond and Teri with Sheila in the middle at Stone on the river Blackwater in Essex.

1952. Teri on his Mobo horse at 86.

1952. Our humble home in Tom Lister's grounds.

287

THE WAY WE WERE

1952. Two more photos of our humble home.

William S. Smith

1952. Mary and I building castles at Friars Cliff beach.

Left: *1952. Irene and Johnny with their two girls.*

Below Left: *1952. Mary holds puppy by Tom Lister's old oak tree.*

Below Right: *1953. Mary holds Barry at Burley in the New Forest.*

THE WAY WE WERE

Top: 1953. Mary lines up children.
Left: 1952. Bill, Sheila and Raymond at Stone on river Blackwater.
Middle Right: 1952. Rear of Robert & Son's before Viking Motors - rough land.
Above Right: 1952. Dorothy and Jack at St Andrews.

William S. Smith

Right: 1952. Front view of Robert & Son's showing house and workshop alongside.

Middle: 1952. Mary's mother Bella with Teri and Barry at the Blue Pool near Corfe Castle.

Bottom: 1953. Mary holding Barry alongside me sitting in Austin FLH283 on forecourt of what is Viking Motors.

THE WAY WE WERE

1953. Motor Auctions.

William S. Smith

Top: 1953. Mary and me on beach with Barry at St Andrews.
Above: 1953. Mary and boys in Glasgow.

THE WAY WE WERE

Top: 1955. Linda, Bonnie, Ciss, Teri, Barry and Mary at Friars Cliff beach.

Middle: 1955. The Chevvy years with Barry, Teri and me.

Left: 1953. Teri and Barry on sands at St Andrews.

William S. Smith

Above: 1952. Teri aged two in siren suit.

Top Right: 1952. Teri in siren suit again.

Right: 1954. Teri, Mary, Bella and Barry in pram, St Andrews.

THE WAY WE WERE

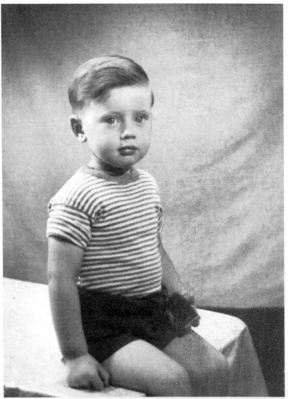

Top: 1954. Barry aged two.

Above: 1955. Mary with Barry sitting in his Jeep on Jack's land at Christchurch.

William S. Smith

1954. Collage of boys (growing up together).

THE WAY WE WERE

Above: 1951. Ken and Dot wedding after fraught journey north. Self, Mary holding Teri, Bella, Pat, Bette and young Derek.

Left: 1951. Bride and groom about to enter car.

William S. Smith

Left: 1925. St Andrews Mary's uncle Peter who took her fishing and whom she called out for as she lay dying!

Below: 1905. Bella and sisters, Maggi, Aggi, Mary, Phemi and Liz.

Bottom Left: 1908. The six sisters again.

Bottom Right: St Andrews Mary with her Gran, Euphemia Black.

THE WAY WE WERE

Top: 1953. Dorothy, Elizabeth, Isabella and Euphemia at No 8 Market Street, St Andrews.

Above: 1954. Irene, Cecilia, Yvonne, Mary, Barry, Bill, Frank, Jack and Johnny at Beach Hut Friars Cliff, Christchurch.

Epilogue

I began these memoirs in 2003 and in a second series I continued to describe our lives as it unfolded, but I have to report that although we accomplished many things and enjoyed wonderful times with members of our family, including six grandchildren, I lost all heart to write further when I lost my dearest Mary in 2007.

Leaving to one side these many words written, I must instead complete the intervening fifty-two years in summary version only, and sincerely hope anyone reading this will forgive me and understand.

After our arrival at Christchurch Jack kindly gave me work at his garage for a couple of years before I managed to gain employment at De Havilland in their Fire Department. When Christchurch Airfield was taken over by the local authority I found a niche on the Air Ministry Fire Service at Eastleigh with an eventual transfer to Bournemouth Hurn Airport.

All during this period I was able to give part-time help to Jack in running his now growing Vauxhall dealership and Mobil petrol outlet, especially where organisation and paperwork matters were concerned (two things Jack hated as he always preferred to be a hands-on man!).

Jack had never been an easy man to please, so when the Air Ministry decided to pull out of Hurn, leaving me in somewhat of a dilemma, I was astounded to say the least when he offered me the managerial position at Viking Motors. Eventually this position became assisted by Jack's brother Bob, who sold his Plaistow shop and moved into a lovely bungalow in Highcliffe.

In 1967 Jack decided to create a partnership for Bob and me with himself and Ciss. Our shares would be purchased from our part of the profits, taking possibly ten years to achieve. This would grant Jack freedom to retire to a new chalet bungalow he was building on land he'd purchased in Matchams Lane. Unfortunately in June 1968 Jack had a terrible accident with a JCB digging machine he had bought and operated himself. Due to previous heavy rain and the sloping nature of the ground the machine slid backwards down the hill as my brother-in-law stood alongside the rear end, working hydraulic controls. Endeavouring to escape the monolith he'd leapt sideways only to be caught by the treacherous undergrowth, allowing the huge wheels to roll over him and the lowered front bucket to drag him downhill. With the aid of ambulancemen I controlled one corner of the stretcher as we struggled to maintain a horizontal position, lifting Jack's conscious person uphill to the waiting ambulance.

He survived six weeks, this tough, self-made man, and it was then I realised how much he thought of me. It was only me he insisted upon seeing, dismissing his poor brother Bob quite abruptly and, I thought, hurtfully. But he needed someone who would get things done in a forthright manner, and I guess I was it! On the night before he died my sister and I had confronted the main surgeon responsible for his inner organs, suggesting transfer to a teaching hospital in London. By this time we had got him both private attention and a room. The answer was a decision for the following morning. On the day, the surgeon passed without acknowledgement, and Jack's eyes appealed to us to sit him up. I hastened to the nurse, who would only attend without my presence, so Ciss and I sat in another room and held hands until they came and told us he'd passed away.

Yes! Jack was a hard task-master but I owed him a lot. He would be appalled by today's world. Within two years I had built the first self-service station in Christchurch and between us Bob and I had enhanced the garage extensively. Jack's beautiful bungalow was completed under my direction, an establishment my sister refused to go near, and who could blame her, but under my guidance only just under half of the ten acres would be sold with the property.

Eventually Christchurch Authority would undertake the development of the old Christchurch Airfield and as it ran on two sides of Viking Motors it would mean a certain encroachment, not least the building of Airfield Way. But as it so happened an approach was made by a Mr Clark looking for a freehold property, and he was a millionaire! The garage was sold and another chapter opened in our lives.

We had been able to retain all the land where our domestic property lay, which was the rear 300 feet, half of Jack's original purchase to which I had now been able to add a further fifty-five feet to the east. This gave us a good three quarters of an acre where Mary and I could create our own Shangri-La.

Over the years I had first built an extra caravan for the explicit use of both the boys and between this had built a bathroom with corridor. However in 1964 I managed to buy under hire purchase a new mobile home called Sun Cottage, built by a firm trading as Paladin Homes. For the first time, Mary had a large lounge and decent kitchen. It is quite true when they say how much more you appreciate things that have only been obtained through sheer hard work and adversity. Mary was over the Moon! Gradually Sun Cottage grew until it became more akin to a ranch-style property with big sun-lounge, studio, annex, dining room, central heating, flushing loos, double glazing, sun canopies and a pitched pan-tiled roof.

After the sale of Viking Motors my younger son Barry (who had become our chief vehicle Repairer and Painter) proceeded, with my assistance to run a new business within my grounds called Carspray.

Here Barry and I worked for the next twenty-three years in complete harmony whilst our eldest son pursued his career in graphic art, going from strength to strength.

Mary loved her life looking after Barry and me for our tea breaks etc. Barry was now married and eventually bought one of the two bungalows Jack had built at the bottom of the grounds, with widowed Ciss remaining in hers, so it was nice having Barry and his wife Anita alongside.

Jack had built two bungalows when he won the services of a panel beater apprenticed back in the days when panels were forged by hand. Bill Brettel purchased his home but sold it to my sister after the sale of the garage, where she promptly installed Dad and second wife Mary in it for free. There they lived until we lost dear Pop at the age of ninety-five, Mary following within two years.

In 1986 Ciss decided to pass the remaining five and half acres of land in Matchams Lane to me although I suggested she include both the boys. She had tried in vain to win permission for property development but to no avail. Only some form of low recreational use could be placed upon it.

After learning to fly and acquiring my own microlight aircraft in 1987 at the age of sixty, I fainted coming in to land at Sturminster Marshall, our local field, and ended up in hospital with a broken wrist. My flying days were over, as there was no way I could subject Mary, or the rest of the family come to that, to such stress!

I then thought to acquire a Rolls Royce and Daimler to go alongside my classic 1935 Ford V8 drop-head to operate a classic wedding car service.

THE WAY WE WERE

Barry and I had renovated this car I'd bought in 1969 and sprayed it in a lovely creamy white to offset its maroon interior and red spoke wheels. This car incidentally had been present at the German Olympics in 1936.

It was while running this service during a game of golf with Barry at the Southampton municipal course that, passing close by its dry ski slope, Barry suddenly asked, "How about building a ski slope at Matchams, Dad?"

It was the glimmer of an idea and after gleaning some knowledge from an acquaintance I decided to build a model for presentation to the local authority. One of the hobbies pursued by my younger son and I had been radio-controlled model aircraft that need exacting tolerances in order to fly, so building a ski centre to scale was child's play in comparison.

My six foot by two foot model took pride of place before the planning committee who endorsed the whole idea enthusiastically. It wasn't easy setting up a partnership including both my sons and two ski experts, but between February and September 1989, without the loss of one working day due to poor weather, our three-quarters-of-a-million-pound project was opened by the Mayor of Christchurch on September 12th 1989.

With my two skiing partners, one of whom was German and a qualified technician as well as instructor, I was able to administer the centre for eleven years. During this period I soon realised we desperately needed a facility to bring in revenue all year round and managed to introduce for the first time in the United Kingdom the sport of ski bobbing. The machines for this new enterprise needed to be of similar or identical construction as one presented to me by one of our ski instructors. He had obtained his from a job lot sold by the Macro superstore outlet at Aldershot, and was called a Snegokat, of Russian origin. Barry and I eventually met two Russian gentlemen on a trade mission in a pub behind Oxford Street who after being shown a picture of the Snegokat felt sure they knew the factory that made them lay just outside Moscow. We clinched the deal there and then and our first ten machines arrived some four weeks later. In all we were to purchase 400 over the next two years with half of them being sold to other dry ski slopes throughout the British Isles.

These machines running on three skids with the front one controlled by a steering wheel were heaven sent for small and not so small children to ride to their hearts content, and made Christchurch Ski Centre into one of the most sought after venues in Christchurch.

Dear Ciss lived to see it all and at her request I had a plaque installed at the Centre recognising her husband Jack's foresight in purchasing the land. But in 1993, approximately one year after introducing my business-saving idea, she died at the age of eighty-six, as did all my three sisters! Almost as if there was a time clock built into their bodies.

At the turn of the millennium, with my age now seventy-three, we were approached by two brothers desperate to become owners of our enterprise. So without ever putting it to the marketplace the partnership decided to go their separate ways. But Barry would stay as one of the new directors and Mary and I would catch up on some sorely needed time together.

It was in early 2006 that my beloved spoke of a slight pain in her side, a pain that was diagnosed as stones in the gall bladder. Not a problem, we were told; keyhole surgery was all that was needed; forty minutes at most. "Let's get it over with," said Mary; "it will mean I can be fine for gardening for the rest of the year."

Mary loved her garden I had taken up working in the greenhouse and produced geraniums, petunias and gazarnias by the hundred and enjoyed it immensely. So we opted to go private and get things over with, we knew many friends who had experienced similar operations.

I phoned at the appropriate time and showed concern when matters were still ongoing. When I saw her later the surgeon said the op had been a little sticky but felt sure there was nothing to worry about, and gave her a little phial of tiny grey stones. Two weeks later he said he was surprised to learn of a growth after the biopsy but would take another scan in six months. Within two weeks Mary was in more pain than previously and I insisted on an immediate appointment.

Finally the penny dropped. Cancer had been found in the gall bladder, and now this dreaded decease had been released into the rest of her body. Mine and Mary's worst nightmares had been realised, and when we next visited the hospital we were told Mary had only months to live. How could it be? I looked at my lovely vivacious wife, it wasn't possible, it couldn't be true, I wouldn't permit it. Surely in this modern technical age with all the mass of intellect there must be an answer. We fought together for a further fifteen months, my darling assuring me she was going nowhere, and I said we would fight this thing and win.

They finally took her away to the Macmillan Unit where she pleaded with me not to let her go, but they insisted I couldn't give her the relief she needed.

THE WAY WE WERE

April had been a glorious month that year. The boys had arranged a helicopter flight with both of them seated behind me as I sat alongside the pilot on the 21st. It was a treat for my eightieth the previous March 18th. Teri's birthday on the 1st had been wonderful weather too.

On our fifty-eighth anniversary on the 25th she got out of bed to see the fifty-eight roses Barry's wife Anita had got for me, and on the 29th, the day of her birthday, she arose and dressed in her summer clothes, insisting on journeying to the lovely venue the family had arranged for her. The very next day, on his own birthday, Barry left for a planned trip to America for ten days; on his return Mary was already in the Macmillan Unit and only just recognised him, so full of morphine was she.

For ten hours a day I sat clasping her hand until she left me forever on the 17th May.

After six months of trying to hold myself together I agreed with both my boys to sell Mary's lovely gardens and move to a high-rise flat overlooking the Stour River somewhere that could also house my 150-year-old reconstituted snooker table.

Sun Cottage was finally obliterated and all the gardens with it. In its place they have erected fourteen attractive looking homes in a very nice close. It is called Wilmar Close in my and her honour.

William S. Smith

Top: 1956. Ciss and Jack silver wedding celebration in garage.

Left: 1956. Jack Rouse.

THE WAY WE WERE

1956. Children at Ciss and Jack's Silver Wedding.

1957. My three sisters with Jack resting outside his new bungalow.

William S. Smith

1957. Viking Motors sign, with Jack (owner), Norman (sprayer), Bill (author).

1957. Family line up near the front of Viking Motors.

THE WAY WE WERE

Left: 1957. St Andrews. Bill and Mary at Lamas Fair.

Below: 1957. Bill and Mary, Stratford-on-Avon.

William S. Smith

Top: 1958. Family picnic at St Andrews.

Above Left: 1958. Teri and Barry as archers.

Above Right: 1958. St Andrews. Mary poses under the arch.

THE WAY WE WERE

Top Left: 1958. Author in De Havillands fire service.
Top Right: 1958. Ken and Dot.
Above: 1958. St Andrews. Lamas Fair. Teri, Barry, Brian and Kathleen.

William S. Smith

1959. Land to rear of Viking Motors showing Irene with youngest daughter Tina.

1959. De Havilland fire crew cup winners at Hatfield.

1960. Bill, Mary and the boys at Ciss's bungalow.

THE WAY WE WERE

1960. Friars Cliff beach rescuing boat with Jack, author, Teri and Barry.

1960. Action at Ciss's bungalow.

1960. Linda, Teri and Barry.

314

William S. Smith

Top: 1960. Teri, Mary, Barry and Bill held in a line - Somewhere in Scotland.
Above: 1960. Dad with stepmum Mary in Ciss's new front garden far end of Jack's land.

THE WAY WE WERE

Top: 1960. Holidays in Scotland with a V8 Pilot & Wolseley.

Left: 1958. Mary models a swimsuit at 34 years of age.

Below: 1964. Mary with Kay at Friars Cliff.

William S. Smith

Top: 1960. Mary and boys.

Left: 1960. Winter snow.

Below: 1959. Viking Motors undergoing extra development with Bill now the proud owner of a V8 Pilot.

THE WAY WE WERE

Top: 1959. Rapide flight from Christchurch Airfield.

Right: 1959. Laughing cowboys.

Below: 1961. Viking Motors.

William S. Smith

Top: 1960. Teri and Barry. St Andrews sand dunes.
Above Left: 1961. Bonnie, Eric and Linda in grounds behind Viking Motors.
Above Right: 1962. Rudi our lovable Poodle joins our Clan.

THE WAY WE WERE

Top: *1962. Devon holiday with Jack's homemade caravette.*

Left: *1963. Mary and I at Spindle Rock, St Andrews.*

Below: *1963. Snow comes to our humble home with Bill, Barry, Teri and Rudi.*

William S. Smith

Top Left: *1964. Clearing the ground for Sun Cottage (note old caravan other side of hedge).*
Top Right: *1964. First half of Sun Cottage comes in!*
Middle Left: *1964. Sun Cottage established.*
Middle Right: *1965. Sun Cottage gains a little terrace with Mary and Barry getting taller.*
Above: *1963. Bill stands on the pier at St Andrews.*

THE WAY WE WERE

Top: 1963. Sister Elsie, Barry and Rudi enjoy the sands at St Andrews.

Right: 1963. Bill and Mary climb the Square Tower - St Andrews.

Below: 1963. St Andrews Craigtown Park. Teri and Barry crab the oars.

William S. Smith

SELF SERVICE PETROL — TREND SETTER FOR FUTURE TRAFFIC

THE first self service petrol station in Christchurch is the proud boast of Viking Motors of Somerford Road. With the most up to date electronic equipment, the system is one of the simplest for the customer to operate.

Said Mr. W. S. Smith, one of the partners owning the firm: "It sets the trend for the fast flow of traffic expected in the future — with the minimum of fuss and the maximum of efficiency."

Viking Motors was founded in Christchurch in 1952 by the late Mr. Jack Rouse. The name was chosen to acknowledge the associations the Vikings had in this area.

From a large, detached three-storey house, with an overgrown garden front and rear, Mr. Rouse transformed the site into an up to date garage and showrooms, with an agency for Vauxhall cars.

Over the years, Viking Motors has gained a reputation for a high standard of car body repairs, under the direction of the equally well known Mr. William Brettell.

Mr. Brettell came to Christchurch from Coventry and began work at Viking Motors soon after it opened. He is still there and is one of the most experienced panel beaters in the area. Amongst his many achievements, probably the most outstanding has been the reproduction of vintage car bodies.

In late 1967, Mr. Rouse made provision for his business to become a partnership, taking in his wife, Mrs. C. Rouse, and his brother and brother-in-law, Mr. W. Rouse and Mr. W. S. Smith.

The garage has always been inclined towards "do it yourself". If more building work had to be done in the garage — then the partners would simply set to and build it. While taking part in one of these self-building operations, in April 1968, Mr. Rouse met with an accident and died some months later. Viking Motors continued to be run by the remaining partners.

They have continued in the same spirit of expansion and progression, still on a "do it yourself" basis. In fact, almost all the work needed to convert to self service has been done by the staff.

Above: 1970. Viking Motors now first self service station in Christchurch complete with canopy and public address system.

Left: 1970. Newspaper cutting First Self Service.

THE WAY WE WERE

Right: 1971. Barry learns his trade doing his own car!

Below Left: 1969. Creating holes by hand for fuel tanks.

Middle: 1967. On board cruise ship Fantasia.

Bottom Right: 1970. Rudi and daughter Cindy in Sun Cottage garden.

William S. Smith

Top: 1976. Mary's brother Ken snaps my 1975 built 4ft 6in wingspan Sopwith One and Half Strutter coming in to land at our local model flying field in Christchurch.

Middle: 1978. Henschell 126 - 6ft 6in scratch built model by Bill and Barry (plans only).

Left: 1978. Peak District with Bill, Sheila and son Geoffrey.

THE WAY WE WERE

Top and Middle: *1979. Bill and Barry prepare the Henschell for flight while grandson Mark looks on.*

Below: *1979. Henschell in flight over marshes.*

William S. Smith

1978. Mary dancing with brother Kenneth.

1981. Bill and Barry with 4ft 6in wingspan Hawker Tomtit that won them the Ripmax Shield.

1980. Sister Elsie's boys all grown up Len, John, Elsie, Rob, Brian, Ron, Derek.

THE WAY WE WERE

1979. Barry working in our new business called Carspray after the sale in 1972 of Viking Motors.

1982. Grandchildren line up on Nan's swing seat: Daniel, Mark, Natalie, Carley.

1982. Bill and Barry study the books outside Carspray.

William S. Smith

1982. Bill acquires a tractor and amuses grandchildren Daniel and Natalie.

1983. Bill and Mary visit Bill and Sheila in the Peak District (last pic of Bill Russell).

1984. Carspray coffee break with Natalie looking the part.

329

THE WAY WE WERE

1984. Daniel watches his Nan and me, Uncle Jack and sister Natalie on swing.

1986. I take up Micro-lighting at the age 59 and buy myself a Pegasus XL in which to solo. Here granddaughter Natalie watches her granddad at his controls!

1987. Grandson Daniel takes the pilot position while Bill stands guard over a tethered machine.

William S. Smith

44 Monday, July 6, 1987

Micro pilot hurt

A MICROLIGHT pilot was rushed to hospital after his machine nosedived into a field at Sturminster Marshall.

Mr. Bill Smith, from Christchurch, was taken to Poole Hospital with a wrist injury after the incident yesterday evening but was not detained.

He was flying with a group of microlight enthusiasts from the Dorset Wings Club when he came down heavily into a field at Newton Peverell Farm.

Mr. Michael Coughlan, of the club, said that Mr. Smith was coming into land with another person on board when it hit the ground heavily.

"The nose wheel fell back. It could have been a rut in the ground that caused it," he said.

Top: 1987. Bill fly's his XL.

Left: 1987. Bill makes newsprint after fainting and crashes back at his flying field in Sturminster Marshall.

Above Middle: Teri draws his Dad's first solo and his Mum's reaction.

Above: Teri draws cartoon of crash to cheer up his Dad.

331

THE WAY WE WERE

Left: 1987. Ciss at 81.

Middle Left: 1987. Bill starts a wedding car service with his V8 drop-head showing a sailor and his bride.

Middle Right: 1988. Classic Car Wedding Service takes off with V8, Rolls and Daimler on display using Barry's address.

Bottom Left: 1988. Granddaughter Natalie takes prime position in front of Rolls.

Bottom Right: 1989. Mary and Bill pose alongside the Rolls.

William S. Smith

Left: 1989. Bill and Barry present the model of Ski Centre in Bill's garden and after presenting it to the local authority, wins approval.

Middle: 1989. Line-up of partners in front of Jack's land now graciously bequeathed by Ciss to Bill and his boys. Showing Bill in the middle with Teri and Barry to his right and partners Martin Westwood and Horst Bergeman to his left.

Bottom: 1990. Ski Centre is completed within 8 months and performing well. Picture shows skiers of various ages on the slopes looking towards artificial lake and surrounding fir trees.

THE WAY WE WERE

Above: 1990. We built it right.

Left: 1990. Bird's eye view of Centre.

William S. Smith

Saturday, July 25, 1992

Ski-bobs give non-skiers a slippery boost

NON-SKIERS can now enjoy the slippery slopes at Christchurch Ski Centre – thanks to the latest American import of ski-bobs.

The Robin Reliants of the Winter Olympics allow visitors to sit down and steer their downhill course in comfort.

Centre director Bob Smith describes the new attraction as a "go-kart on skis."

"It's a good little fun machine. You don't need any experience, you just get on and go," he said.

The new addition should boost summer business at the Matcham's Lane centre.

"We were wondering what else we could do with the slopes and at first we thought of toboggans," said Mr Smith.

One of his staff aquired a similar Russian machine two years ago and gave Mr Smith the idea for the three-ski fun ride.

He now has 12 American Snofox machines and is waiting for a delivery of 10 Russian Snegokats.

Emma Cary, aged 10, on a ski-bob at Christchurch   Picture: Duncan Lee

Right: 1992. Bill introduces Ski Bobs after tying up a deal with two Russian gentlemen in London. Picture shows girl on Bob with caption alongside.

Below: 1994. Mary tries out a Bob on her own.

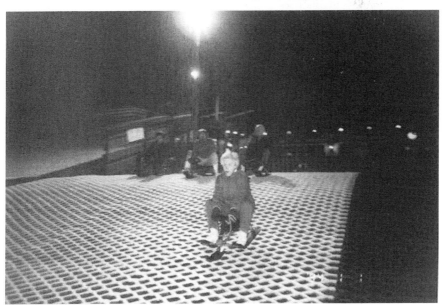

THE WAY WE WERE

Top: 1994. Bill (author) stands with Dakota at Bournemouth Airport.

Above: 1998. After nearly 26 years of voluntary work for the Red Cross and Macmillan Unit. Mary, alongside her friend Patricia Cooling, are invited to Buckingham Palace and gets to meet Prince Philip. Photo is taken outside Bournemouth Hospital with Pat and Mary front centre.

William S. Smith

*Throughout our life together
you have never left my side,
My constant guiding angel
in whom I could confide*

*Oh! what would I be
where should I have gone,
Without this lovely lady
to devote my life upon*

*You give such joy and pleasure so
my poignant partner, doting dove,
For fifty years we,ve sung our song
and its all because of YOU MY LOVE*

1999. Our Golden Anniversary year and I write a poem to my beloved. Picture shows a silver wallet open with poem on left and Mary and myself on the right. You My Love *was a favourite song of ours sung by Doris Day in our youth. (On the left is the poem enlarged for clearer reading.)*

THE WAY WE WERE

2002. Mary and I celebrate my 75th birthday with our two sons.

2002. Xmas Day potters.

2002. Mark, Carley and Dan - all grown up.

William S. Smith

2003. William and Mary.

2006. Picture of Mary in hospital the morning after the gall bladder operation.

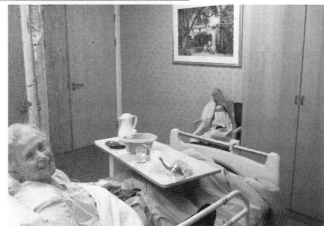

2007. Picture of Mary wearing her wig I bought her because her hair had become poorly with the chemotherapy, with our sons, one each side of her on April 29th, her 83rd birthday, which she desperately wanted to attend come what may! Eighteen days later on the 17th May, she died in the very Macmillan Unit she had so tirelessly worked in and begged me never to let her go to, but matters were taken out of my hands and for the first time I was not in control!

THE WAY WE WERE

2007. Pictures of Sun Cottage and Gardens.

William S. Smith

2007. Pictures of Sun Cottage and Gardens.

THE WAY WE WERE

2010. Wilmar Close.

2010. Part of Wilmar Close development.

2011. Author William at Christmas time with his six grandchildren and three great grandchildren.